FIVE PION

CW00969626

FIVE PIONEER MISSIONARIES

David Brainerd

William C. Burns

John Eliot

Henry Martyn

John G. Paton

THE BANNER OF TRUTH TRUST

THE BANNER OF TRUTH TRUST
3 Murrayfield Road, Edinburgh EH12 6EL
PO Box 621, Carlisle, Pennsylvania 17013, USA

*

© The Banner of Truth Trust 1965
First published 1965
Reprinted 1987
Reprinted 1993
ISBN 0 85151 117 1

*

Printed and bound in Great Britain by
BPCC Paperbacks Ltd
Member of BPCC Ltd

Contents

Maps and illustrations appear
between pages 176 and 177.

EDITOR'S INTRODUCTION

The Bible is essentially a missionary book. It shows that the entire world population sprang from a primeval God-created pair who were commanded to be fruitful and to multiply. Its survey of human affairs, while focused chiefly on Palestine and the people of Israel, takes in all nations 'that see the light or feel the sun'. As the story of grace and divine goodness reaches its marvellous climax in the closing book of Scripture, it is revealed that the company of the redeemed includes folk 'of all nations, kindreds, and people, and tongues', even as, in the commencement of the unfolding of the divine purpose, it was said to Abraham, 'In thy seed shall all the nations of the earth be blessed'.

Confirmation of God's 'eternal purpose which He purposed in Christ Jesus our Lord' was given when, in the fulness of the days, the risen Son of God directed His disciples to 'go into all the world, and preach the Gospel to every creature', a commission as wide in its geographical scope as it was significant in its requirement of obedience. More specifically, the Lord instructed the called ones that the preaching of the glad tidings was to begin at Jerusalem, and then to proceed in ever-widening circles until 'the uttermost part of the earth' had learned Messiah's Name. The Acts of the Apostles opens with this graphic charge; it closes with an account of the penetration by the Gospel of a world city, after having shown how the testimony to the truth as it is in Jesus had been confirmed with 'signs following'. Galilean fishermen, a tax collector, a learned rabbi, and many others had borne their witness to the power and grace of their crucified and risen Master, not by any ability of their own, but in the power of the Holy Ghost sent down from heaven. The winged seed of truth blown hither and thither by the winds of the Spirit, had already found lodging and root in a multitude of human hearts. It was taking root downward and bearing fruit upward (Isa. 37. 31). The harvest was great even though the labourers were, comparatively, few.

Missionary work of this humble yet exalted character was a new thing in the earth. Certainly, a disobedient prophet had long before fulfilled his commission to preach to another world city, and, sinner that he was, he had sorrowed over the success of his message. Here and there, too, individual Gentiles had reached out to gather the good fruit brought forth by the branches which ran over the Jewish wall. Even so, some may be inclined to say that the Old Testament, despite its references to Gentile nations and to Gospel blessings in the womb of the future, can scarcely be described as a missionary book. The Messiah Himself, it may be said, when He came to open men's eyes and to turn them from darkness to light, confirmed that He was not sent but to the lost sheep of the house of Israel. He was, in the first instance, 'a minister of the circumcision for the truth of God, to confirm the promises made unto the fathers' (Rom. 15. 8). But remarkably, the apostle who makes this assertion follows it immediately by the quotation of four Old Testament passages which speak unmistakably of Heaven's blessing destined for Gentile peoples. And in the middle of the Book of Acts, in the account of the first missionary crisis in the apostolic church, Peter and James combine to give delightful emphatic testimony to the missionary forecasts contained in the ancient writings.

It is not for us, in this brief Introduction, to attempt to record the story of the world's penetration by the Gospel in post-apostolic days. We concentrate attention on modern times. The corruption of Christianity in the pre-Reformation period augured ill for missionary enterprise. And even when purer light marked the road of the Church and brought it nearer to the Lamb (to adapt the phrases of one of Cowper's hymns), it was long before the Protestant missionary was seen at work. To some extent the Roman Catholic Church shamed the Reformed Churches by sending out its emissaries to many lands unvisited by the preachers of the true Gospel.

By slow degrees at first, but with increasing rapidity once the tide turned, evangelical missionary effort commenced. The zeal of the obscure Moravians, the ardour of the early Methodists, and the spirit of consecrated endeavour which, in England, God put into the hearts of individuals rather than of the long-established Churches as a whole, opened the way to a missionary outreach which ultimately earned the admiration of the Western peoples. Even a Darwin was constrained to call the 'lesson of the missionary' (as illustrated by results) 'the wand of the enchanter'.

Charles Wesley, the great poet of the Methodist revival and God's gracious gift to the entire Christian Church, could sing:

> 'See how great a flame aspires,
> Kindled by a spark of grace!
> Jesus' love the nations fires,
> Sets the kingdoms on a blaze.
> To bring fire on earth He came,
> Kindled in some hearts it is,
> O that all might catch the flame,
> All partake the glorious bliss!'

Doubtless by 'the kingdoms' Wesley meant the British Isles and the linked settlements on the eastern seaboard of North America. He is fully correct in his claim that a spark can set kingdoms ablaze. It is simply another way of saying that a few people, small and despised by the mass of mankind, can blossom and bud and fill the face of the world with fruit (Isa. 27. 6).

Accompanying the Methodist revival in the Established Church were less noticeable stirrings in the Nonconformist bodies, and wrapped up within them in sundry obscure places was the desire to terminate the lassitude which had too long caused the people of the Lord to despise and even oppose missions to the heathen. 'Young man, sit down, sit down; you're an enthusiast', an 'old hand' had said to William Carey. 'When God pleases to convert the heathen, He'll do it without consulting you or me. Besides, there must first be another pentecostal gift of tongues'. Paralleled by this is the 'crowning argument' addressed repeatedly by 'a dear old Christian gentleman' to John Paton: 'The cannibals!

You will be eaten by cannibals!' But God willed not so. He gave the Word; great was to be the company of those who published it. New and abundant evidence was supplied that wisdom is justified of all her children. The missionary enterprise of modern times had begun.

Such work has its prospectors and its pioneers. Beginnings have to be made. Lands to be possessed for the Lord have to be surveyed and charted in a manner set by the Lord. And it is often the beginnings which, in retrospect, supply the interest and the colour which later developments may lack. The early struggles of men and women who brave the terrors of the wilderness, their resolute efforts to overcome the hindrances in the homeland and the home churches, their steady march 'breast forward, never doubting clouds would break', their isolation and their disappointments, their heart searchings when fruit was scanty or depressingly absent, their grappling with the forces of the enemy in terror-striking situations – these and similar factors supply the work of the pioneers with a compelling interest which a mature and more settled work of God does not always produce. Indeed, in the annals of the modern Church, the records of pioneer missionaries who jeoparded their lives to the death in the high places of the field furnish as graphic and colourful a story as the heart and mind of the Christian could wish. It is one which should stir his blood and re-kindle his devotion to the Lord. Of them the witness is borne, 'Known unto God are all His works from the beginning of the world'.

To familiarize the Christian Church in the present day with the records of such outstanding men of God, and also with the lesser though not unworthy purpose of searching out men and women of literary gift, the Banner of Truth Trust in 1962 advertised an Open Competition for the writing of short biographies of pioneer missionaries. A prize of £100 was offered for the best essay submitted; there was to be a second prize of £50, and five of £10. The missionaries selected were John Eliot and David Brainerd (of North America), William Carey and Henry Martyn (of India), Robert Morrison and William Chalmers Burns (of China), Adoniram Judson (of Burma) and John G. Paton (of the New

Hebrides). In the outcome, essays were received from seventy-two competitors, and of these the judges were of the opinion that five were worthy of publication. The premier award went to Mr. R. T. France, M.A., B.D., of Tyndale Hall, Bristol, for his biography of Henry Martyn. Second place was secured by the Rev. John Thornbury, B.A., Baptist minister in Ashland, Kentucky, U.S.A., who wrote on David Brainerd. £10 awards went to the Rev. R. Strang Miller, B.A., LL.M., B.D., Presbyterian minister of Blenheim, New Zealand, for his essay on William Chalmers Burns; to the Rev. N. B. Cryer, M.A., vicar of Addiscombe, Croydon, for his biography of John Eliot; to the Rev. John D. Legg, B.A., B.D., of Reeth, Richmond, Yorkshire, for a Life of John G. Paton; to Mr. W. G. How of Hailsham, Sussex, for a Life of Henry Martyn; and to the Rev. J. T. Orrell of Liverpool for a Life of John Paton. Thanks are due to Mrs. H. F. R. Catherwood for her kind assistance in the work of adjudicating the competition.

Five of these seven biographies are here printed. They supply portraits of men who walked with God, and who threw themselves, body and soul, into the work to which God had called them. They shame much of our easy-going present-day Christianity. Whereas, in this soft modern age, we regard luxuries as necessities, they, in their harder times and sterner habits, esteemed necessities as non-essentials, if only they could preach the Word where Christ had not previously been named or known. Their meat and their drink was to do the will of Him who had sent them, and to finish His work. In them, therefore, within the limits set by human frailty and human incompleteness, we have portraits of Christ Himself. As Christians we have long grown accustomed to the thought that we are to be conformed to the image of God's Son. From the angle supplied by the missionary cause, let the question present its challenge to us in reverse. Said an African chief to a missionary, 'Is Jesus Christ like you?' The reply to the question is not recorded. Let us make the query personal, and as we read of the exploits of the Lord's own 'men of renown', and contrast our own littleness with their greatness, let us seek grace to humble ourselves in the dust for our innate selfishness and love of ease in the divine service; and let this be accompanied by the strong conviction that, in the strength of the Lord and by His mighty power, we too shall become followers of the Lord's servants in the holy war, even as they themselves were followers of Christ.

Dr. Arthur T. Pierson, writing at the commencement of the present century, asserts that 'we are living in days when men are strangely bent on denying the supernatural element in history, and even in the Bible; and God has supplied, in the record of Christian missions, a corrective to this tendency. Those who see this Burning Bush call others to turn aside and see this great sight. Here historic events and human instruments are lit up with a new lustre'.

Indeed they are! By their means individual believers and the home churches as a whole have, in the wisdom of God, received great good. We close with the sage remark of a much-honoured missionary, which is also a note of warning: 'The church that is no longer evangelistic will soon cease to be evangelical'.

S. M. Houghton

March, 1965

DAVID BRAINERD

(Missionary to the Red Indians of North America)

by

JOHN THORNBURY, B.A.

Introduction

Two and a half centuries ago, most of what now comprises the states of New England had been touched only slightly by civilization. Although thriving colonial towns, with their transplanted English culture, dotted the Atlantic coast and the inland waterways, stretching between these settlements were miles of wilderness the beauties and dangers of which few white men had experienced. Where now veins of modern highways and railroads connect sprawling industrial centres, then nothing but rivers and streams threaded the valleys, and pioneer trails penetrated the thick forested hills; where now farms and houses adorn the hill sides, then nature ruled undisturbed by the ox and the plough; where now children play and livestock graze, then the wolf and the deer roamed freely.

The only human inhabitants of this no man's land were tribes of aborigines, the American Indians. Since time began there have been few peoples more backward, abject, and steeped in paganism than they. Politically, they had no national or military bond; economically, they used the most primitive methods in eking out a miserable existence; socially, their customs were extremely barbarian; and religiously, they were sunk in an appalling blindness characterized by strange superstition and demon worship.

It might have been expected that the highly-civilized people who landed on their shores from the sixteenth century onwards would have shown pity on these benighted savages and exercised a measure of restraint when moving into their territories, but from the beginning the Indians experienced little but treachery and abuse from their European neighbours. In fact, most of the 'Christian' Englishmen, with whom they came into contact, taught them to shoot instead of read, and drink instead of pray. Far from instilling in their minds the principles of Christian honesty, they cheated them out of their furs and ornaments, and instead of teaching them to love their fellow men, they drove them like beasts from their homelands. There were, happily, notable exceptions, for some, recognizing the dignity of the human soul, sought to lead them from their spiritual darkness to the Light of the world. To David Brainerd, one of the most heroic of these exceptions, we are now to give our attention. But first a word about one who preceded him.

The first significant effort toward converting the American Indians was undertaken in the mid-seventeenth century by John Eliot (1604–90). A native of Hertfordshire, England, this scholarly man migrated to America in 1631 where he was appointed to the pastorate of a Presbyterian church in Roxbury, Massachusetts. An indefatigable labourer, Eliot combined his work as a pastor with evangelistic work among the Indians. He translated both the Old and New Testaments into the Mohican dialect, published several English theological works for the use of the Indians, and edited an English grammar and primer in their behalf as well. Before Eliot died he had gathered a considerable community of believers from among the savages.

In some respects, Brainerd's labours cannot be regarded as so significant as those of his illustrious predecessor. For one thing, his career was much shorter: only four years as compared to the half-century of Eliot. Furthermore, unlike Eliot, Brainerd never lived to make such scholarly contributions as the translation and publication of books in the Indian languages. It must also be admitted that, were we to judge solely by the number of converts each succeeded in making, Brainerd's measure of success cannot compare with that of Eliot. But in other ways, which the succeeding life will seek to delineate, the career of Brainerd not only eclipses in glory that of the Roxbury pastor but shines brightest of all in the great galaxy of missionary stars.

I. David Brainerd:
His Birth and Early Life (1718–38)

David, the third son of Hezekiah and Dorothy Brainerd, was born
April 21, 1718, at Haddam, Connecticut, a quiet little colonial
village seated on a shelf of land beside the Connecticut river,
25 miles north-east of New Haven. Since his ancestry is not without interest, and his family connections are by no means insignifi-
cant as they relate to his life-work, it will be well to look for
a moment at the stock from which the future missionary
sprang.

His father, says Jonathan Edwards, who edited his diary, was
one of the council members in Connecticut, appointed by the
English king. Hezekiah Brainerd was the son of one Daniel
Brainerd, a justice of the peace, and deacon in the church at
Haddam. More impressive, for our present purpose, is Brainerd's
maternal ancestry. Rev. Peter Hobart, his great-grandfather, was
a Puritan minister who once held a charge at Hingham, Norfolk,
but during days of persecution he crossed the Atlantic and spent
the rest of his life preaching on the American continent. Hobart
had five sons, four of whom were preachers, including Jeremiah,
Brainerd's grandfather. Jeremiah Hobart married the daughter of
the Rev. Samuel Whiting, a minister, first at Boston in Lincoln-
shire and later in Lynn, Massachusetts. Dorothy, the offspring of
the marriage, becoming wife to Hezekiah linked together the
Hobart, Whiting, and Brainerd families.

The religious bias of David Brainerd's forefathers took strong
root in his own immediate family. Of the five male children of
Hezekiah and Dorothy Brainerd, four of them – Nehemiah, John,
Ishmael and David – devoted their lives to preaching the gospel.
Nehemiah ministered at Eastbury, Connecticut, but died of
consumption at the early age of twenty-seven. Ishmael died about
six years later while a student at Yale, and John, David's successor

as Indian pastor, lived to see his sixty-first birthday before going to be with his long-deceased brothers.

Evidently, therefore, the religious tradition to which David Brainerd fell heir was deeply rooted in the Puritanism which had developed in England since the days of Reformation, and which had retained all its native strength when transplanted to American soil.

Primarily due to the lack of reference in his own Diary, our main source of information, we know very little about Brainerd's early years. Other than the death of his father when David was only eight, nothing important happened to him as far as outward circumstances are concerned. But we are, after all, more interested in the spiritual experiences of the youth; and here our curiosity is gratified, because the first entry in the account of his early life informs us that its author was, from his youth, 'somewhat sober and inclined to melancholy'. Brainerd's first comment on his own spiritual history is pregnant with meaning and is, in fact, almost prophetic, for much of his life can be comprehended only in the light of the two qualities which characterized him through all his twenty-nine years: a strict sobriety and an extreme tendency to melancholy. No doubt the majestic, awe-inspiring truths of the Westminster Confession, which he certainly was familiar with quite early, contributed to his 'sobriety', and probably his melancholy disposition was simply an innate trait of character. At any rate, the pensive, sober and meditative youth of Haddam seemed destined to a devout life almost from the start.

When a child of only seven or eight, the solemn truths of religion began to make deep furrows in his heart. At this time he became greatly concerned about his lost condition. Thoughts of death terrified him and spoiled his pleasurable pastimes. Though these extreme early convictions soon wore off, he was driven to a strict performance of religious duties, in which he consistently walked until he was thirteen. Then the waves of conviction swept over him again, and he gave himself up to an even more diligent pursuit of spiritual matters. He describes himself as follows, 'I was frequent, constant, and somewhat fervent in duties; and took delight in reading, especially Mr. Janeway's *Token for Children*.

I felt sometimes much melted in the duties of religion, took great delight in the performance of them, and sometimes hoped that I was converted, or at least in a good and hopeful way for heaven and happiness; not knowing what conversion was. The Spirit of God at this time proceeded far with me. I was remarkably dead to the world; my thoughts were almost wholly employed about my soul's concerns; and I may indeed say, "Almost I was persuaded to be a Christian".'

The seeker's anxiety during this period was considerably increased by the second major tragedy in his already tempest-tossed life, the death of his mother. This shock was followed by a period of decline in his spiritual concern, and he fell into a state of carnal security. His fifteenth year found him in a rather un-happy condition. He was now an orphan, destitute of parents' love, and a lost sinner, walking in the outward forms of religion but without any real peace of mind and heart.

Slightly over a year after his mother's death, Brainerd left his father's house at Haddam and went to East Haddam, another Connecticut river village a few miles to the south, where he lived with friends. The four years he spent there were apparently uneventful, though he records some interesting facts about his soul conflict. With his typical pessimism, he describes himself as one who continued in a 'round of sacred duty', separating him-self as far as possible from the company and amusements of the young, and seeking to please himself with 'good frames' – but all the while 'without God in the world'. He says that his conscience constantly harassed him with guilty feelings because he failed to live up to the moral code he had framed for himself, but concludes that these strivings and strugglings were, after all, worthless since they were self-righteous – not springing from the desire to glorify God.

When he was nineteen, Brainerd made another change of residence. In April, 1937, he left East Haddam and moved to Durham to work on his own farm, evidently a patrimony. For some months, his daylight hours were spent in bodily labour, tilling and cultivating the rich Connecticut soil, but his mind was now soaring to more noble ambitions. He began to dream of a college education, presumably at Yale, which was but a short distance from his farm.

At the age of twenty, David Brainerd was a studious and serious young man of thorough religious conviction. For an unconverted religionist (as he later viewed it) his outward sanctity was remarkable. He says, 'I became very strict and watchful over my thoughts, words, and actions; and thought that I must be sober indeed, because I designed to devote myself to the ministry, and imagined that I did dedicate myself to the Lord.'

It was probably due to his secret purpose of entering the ministry that he left his farm after less than a year and returned to the town of his birth. The pastor of the church at Haddam was then Thaddeus Fiske, a devout Congregationalist, who took an interest in David and invited him into his home. Under the tutelage of his elderly counsellor, his life reached an even higher peak of religious devotion. He abandoned the company of those of his own age and associated himself with 'grave, elderly people'; he spent much time every day in prayer and other secret duties, reading the Bible more than twice through in less than a year; he gave great attention to the public preaching of the gospel and tried to retain all he could from his pastor's sermons. On sabbath evenings, he met with other young people to engage in 'religious exercises', and as soon as the meetings were over he would 'repeat the discourses of the day' to himself. At the end of the Lord's day he strove to meditate on all he had learned during the day, and Monday evenings found him 'recollecting' the same themes. He 'experienced a considerable degree of enjoyment in (religious) duty and had many thoughts of joining the church.'

Had he lived in this day of shallow religious profession, David Brainerd would no doubt have been considered the epitome of true piety during these years when he was still unconverted; perhaps he would have been given the honourable title of 'religious fanatic'. Even those of us who sympathize with his doctrinal views may indulge the speculation that he was a true believer long before the time when he had what he regarded as his conversion experience. But in his own day the church demanded and experienced deep religious feelings and great skill was required in discerning between an 'enlightened' or 'awakened' sinner and a truly converted soul.

Before we judge too hastily in the matter, however, let us remember that Brainerd, more than anyone else, should have known his own heart; and besides, the Bible makes it clear that there are some who have a name to live but are dead. Brainerd says that during this period of religious activity he was not really trusting Christ but was resting solely on his duties and good frames. This being the case, he certainly was not really saved. But whatever was his spiritual state at this period, the appointed time was at hand when the great Redeemer was to capture completely the heart of the Connecticut farm boy and set him forth on his meteoric career, a career making up for its brevity by its burning intensity.

II. His Conversion (1738–39)

There is one basic change which all who receive salvation experience, but God uses a variety of means to lead His chosen into it. It does not come in the same way to all. Many have a violent and stormy experience of conviction, while, to others, God speaks not in the whirlwind, the earthquake, or the fire, but in the still small voice. The strange thing is that the intensity of conviction does not always bear a direct relation to the degree of outward wickedness on the part of the subject. The profligate slave trader, John Newton, testifies that his convictions for sin were comparatively moderate, while the conflict of Bunyan, who certainly was not an abandoned sinner, was, as is well known, extreme. Brainerd seems to have been one of many whose deep convictions had no apparent relation to a past life of great moral deviation. Although given up, more or less, to strict outward piety all his life, the period preceding his conversion, which Bunyan called the Slough of Despond, was unusually painful.

When the pastor of the Haddam church died in November,

1737, David returned to the Brainerd farm and continued religious studies in company with his brother John. Adjacent to his farm were fields and woods where he often resorted for meditation and prayer. He loved to wander out in the open where he could be alone with God. Early in the winter of 1738, he was taking his accustomed walk for prayer when he was overwhelmed with a sense of his danger and the wrath of God. 'I was much dejected', he said, 'kept much alone; and sometimes envied the birds and beasts their happiness, because they were not exposed to eternal misery, as I evidently saw that I was.' This was the beginning of a period of intense inward turmoil which lasted till he walked out into the light of assurance in July of the following year. During this time, he laboured constantly under an opinion which was a source of considerable anguish to his soul. This notion was that there were certain qualities of mind which he had to possess before God would have mercy upon him. It appeared to him that only if he were sufficiently melted because of sin, humble, affectionate in prayer, submissive to God's just disposal of him, and resigned to the doctrines of Scripture could he presume to lay a claim to salvation. Unhappily, however, he arrived at the opinion, though somewhat unconsciously, that were he properly affected, as he called it, God was actually obliged to hear his 'sincere cries'. Of course this view of things turned his eyes inward and drove him to a careful and exacting introspection. He would spend whole days fasting and pleading with God to reveal to him the evil of sin and to break his rebellious heart.

Occasionally he concluded that he had actually reached his goal, being, in his own opinion, quite humble, submissive, affectionate and therefore qualified for saving mercy. But then, to his amazement, he could still find no real comfort. When his distress remained in spite of all his fastings, strivings, meltings and other efforts, a spirit of bitterness would arise in his heart because it appeared that God was dealing hardly with him. This only plunged him more deeply into despair for he knew that such feelings were very displeasing to God.

Sometimes he lost the intensity of his convictions and grew listless and dead, but always he became alarmed and his former convictions returned. 'One night,' he declares, 'I remember in particular, when I was walking solitarily abroad, I had opened to me such a view of my sin, that I feared the ground would cleave asunder under my feet, and become my grave; and would send my soul quick into hell, before I could get home. Though I was forced to go to bed, lest my distress should be discovered by others, which I much feared, yet I scarcely durst sleep at all, for I thought it would be a great wonder if I should be out of hell in the morning.' When these strong convictions increased, he tended once again to rest in them and he became complacent as before. Thus he continued to vacillate between carnal security and despair.

One of the most remarkable elements in Brainerd's early struggle was his attempt to become intellectually reconciled to some of the fundamental doctrines of the Bible. As previously stated, he had an abiding conviction that it was impossible for him to be saved until he possessed certain emotional qualities to prepare him for eternal life, especially a hearty acquiescence in the truths revealed in Scripture pertaining to salvation. Having been a student of the Bible since childhood, he had clear views of what the Scriptures taught on the great themes of sin and salvation. But, to his dismay and consternation, instead of finding these truths pleasant and agreeable to him, his heart was quite 'irritated' when he reflected on them. Three doctrinal facts, especially, he found himself quite opposed to, in spite of all he could do. These were the strictness of the law of God, the fact that faith alone was the condition of salvation, and the sovereignty of God. The first vexed him greatly because he could not, try as he might, live up to the law's demands. This caused him to quarrel with God because of the strictness and rigidity of His law. The second troubled him because he could not find out what faith was and how he could obtain it. But it was the doctrine of divine sovereignty against which he especially rebelled. On this he said, 'I could not bear that it should be wholly at God's pleasure to save or damn me, just as He would. That passage, Rom. 9. 11–23 was a constant vexation to me, especially verse 21. Reading or meditating on this, always destroyed my seeming good frames; for when I thought I was almost humbled, and almost resigned, this passage would make my enmity to the sovereignty of God appear.'

In the summer of 1739, while taking one of his walks in a 'solitary place', his views on some things which had perplexed him became considerably altered. First, he became completely convinced that salvation lay completely beyond his own power. Although he thought he had believed this before, since he had entertained a feeling that he could merit the favour of God by reaching a certain pitch of religious fervour, it is evident that he had not. He now regarded himself as hopelessly lost, believing that nothing he could possibly do could alter his state. Secondly, he reached the conviction that all his past activities in praying, fasting and other exercises were all completely worthless because they were based solely on self-interest and had no respect to the glory of God. He now realized that there was no more virtue or goodness in them – as far as putting God under an obligation to save him was concerned – than 'paddling with his hand in the water' (his own expression). When these feelings emerged he was considerably eased of the distressing struggles which had plagued him for months past.

Finally, on Friday, July 12, 1739, as he was walking in the same solitary place, the light of heaven broke upon his soul. It seems inappropriate to do other than quote his own words: 'Having been thus endeavouring to pray – though, as I thought, very stupid and senseless – for near half an hour; then, as I was walking in a dark thick grove, *unspeakable glory* seemed to open to the view and apprehension of my soul. I do not mean any external brightness, for I saw no such thing; nor do I intend any imagination of a body of light, somewhere in the third heavens, or any thing of that nature; but it was a new inward apprehension or view that I had of God, such as I never had before, nor any thing which had the least resemblance of it. I stood still, wondered, and admired! I knew that I never had seen before any thing comparable to it for excellency and beauty; it was widely different from all the conceptions that ever I had of God, or things divine. I had no particular apprehension of any one person in the Trinity, either the Father, the Son, or the Holy Ghost; but it appeared to be

Divine Glory. My soul rejoiced with joy unspeakable, to see such a God, such a glorious Divine Being; and I was inwardly pleased and satisfied that He should be God over all for ever and ever. My soul was so captivated and delighted with the excellency, loveliness, greatness, and other perfections of God, that I was even swallowed up in Him; at least to that degree, that I had no thought (as I remember) at first, about my own salvation, and scarce reflected that there was such a creature as myself.'

Immediately after this experience, Brainerd was brought to a 'hearty disposition to exalt the Lord', i.e. 'to aim at His honour and glory as the King of the universe'. A feeling of peace and joy filled his heart till 'near dark', and he was 'sweetly composed' in mind all the evening following. The way of salvation through the grace of God, which formerly had been very unattractive to him, now became his soul's delight. 'I was amazed,' he writes, 'that I had not dropped my own contrivances and complied with this lovely, blessed, and excellent way before.' Like Paul, he realized that all his self-righteousness was merely so much dung, and he marvelled that all men did not seek salvation through the righteousness of Christ.

Thus it was that David Brainerd's long search for spiritual peace came to an end. From that moment till his death eight years later, he had little doubt as to his interest in divine saving mercy. He would bear many physical hardships; he would often groan because of his deep feeling of inward corruption; he would spend many dark hours when the face of his Beloved was hidden, but never again did he experience the bitter struggles that preceded his hour of deliverance. The great doctrines of grace, which he had previously despised, now became the source of his most delightful meditations, and from the time the 'unspeakable glory' flooded his spiritual sight, his desire to promote the honour of his Redeemer never abated.

'Unspeakable glory!' We might well remember these words since they are the sum and substance of Brainerd's theology and the driving force of his subsequent life.

III. His College Career (1739–42)

The 1739 Freshman class at Yale (New Haven) listed one David Brainerd, age: 21, home town: Haddam, Connecticut. The chances are that he stood out among his associates from the very first. There was, as far as we know, nothing really extraordinary about his physical appearance; but certain other traits, such as his quiet demeanour and far-off look, undoubtedly made him somewhat peculiar upon close observation. Possibly his extreme shyness and strictness of life and speech made him seem almost effeminate. Some of his favourite expressions, such as 'sweet relish of Christ', 'precious discoveries of God', 'comfortable frame of soul', and 'dear ministers', sound rather odd today to the vast majority, but even in his own time they probably got for him the reputation of being super-pious and affected. But whatever his associates thought of him, the ploughboy from Haddam was in dead earnest.

Brainerd had been very reluctant to enter college, for he feared that amid its many temptations he would be unable to lead a strict religious life. In the months preceding his entrance into college, the Lord had given him some wonderful manifestations of His love. He spoke of God's shining into his heart, refreshing him with divine and heavenly enjoyments, and opening sundry passages of Scripture to him with clearness, power and sweetness. But to his delight the experiences never left him after he went to college. 'I enjoyed considerable sweetness in religion all the winter following,' runs the Diary.

Only a brief bout of the measles in January, 1740, interrupted Brainerd's first year at Yale. His daily schedule included many hours of hard study and, of course, his customary walks in retirement. Shortly before he was taken ill, while engaged in meditation and prayer, he enjoyed a 'sweet refreshing visit from above'. At this time his soul was quite lifted above the fears of death, in fact he experienced a feeling then which returned to him countless times afterwards, only in a much stronger degree: a real longing to leave the world of sin and sorrow and go to be with his Lord.

This delightful season, in his opinion, far exceeded all the joys and pleasures earth could afford.

In June, 1740, while walking in the fields some distance from the college, he again found 'unspeakable sweetness and delight in God'. He thought that if he must continue in this evil world 'he wanted always to be there to behold God's glory'. These tender feelings reached outwards also. He 'dearly loved all mankind and longed that they should enjoy what he enjoyed'. The entire experience is described by Brainerd as 'a little resemblance of heaven'. However, his ambition and diligence in studies curtailed somewhat the frequency of such times alone with God. This was one thing about college which began to vex him.

Another source of grief to him was the carelessness and spiritual apathy of his fellow students. Once his heart was refreshed while partaking of the Lord's supper. When he arose from the communion he thought of the worldliness of his classmates and marvelled that they should conduct themselves so irreligiously.

In August, 1740, a close application to books began to prey on his delicate physical constitution. He became so weak that he began to spit blood, the first sign of the disease that would eventually bring him to a premature grave. Heeding the advice of his tutor, he headed back again for his home on the Haddam farm, determined for the time being to lay aside his studies. He returned to college on November 6.

During his brief retirement, God continued to reveal to him the heinousness of sin and the perfection of the Divine excellencies. On October 18, he made this entry in his Diary: 'In my morning devotions, my soul was exceedingly melted, and bitterly mourned over my exceeding sinfulness and vileness.' But such crushing sights of his own corruption were counterbalanced by joyous transports of fervent affection toward God. 'My soul was carried forth in love to God, and had a lively sense of God's love to me.' 'And this love and hope', he added, 'at that time, cast out fear.' On another occasion, while looking on the sacramental elements and reflecting on the fact that soon Jesus Christ would be 'set forth crucified before him', his soul was almost in ecstasy, causing his body to be so weak that he could hardly stand. 'My soul and all the powers of it seemed, as it were, to melt into softness and sweetness', he writes. So wonderful were these times of retirement that he almost dreaded the return to college. He said, 'I now so longed after God, and to be freed from sin, that when I felt myself recovering, and thought I must return to college again, which had proved so hurtful to my spiritual interest the year past, I could not but be grieved, and I thought I had much rather have died; for it distressed me to think of getting away from God.'

Brainerd's entrance upon his final year at Yale in the Autumn of 1741 was auspicious enough. His mental keenness and hard study had earned for him the topmost position in his class, and though his health remained uncertain, the prospects of his graduating in 1743 could not have been brighter. But alas, how uncertain are the affairs of this earth, where the fondest hopes may soon fade and the brightest schemes can be quickly dashed in pieces! Certainly Brainerd was to learn by bitter experience of the vicissitudes of temporal circumstances, for in the winter of 1741–2 he became the unwilling, and largely undeserving, victim of a tragic misfortune. None could have foreseen the humiliating setback which awaited the prayerful student, the galling effects of which never fully left him.

The indirect cause of Brainerd's expulsion from College was the extraordinary religious upheaval which shook New England in the late 1730's and the early 1740's. It began in Northampton, Massachusetts, in 1734 under the ministry of Jonathan Edwards. The Spirit of God worked so mightily there that virtually the entire town became baptized in a holy flame of supernatural influence. This awakening spread rapidly to many other places in the colonies. It broke out in New Jersey in 1736 in connection with the labours of William and Gilbert Tennent. Revivals also visited such places as Newark (1738) where Jonathan Dickinson preached, and Harvard (1739) with John Seccomb leading the way.

But the great impetus to these somewhat disjointed and isolated outbreaks came in the winter of 1739 when the seraphic George Whitefield visited the colonies. All the tiny streams of spiritual fervour seemed, under his ministry, to converge, as it were, into a torrent of divine power. As he went up and down the colonies, multitudes were charmed by his sacred oratory and thousands received salvation. Scarcely a spot in the English settlements was left untouched by this mighty man of God.

Inevitably the awakening had an impact on the college at New Haven. Several of the students began to attend the preaching of men like Gilbert Tennent and were greatly affected. A general concern for the soul's interests spread among the student body, resulting in increased sobriety and a remarkable transformation of manners. As might have been expected, Brainerd took a great interest in the awakening among the students and soon became one of its most ardent supporters.

Unfortunately, some of the tutors in the college were not sympathetic toward the stirring in their midst. This was especially true of the newly-appointed Rector, Thomas Clap. He was thoroughly opposed to these 'wild fire enthusiasts' and especially disliked their standard-bearer, George Whitefield. When the spirit of revival invaded the campus, the rigid head of the college tried to squelch it by forbidding the students to attend any of these separate 'revival' meetings.

Judicious students of the awakening have conceded that though it was based on sound principles, broadly speaking, and though it produced many wholesome and abiding effects on the community at large, it was attended with a measure of excess in some places. Jonathan Edwards, than whom none was better qualified to judge in the matter, said that 'an intemperate, imprudent zeal, and a degree of enthusiasm soon crept in, and mingled itself with that revival of religion.' For example, it became common, apparently, for some of the more unskilled friends of the revival to denounce certain other professors of Christianity with an unbecoming sharpness. This was a misdemeanour into which Brainerd himself fell.

When the awakening was at its height at Yale, some of the students, Brainerd included, often met together for religious conversation. On one occasion a certain tutor named Whittelsey, sensing the revival spirit in the college, attempted, it seems, to appear quite moved and overwrought while leading in prayer in chapel. After the service, a few in attendance remained to discuss religious affairs, when Brainerd was asked by a fellow student what he thought of the one who had just prayed. His answer, 'He has no more grace than this chair' (as he pointed to one of the seats in the hall) was sincere but unfortunate, for it soon reached other ears. The enraged rector, already in a bad mood because of the revival and probably looking for some specific incident upon which to vent his wrath, summoned the offender into his presence. He extorted from Brainerd all the details of the offence and then demanded of him a public confession and show of repentance before the whole college. When Brainerd not only refused to do this but persisted in attending forbidden meetings, he was summarily dismissed.*

Whether the chapel chair actually had as much grace as tutor Whittelsey is a matter of no consequence to us today, but it is certain that Brainerd should not have divulged his opinion, even in private. In fact, he later felt that his spirit and conduct in the whole affair was unchristian. But assuming that he was guilty of a rash and, as Edwards would say, 'intemperate' remark, candour forces us to ask whether the severity of the punishment was not altogether disproportionate to the nature of the offence. For one thing, the statement was not made in public, and who could stand if all secret utterances were noised abroad? Why should Brainerd have been required to humiliate himself before the entire college when at worst it was but a private offence? As it fell out, for better or for worse, Brainerd's college career was forever at an end.

IV. Interlude:
Preparation for Mission Work (1742-43)

The misfortune of February, 1742, was a crushing blow to the soul of one who already, as Edwards put it, 'was by constitution and temper prone to melancholy and dejection of spirit.' More than once his Diary reveals the bitter grief caused to Brainerd by the loss of his college status. On July 3, 1742, he wrote, 'The disgrace

*Also entering into the dismissal was a charge that Brainerd had said some uncomplimentary things about the rector himself. Brainerd denied the charge.

I was laid under at College seemed to damp me, as it opens the mouth of opposers. I had no refuge but in God.' Edwards, who knew him as a father knows a son, said that his subsequent gloominess during his missionary labours was due in no small measure to this.

The story of Brainerd's relation to the college took an even sadder turn after his dismissal. On several occasions he actually went back to New Haven and tried to effect a reconciliation with the offended governors, but in vain. A number of prominent ministers including Aaron Burr, Ebenezer Pemberton, and a group from the Hartford, Connecticut association also interposed in his behalf, but with a similar lack of success. At length Brainerd sent a full and formal apology in which he confessed that 'he had sinned against God, acted contrary to the rules of His word, and injured Mr. Whittelsey', conceding that his 'behaviour did not become a Christian – that it did not savour of the humble respect he should have had toward the tutor.' 'Reflecting with grief on the act', he 'was willing to be low and abased before God and man' for it. In this apology, he 'humbly asked the forgiveness of the governors of the college and of the whole society, and especially Mr. Whittelsey.' Eventually, after Brainerd had become quite involved in his mission work, the heads of the college seemed willing to take him back; but then it was too late. Seldom has anyone suffered so intensely and been dealt with so severely over so trifling an offence.

But He who 'maketh the wrath of man to praise him' designed good for His servant in this affair, for it caused his mind to be turned toward that sphere of labour to which the remainder of his life was devoted. In the outcome he made an indelible mark in the history of Christian missions and attained a fame far excelling the honours which would no doubt have been conferred upon him as one of the ablest students of the year.

In the spring of 1742, for the second time in his life, Brainerd found shelter with the family of a minister, this time Jedediah Mills, himself a Yale graduate and a true man of God. In the quiet confines of this pastor's home, he pursued his favourite pastimes: reading, prayer, fasting and meditation. In the Journal, under the date May 11, another of those statements appears which are so indicative of the set of his soul: 'Alas! I cannot live in the midst of a tumult. I long to enjoy God alone.'

These times of retirement deepened his commitment to Christ and acquainted him more fully with the laws of spiritual growth. His devotion reached an advanced stage. April 14, 'My soul longed for communion with Christ, and for the mortification of indwelling corruption, especially spiritual pride.' April 27, 'O my sweet Saviour! O my sweet Saviour! whom have I in heaven but thee? and there is none upon earth that I desire beside thee. If I had had a thousand lives, my soul would gladly have laid them all down at once, to have been with Christ.' June 18, 'My soul seemed to breathe after holiness, a life of constant devotedness to God.'

His sense of undoneness and unworthiness increased. April 10, 'I am made to possess the sins of my youth, and the dreadful sin of my nature. I am all sin; I cannot think, nor act, but every motion is sin.' April 13, 'I saw myself to be very mean and vile; and wondered at those that showed me respect.' July 22, 'Journeying from Southbury to Ripton, I called at a house by the way, where being very kindly entertained and refreshed, I was filled with amazement and shame, that God should stir up the hearts of any to show so much kindness to such a dead dog as I.' Such self-abasement seems to follow the pattern of one of old who said, 'I am the chief of sinners.'

July, 1742, found Brainerd at Danbury, Connecticut, where he was examined by an association of Presbyterian ministers on his doctrinal views and acquaintance with experimental religion; and, passing all the tests they applied, he was licensed to preach the gospel.

During the summer and autumn of this year, he spent a considerable time in the fellowship of Christian friends, among whom was the well-known Joseph Bellamy, minister at Bethlehem, Connecticut, and in preaching the gospel in various places, sometimes with considerable effect. The college affair showed another of its seamy aspects in September, for on the sixth, Brainerd was informed that some were lying in wait to arrest and imprison him for preaching, as he had done recently, at New Haven. Fear of being jailed kept him from attending the yearly 'commencement exercises' where he could have seen some of his old friends. He stayed in the woods instead.

Shortly after he took up residence with Mr. Mills, Brainerd's heart began to yearn for the salvation of the Indian tribes scattered along the colonial trails in his homeland and in the vast expanses further west. On April 8 he wrote, 'Had raised hopes today respecting the heathen. Oh that God would bring in great numbers of them to Jesus Christ! I cannot but hope that I shall see that glorious day.' He began to take great delight in praying for their conversion, in fact he found the thought of personally undergoing the greatest sufferings – even banishment from his native land – for the spiritual well-being of the Indians, very pleasant to his mind. One afternoon he so agonized in prayer for the advancement of Christ's kingdom among the heathen that he was quite wet with perspiration. In the following months, purposes of dedicating himself to the task of Indian evangelism rapidly crystallized.

Brainerd's moment of opportunity came on November 19 (1742), when he received a letter from a certain Ebenezer Pemberton of New York who requested that he come immediately to discuss the possibility of his engaging in work among Indians and to meet a few deeply interested persons. Pemberton was the 'Secretary of the Correspondents in New York, New Jersey, and Pennsylvania' of *The Society in Scotland for the Propagation of Christian Knowledge*. This enterprising society originated in Edinburgh in 1709 and was one of several British missionary societies which supported evangelistic enterprises in the backwoods of America. Thirty years later, several American ministers, among whom were Ebenezer Pemberton, Jonathan Dickinson of New Jersey, and Aaron Burr of New Jersey, petitioned the society to undertake work on behalf of the Indians. Immediately a response came. Funds were appropriated for two missionaries, and Correspondents were appointed to inspect and report on the work as it developed. Pemberton was appointed secretary and Burr treasurer, and gospel work among the Redskins was inaugurated forthwith. The first chosen to this business was Azariah Horton who was directed to labour among the Indians at Montauk on Long Island.

The Correspondents then went about finding another to engage in Indian evangelism. Aaron Burr, having some acquaintance with Brainerd, and recognizing his ability and interest in the heathen, proposed to his friends that he should be summoned to New York to be interviewed.

As might have been expected, Brainerd, at the time of his interview, felt himself to be quite unfit for the task. While willing to respond to the invitation, he looked upon himself as ignorant and unworthy – the worst wretch that ever lived. The examiners had a better opinion of him, however. His humility, his thorough acquaintance with doctrine, and his obvious zeal for the salvation of the lost quickly obtained for him a favourable verdict.

For some time the commissioners of the Scottish society had been interested in thousands of unevangelized Indians residing in North-western Pennsylvania. There were several tribes living near the forks of the Delaware river, and others further west on the banks of the Susquehanna, who had never heard the good news of salvation. Brainerd's original commission in the autumn of 1742 was to work among these groups. It was at first the intention of the Society, in fact, to send him immediately; but the winter being extremely severe, it was decided to defer the undertaking till the following March. This would give Brainerd time to settle his personal affairs, bid farewell to his friends, and gain some acquaintance with Indian mission work by conferring with his senior colleague, Azariah Horton, on Long Island.

Between November, 1742 and March of the following year, Brainerd made final preparations for his life-work. Travelling alone on his horse, sometimes through bitter cold and blinding snow, he went from place to place, visiting his friends, whom he never expected to see again, disposing of his personal belongings,*

*One interesting thing here deserves at least a note. Expecting to spend the rest of his life among the Indians, he decided to sell his estate, which he had received from his father, and use the money in the most profitable way. He felt that it could be best used to finance a promising young minister through college. Such a young man was chosen and the money appropriated for that purpose.

[34]

preaching wherever he had opportunity, and generally condition-
ing himself for the toils that lay ahead. He eagerly anticipated
the time when he could speak of Christ's redeeming love to the
Indians, but he was not ignorant of the difficulties he would
encounter. He knew that untold hardships – hunger, cold, loneliness, perhaps death – lay ahead. But his mind was made up.
God had called him; he must follow.

After preaching his farewell sermon in East Haddam 'at the
house of an aged man, who had been unable to attend on the
public worship for some time', and spending a few days with the
Indians at Montauk, he went to Woodbridge, New Jersey, for
his final conference with the commissioners. But since he last saw
them, there had been new developments. Contention had arisen
between the white people and the Indians at the Delaware, which
did not augur well for a missionary enterprise there.

But another door was opening. John Sergeant, who had a mission outpost at Stockbridge, Massachusetts, informed the correspondents that the prospects were bright for a successful attempt
at converting a community of Indians at Kaunaumeek, New York.
Brainerd was reassigned this place as the field of his incipient
missionary endeavours.

V. Kaunaumeek (1743–44)

It seemed providential that Brainerd should go to New York
rather than Pennsylvania. Since Stockbridge was only twenty
miles from Kaunaumeek, while stationed there he would have an
opportunity of frequent conference with John Sergeant, an experienced missionary who could give him helpful instruction on
various aspects of Indian evangelism. Also, fellowship with Sergeant and his wife would alleviate the hardships of his work.

Eight days of hard riding brought the missionary to Stockbridge on March 21. After a visit to the Sergeants lasting barely
two days, he headed into the forests toward Kaunaumeek with a

few clothes, enough food for his trip, a Hebrew lexicon, and a heart filled with love for God and immortal souls.

Brainerd's residence for the time being was to be at the home of the McGinlays, Scottish pioneers who lived a short distance from the Indian village. Their cabin was nothing elaborate – barely shelter in fact, but at least it was a place where he could get alone with God and be protected from the elements. A twenty-mile ride through very wild country brought him to their door.

Brainerd's attempts to minister to the Indians were soon begun. On April 10, he 'rose early in the morning, walked out and spent a considerable time in the woods in prayer and meditation' and then went to the Indians. He preached twice with the following results recorded: 'They behaved soberly in general; two or three in particular appeared under some religious concern; with these I discoursed privately; and one told me, "her heart had cried, ever since she heard me preach first".'

A few encounters with the Indians convinced him of the difficulties of his work. On April 16, after preaching, he was quite discouraged, 'I feared that nothing would ever be done for them to any happy effect', he wrote. One problem was his difficulty in communicating with the Indians. He needed an interpreter greatly. In May he secured a Christian Indian named Wauwaum-pequunnaunt who had been instructed by Mr. Sergeant to convert his messages into the Indian dialect. This was a considerable assistance.

Not only were the difficulties of preaching to the Indians great, but he soon felt the pinch of loneliness and poverty. A letter to his brother John, then a student at Yale, dated April 30, gives a touching insight into his temporal circumstances. In it he said, 'I live in the most lonely melancholy desert, about eighteen miles from Albany; . . . I board with a poor Scotchman; his wife can talk scarce any English. My diet consists mostly of hasty-pudding, boiled corn, and bread baked in the ashes, and sometimes a little meat and butter. My lodging is a little heap of straw, laid upon some boards, a little way from the ground; for it is a log room, without any floor, that I lodge in. My work is exceeding hard and difficult: I travel on foot a mile and a half, the worst of ways, almost daily, and back again; for I live so far from my Indians. I have not seen an English person this month. These, and many other circumstances, equally uncomfortable, attend me; and yet my spiritual conflicts and distresses so far exceed all these, that I scarce think of them, or hardly observe that I am not entertained in the most sumptuous manner. The Lord grant that I may learn to "endure hardness, as a good soldier of Jesus Christ!"'

Brainerd's interpreter did so well that he decided to start an Indian school at Kaunaumeek and employ him as schoolmaster. In connection with this enterprise, he made a number of trips to New York to consult with the correspondents. These trips occasioned considerable hardship. Once he was lost in the woods and had to lie out in the open air. These outward adversities, combined with his inward conflicts, depressed him greatly. His trials so crushed his spirit that sometimes he wished that, while travelling through the thick brakes, he could 'drop . . . into everlasting oblivion'.

In September, 1743, Brainerd journeyed to Yale at 'commencement time', partly in order to enjoy 'religious and spiritual conversation', and partly to seek better relations with the college officials. He trembled at the thought of witnessing his classmates receive their degrees*; but when the time came, the Lord gave him 'more comfort than he expected'. This was a very important visit for Brainerd because, while at New Haven, he became personally acquainted with Jonathan Edwards of Northampton, Massachusetts, who was also there. Edwards had learned of Brainerd's troubles, and was one of the many influential persons who were interested in removing the stigma the college had put on him. The missionary sought the counsel of Edwards about these matters and found in him a kind and faithful friend. This was the beginning of a firm friendship between the two. The great theologian was destined to exert an immense influence over the life and character of Brainerd.

*Jonathan Edwards comments, 'His trial was the greater, in that, had it not been for the displeasure of the governors of the college, he would not only on that day have shared with his class-mates in the public honours which they then received, but would, on that occasion, have appeared at the *head* of that class; which, if he had been with them, would have been the most numerous of any that ever had been graduated at that college.'

In spite of such trials as the physical hardships connected with his preaching, an overwhelming sense of his personal unworthiness, times of hidings of God's face, and distress over his college disgrace, Brainerd possessed a meek, patient, and elevated spirit. Amid his many difficulties, he said, 'It is good for me to be afflicted that I may die wholly to this world.' Again he wrote, 'I felt contented with my circumstances, and sweetly resigned to God. In prayer I enjoyed great freedom, and blessed God as much for my present circumstances as if I had been a king, and thought that I found a disposition to be contented in any circumstances. Blessed be God.'

Another letter he wrote to his brother John in December is interesting because it reveals something of his contempt for the comforts of the world and the high standard he set for Christians, especially ministers. He wrote, 'The whole world appears to me like a huge vacuum, a vast empty space, whence nothing desirable, or at least satisfactory, can possibly be derived; and I long daily to die more and more to it; even though I obtain not that comfort from spiritual things which I earnestly desire. Worldly pleasures, such as flow from greatness, riches, honours, and sensual gratifications, are infinitely worse than none. May the Lord deliver us more and more from these vanities. ... I find nothing more conducive to a life of Christianity, than a diligent, industrious, and faithful improvement of precious time. Let us then faithfully perform that business, which is allotted to us by divine Providence, to the utmost of our bodily strength and mental vigour. Why should we sink and grow discouraged with any particular trials and perplexities we are called to encounter in the world? Death and Eternity are just before us; a few tossing billows more will waft us into the world of spirits, and we hope, through infinite grace, into endless pleasure, and uninterrupted rest and peace.'

After a year at Kaunaumeek, Brainerd's accomplishments were not impressive, but he had at least gained a sample of the lot of a missionary to the Redskins. He had built himself a hut to live in, successfully maintained sustenance for himself and his horse, disciplined himself to riding in inclement weather and sleeping on straw, and learned the Indian language well enough to converse in it with considerable freedom.

As the spring of 1744 approached, the situation at Kaunaumeek did not look encouraging. For one thing, there were few Indians left. White men were stealing their lands and frightening them into a westward retreat. It now seemed that the best thing to do would be to persuade the few remaining Indians to move to Stockbridge where they could be under the teaching of Mr. Sergeant.

When Brainerd informed the Indians that he planned to leave them, they were very sorrowful and tried to persuade him to remain. They urged that they had now heard so much about their souls' concerns that they could not bear the thought of being without a minister. When he reminded them that others in far distant regions needed the gospel also, they replied that those Indians were not willing to become Christians as were they. Such importunity is evidence that his ministry at Kaunaumeek had not been without some good effect. At length they consented to move to Stockbridge, and Brainerd set out for New Jersey to receive further instructions from the Correspondents.

VI.   The Forks of the Delaware (1744-45)

While travelling eastwards in March, 1744, Brainerd encountered circumstances which, had he not been singularly dedicated, could easily have dissuaded him from further Indian mission work. In Sheffield, Massachusetts, he met a messenger from East Hampton on Long Island who had been commissioned unanimously by the townspeople to invite and urge Brainerd to labour among them as their minister. According to Edwards, this invitation had come from one of the largest and most wealthy parishes of an island famous for its beauty and prosperity. Humanly speaking, this was a golden opportunity for him to relinquish his design of continuing in his Indian work, which he knew would only bring greater misery, and settle down in a pleasant community to minister among a devoted and appreciative people.

Only three days later, he received news of a second congregation which was anxious to secure his services as pastor. Feeling himself definitely called to a life of self-denial in ministering among the Redskins, however, he never gave these attractive offers a moment's serious consideration. He was determined to forsake all earthly comforts and spend his life in the waste places of the earth.

His new assignment was the one which had been originally given him: to evangelize the Indians on the Forks of the Delaware. After making a final check at Stockbridge to see that the Indians there were well cared for, he promptly started in that direction. On May 8, after a ride of forty-five miles, he reached Fishkill, in New York State, a town located on the east side of the Hudson river near modern Beacon. The next day he crossed the Hudson and travelled one hundred miles almost due west through the same State. As his homeland removed further behind him, the wilderness more and more took on a 'desolate and hideous' aspect. It is no wonder that when he thought upon the difficulties of going alone into the wilds of the Delaware region his heart was ready to sink. But he remembered that others of God's children had 'wandered about in caves and dens of the earth'. Also, he thought of Abraham who, when he was called to go forth, went out, not knowing whither he went. This comforted him.

Several times during this trip, he visited Indians and had opportunity to discourse with them about Christianity.

On Saturday, May 12, he came upon a settlement of Irish and Dutch twelve miles above where the Delaware river divides. The next morning, his beloved Lord's Day, he found the settlers going about their ordinary business and the children at play. How different this was from the delightful Sabbaths he had spent at Haddam! His spirits were damped further by an unsuccessful attempt to secure an interpreter and the news that the Indians were quite scattered in that vicinity.

The lone prophet lost no time in applying himself to the work of ministering to the Indians. All day long he rode from place to place collecting audiences and telling them of the grace of God, while never neglecting his own daily seasons of necessary retirement. He also found opportunity to preach to the Irish settlers. Although much dejected by the heathenism and irreligion of those among whom he was dwelling, and though frequently lonely and disconsolate, Brainerd was happy to be where God had placed him. He rejoiced that God was his portion, and sometimes he was enabled to rely confidently on God to do a mighty work among the pagan tribes. Often he preached with considerable freedom and power, and his hearers showed much concern for their souls.

At this juncture, when he had scarcely settled down in his new quarters, the Correspondents who had directed him decided that he needed to be ordained. It took two days of hard riding in the hot, sultry June weather before he reached Newark where the ordination was to take place. After an examination, a probation sermon on the assigned text, Acts 26. 17–18, another examination – the subject: his experimental acquaintance with Christianity – and an ordination sermon the next day, the weary traveller was again sent on his way.* By June 24, though extremely feeble and scarcely able to walk, he was back among his Indians in the Forks of the Delaware.

Brainerd's Diary during this period reveals something of his greatness as a missionary and gives a clue to the reasons for his eventual wonderful success. For one thing, it is evident that his work thus far among the Indians had increased his desire that Christ should set up His kingdom among them. A continual viewing of these people in their utter spiritual blindness and degradation only make him more determined to strive for their salvation. On July 6, 1744, he said, 'Last year, I longed to be prepared for a world of glory, and speedily to depart out of this world; but of late all my concern almost is for the conversion of the Heathen; and for that end I long to live.' On July 21, he wrote,

---

* Ebenezer Pemberton, who preached the sermon at the ordination, told the missionary society in a letter that Brainerd was universally approved and uncommonly qualified for the work of the ministry. He said, 'He seems to be armed with a great deal of self-denial and animated with a noble zeal.'

'I exceedingly longed that God would get to Himself a name among the heathen.' The trials he had to endure seemed nothing when viewed in the light of the glorious goal before him, as the following entry shows: 'I had no notion of joy from this world; I cared not where or how I lived, or what hardships I went through, so that I could but gain souls for Christ.'

And yet, how difficult, even impossible, this seemed from a human standpoint! Problems were endless; earth and hell seemed combined to prevent the spiritual transformation of the Indians. They were so scattered throughout the region that only by riding from one camp to another could he preach to them in any substantial numbers. Their devotion to idolatrous feasts and dances seemed unbreakable. Religious teachers known as powwows* threatened to enchant and poison the Indians if they accepted Christ. Add to this the difficulties involved in the translating of Christian teachings and terminology into languages the Indians could understand, and one can see why he was faint of heart. No wonder he remarked, 'To an eye of reason, everything that respects the conversion of the Heathen is as black as midnight'!

How did he deal with these problems? The weapons of his warfare were not carnal but spiritual. First, he had great confidence in and reliance on the power of God for the salvation of the Indians. As he reflected upon the greatness and the difficulty of his work, he found great comfort in relying wholly upon God for success. He 'saw with the greatest certainty, that the arm of the Lord must be revealed, for the help of these poor Heathen, if ever they were to be delivered from the bondage of the powers of darkness'. So far from sinking into despair, he 'had strong hope that God would bow the heavens and come down and do some marvellous work among the Heathen.' As he considered the greatness and the power of God, no obstacle seemed insurmountable. 'It seemed to me', he once said, 'that there could be no impediment sufficient to obstruct that glorious work, seeing the living God, as I strongly hoped, was engaged for it.'

But Brainerd did not expect that God would do this work apart from the use of means. He laboured constantly under a

---

* More will be said later about one of these strange persons.

sense of his obligation to use to the fullest the means which God normally employs in saving sinners, particularly that of prayer. Since the conversion of the Indians lay wholly beyond the power of any created arm, and since it was God alone who could accomplish this work, he travailed long hours in intercessory supplication. He habitually poured out his soul to God alone in the forest that He would make bare His arm for the salvation of the Indians. While riding alone on the wooded trails he persistently 'lifted up his heart for assistance' in his momentous undertaking. It was nothing for him to go whole days without food as he agonized over souls. A diary entry dated June 28 (1744) records a typical illustration of his practice of intercession: 'Spent the morning in reading several parts of the Holy Scripture, and in fervent prayer for my Indians, that God would set up His kingdom among them, and bring them into His church.' He was determined (if we may adapt the words of Isaiah the prophet) to give the Almighty no rest till He had made the Indian settlements a praise in the earth.

Yet after a year's labour at the Forks of the Delaware, Brainerd seemed to have done little more good than he had done at Kaunaumeek. He had succeeded in causing many of the Indians to abandon some of the worst excesses linked with their heathen customs, and often considerable crowds had listened with solemn faces and wet eyes as he pointed them to Christ, but up to the middle of June, 1745 – two full years after he had begun his mission work – he had failed to make a single convert. About this time, he began to regard himself as a burden to the missionary society which had commissioned him, and he entertained serious thoughts of giving up his position should he not see more success in the coming year.

VII. Crossweeksung (1745)

'We are now come to that part of Brainerd's life, wherein he had his greatest success in his labours for the good of souls, and in his particular business as a missionary to the Indians. Long had he agonized in prayer, and travailed in birth for their conversion. Often had he cherished the hope of witnessing that desirable event, only to find that hope yield to fear, and end in disappointment. But after a patient continuance in prayer, in labour, and in suffering, as it were through a long night, at length he is permitted to behold the dawning of the day. "Weeping continues for a night; but joy comes in the morning." He went forth weeping, bearing precious seed; and now he comes rejoicing, bringing his sheaves with him. The desired event is brought to pass at last; but at a time, in a place, and upon subjects, that scarce ever entered into his heart.' These words are those of Jonathan Edwards, the editor of Brainerd's Diary. They are a fitting introduction to the most fruitful period of his life.

When Brainerd first heard about the Indians residing some eighty-five miles south of the Forks of the Delaware, he immediately considered going there to preach. Although a year at Kaunaumeek and over a year at the Forks had yielded little fruit, he still entertained hopes that God would set up His kingdom among them. With mingled hopes and fears he began his journey.

He arrived at Crossweeksung on June 19 and met with a different reception almost immediately from the Indians located there. Though at first disappointed at the way they were scattered about, there being only a few families in each place, he found them well disposed to listen to the preaching. They were serious and attentive and not inclined to cavil and object as the Indians elsewhere had done. The few women and children who formed his first congregations were so much interested that they travelled as far as fifteen miles in a day to tell others of the white man who spoke of Jesus the Saviour. Brainerd likened them to the woman of Samaria, since they 'seemed desirous that others should see the man who had told them what they had done in their lives past and the misery that attended their idolatrous ways'.

Interest in his preaching began to increase in every direction like a spreading flame. Three days after he had arrived, the hearers had increased from seven or eight to nearly thirty. All were very solemn and appeared impressed with the message. The power of God was obviously accompanying the word. Several of the hearers were brought under deep concern for their souls; 'they wept, and wished that Christ would save them.' Indians began now to come from all points of the compass to hear the 'new thing', requesting Brainerd to preach twice a day. Greatly encouraged, he cheerfully complied with the invitation.

On July 2, he informed them that he felt it his duty to visit once again the Indians at the Forks of the Delaware. When they heard this, they enquired earnestly when he would return and promised that if he would come again they would all meet and live together so as to be able to benefit further from his instructions. They also said they would try to induce Indians in more remote areas to come and hear the gospel.

Upon his departure, several in particular were much exercised over their souls. One woman with many tears said 'that she wished God would change her heart'; another, that 'she wanted to find Christ'; and an old chief wept bitterly because of his lost condition. After warning them not to stifle their convictions or lose their good impressions, he left, promising to return as soon as his health and business in other places would allow.

Since the beginning of his mission work at Kaunaumeek, Brainerd had frequently seen his expectations for a work of God among the Indians disappointed. Time and time again his courage had been severely tried because the convictions manifest among his hearers had proved to be like the morning cloud. For this reason, he scarcely dared hope that the good signs at Crossweeksung would continue. While the enlargement of Christ's kingdom was the all-consuming passion of his soul, he had experienced so many futile attempts at attaining that end that when the awakening began at Crossweeksung, much in the manner of Job he cried, 'If I had called, and he had answered me, yet would I not believe that he had hearkened unto my voice'. But now he was not to be denied. Jacob-like, he had prevailed.

It was on his return to the Forks of the Delaware in July, 1745, that Brainerd saw the first-fruits of an Indian harvest. The Spirit of God was manifestly at work, and the results of two and a half years of toil began to appear. The history of Moses Finda Fautaury

– for such was the interpreter's name – is highly interesting though space permits only a brief summary. At the time of his conversion, he was about fifty years of age. He had originally been a drunkard, but after hearing Brainerd a few times he was awakened to see his need of salvation. In August, 1744, his convictions so prevailed that he could scarcely sleep. He described his experiences as one who was pressing towards heaven, but 'his way was hedged up with thorns so that he could not stir an inch further'. He soon sank into a state of hopeless despair, feeling that it was 'impossible for him ever to help himself through this insupportable difficulty'. 'It signifies just nothing at all,' he lamented, 'for me to strive and struggle any more.' But feeling himself totally beyond the strength of any created arm, he fell helpless into the arms of Christ who spoke, as it were audibly, to him saying, 'There is hope, there is hope!' He received that hope and became a devout Christian.

But back to Crossweeksung. When Brainerd left in July he had caught little more than a glimpse of 'a cloud like a man's hand'; upon his return a few weeks later, the heavens were showering blessings, and the winds of revival were blowing with ever-increasing strength. The first week of his return saw an intensification of the concern apparent formerly. As Brainerd preached of the love of Christ and admonished sinners to come to Him, his voice was almost drowned in the sobs and groans of souls in travail. Whereas before, his most earnest pleadings and importunate warnings were apparently without result, now the simplest word about the grace of God in Christ fell upon the hearts of the Redskins with crushing power. On August 7, many were affected bodily by the arrows of the Almighty. So distressed were some that they fell upon the ground like the wounded in battle, crying incessantly for mercy. People who journeyed from remote places were seized with concern as soon as they came to the meetings.

But these were mere mercy drops. On August 8, a deluge of pentecostal power broke upon the Indians. Brainerd's own words alone can give an adequate description of events. 'There was much visible concern among them, while I was discoursing publicly; but afterwards, when I spoke to one and another more particularly, whom I perceived under much concern, the power of God seemed to descend upon the assembly "like a rushing mighty wind", and with an astonishing energy bore down all before it. I stood amazed at the influence that seized the audience almost universally, and could compare it to nothing more aptly than the irresistible force of a mighty torrent or swelling deluge, that with its insupportable weight and pressure bears down and sweeps before it whatever is in its way. Almost all persons of all ages were bowed down with concern together, and scarce one was able to withstand the shock of this surprising operation. Old men and women who had been drunken wretches for many years, and some little children not more than six or seven years of age, appeared in distress for their souls, as well as persons of middle age. And it was apparent that these children, some of them at least, were not merely frighted with seeing the general concern; but were made sensible of their danger, the badness of their hearts, and their misery without Christ, as some of them expressed it. The most stubborn hearts were now obliged to bow.'

The depth of concern manifest in the assemblies did not subside after the people dispersed. There were mourners in every house, pouring out their souls to God. The Crossweeksung Indian village, with fathers and mothers, as well as little children, praying to God individually began to appear to Brainerd like another Hadadrimmon – each soul 'mourning apart'. (Zech. 12. 10–12.)

There were many outstanding cases of God's work in specific individuals. One instance cannot be passed over. A young Indian woman, who, according to Brainerd, had never before heard that there was such a thing as the soul, hearing that there was something strange going on among the Indians, came to a meeting, apparently out of curiosity. While he was preaching, she cried out with distress as though her heart would break. After the service, she lay upon the ground many hours crying out, 'Guttummaukalummeh wechaumeh kmeleh Ndah', meaning, 'Have mercy on me and help me to give you my heart'. 'This was indeed a surprising day of God's power', says Brainerd, 'and seemed enough to convince an atheist of the truth, importance, and power of God's word.'

All this was but the beginning of the work effected by God's Spirit. Before the month was over, twenty-five persons had professed faith in Christ and given solid evidence of a genuine change of heart. On August 25, with a considerable crowd of Indians and whites looking on, Brainerd baptized the converts. After the spectators were gone he reminded the new-born souls of the solemn obligations they were now under to live to God, and warned them of the dangerous consequences of careless behaviour after a profession of faith. The evangelist was now becoming the pastor of a believing flock.

VIII. Crossweeksung Continued (1745–46)

The unusual manifestation of divine power just described was the prelude to what proved to be a thorough work of God among the Indians at Crossweeksung. In the ensuing months, Brainerd's ministry continued to be attended with uninterrupted success. Day after day his messages came not in word only but in power and demonstration of the Holy Spirit. The entries in his Journal, containing the record of the moving of the Spirit of God, might well be the envy of any pastor or missionary. The following are typical of the whole:

'August 26, (1745). Preached to my people from John 6. 51–55. . . . Opened to them the persevering nature of those consolations which Christ gives His people, and which I trusted He had bestowed upon some in that assembly; showed them that such have already the beginnings of eternal life, and that their heaven shall speedily be completed. . . . I no sooner began to discourse in this strain, than the dear Christians in the congregation began to be melted with affection to, and desire of the enjoyment of Christ, and of a state of perfect purity. They wept affectionately, yet joyfully; and their tears and sobs discovered brokenness of heart, and yet were attended with real comfort and sweetness.

'Lord's day, October 6. In the evening, expounded Acts 20. 1–12. There was at this time a very agreeable melting spread through the whole assembly. I think I scarce ever saw a more desirable affection in any number of people in my life. There was scarce a dry eye to be seen among them . . . I could not but earnestly wish that numbers of God's people had been present at this season to see and hear these things, which I am sure must refresh the heart of every true lover of Zion's interest. To see those, who very lately were savage pagans and idolaters, "having no hope, and without God in the world", now filled with a sense of divine love and grace, and worshipping the Father in spirit and in truth was not a little affecting.

'November 4. Discoursed from John 11. Divine truths made deep impressions upon many in the assembly. Numbers were affected with a view of the power of Christ manifested in His raising the dead. . . . One in particular, who not long since came half drunk, and railed on us, and attempted by all means to disturb us while engaged in divine worship, was now so concerned and distressed for her soul, that she seemed unable to get any ease without an interest in Christ.

'November 26. I discoursed publicly among them from John 5. 1–9. I was favoured with some special freedom and fervency in my discourse, and a powerful energy accompanied divine truths. The influence which seized the audience appeared gentle, and yet pungent and efficacious. . . . It seemed like the gentle but steady showers which effectually water the earth, without violently beating upon the surface. . . . The persons lately awakened were, some of them, deeply distressed for their souls, and appeared earnestly solicitous to obtain an interest in Christ.

'November 28. Opened and made remarks upon the sacred story of our Lord's transfiguration, Luke 9. 28–36. . . . Observed some, that I have reason to think are truly God's people, exceedingly affected with an account of the glory of Christ in His transfiguration, and filled with longing desires of being with Him that they might with open face behold His glory. After public service was over, I asked one of them who wept and sobbed most affectionately, What she now wanted? She replied, "O, to be with Christ. I do not know how to stay".

'Lord's day, December 22. Discoursed upon the story of the young man in the Gospel, Matthew 19. 16–22. . . . This was a season of comfort to some souls, and in particular to one . . . who never before obtained any settled comfort, though I have abundant reason to think she had passed a saving change some days before. She now appeared in a heavenly frame of mind, composed, and delighted with the divine will. When I came to discourse particularly with her, and to inquire of her how she obtained relief and deliverance from the spiritual distresses which she had lately suffered, she answered in broken English, "Me try, me try save myself, last my strength be all gone; (meaning her ability to save herself) could not me stir bit further. Den last, me forced let Jesus Christ alone, send me hell if He please." I said, "But you was not willing to go to hell, was you?" She replied, "Could not me help it. My heart, he would wicked for all. Could not me make him good," (meaning, she saw it was right she should go to hell, because her heart was wicked, and would be so after all she could do to mend it.) . . . She could not readily be convinced but that she was willing to go to hell if Christ was pleased to send her there; although the truth evidently was, that her will was so swallowed up in the divine will, that she could not frame any hell in her imagination which would be dreadful or undesirable, provided it was but the will of God to send her to it.

'Lord's day, December 29. Preached from John 3. 1–5. The discourse was accompanied with power, and seemed to have a silent but deep and piercing influence upon the audience. Many wept and sobbed affectionately. . . . After public worship was over, I went to my house, proposing to preach again after a short season of intermission. But they soon came in, one after another, with tears in their eyes, to know "what they should do to be saved". The divine Spirit in such a manner set home upon their hearts what I spake to them, that the house was soon filled with cries and groans. They all flocked together upon this occasion; and those whom I had reason to think in a Christless state were almost universally seized with concern for their souls. It was an amazing season of power among them and seemed as if God had bowed the heavens and come down. So astonishingly prevalent was the operation upon old as well as young, that it seemed as if none would be left in a secure and natural state, but that God was now about to convert all the world. I was ready to think then, that I should never again despair of the conversion of any man or woman living, be they who or what they would.'

Any devout person who reads this account of the divine work among the Indians at Crossweeksung can only exclaim, 'This is the Lord's doing; it is marvellous in our eyes.' Who could have dreamed that so unpromising a spot, where Satan's power seemed enthroned, should become the scene of penitential tears and holy affections? The desert of pagan darkness was indeed made to blossom like the rose. It seemed that the oracle of Isaiah had been fulfilled in the wilds of colonial New Jersey: 'I will open rivers in high places, and fountains in the midst of the valleys; I will make the wilderness a pool of water, and the dry land springs of water. I will plant in the wilderness the cedar, the shittah tree, and the myrtle, and the oil tree; I will set in the desert the fir tree, and the pine, and the box tree together: that they may see, and know, and consider, and understand together, that the hand of the Lord hath done this, and the Holy One of Israel hath created it.' (Chapter 41, 18–20).

As Brainerd's success at Crossweeksung occupies such a prominent and important place in his life-story, it seems appropriate that some consideration should be given to the character of the work. Although much more could be said, certainly the awakening, viewed not only in its initial but in its over-all aspects, bore at least four characteristics.

First of all, it was undoubtedly *divine in its origin*. The wonderful results which were accomplished lay wholly beyond all human power. Brainerd did not have the dubious assets of certain modern evangelists with their charming, trained voices, glamorous clothes, impressive advertising, entertaining music, and much else; in fact he did not even have the advantage of an audience sufficiently educated to understand simple English. His only resource was the power of the Holy Spirit. When God began to work, none could deny that something supernatural was taking place, and Brainerd was never disposed to take any credit for the results to himself. In fact he seemed in his own eyes to be but a bystander watching the Indians transformed before him. He said once, after witnessing a powerful display of the Spirit's operations, 'I seemed to do nothing, and, indeed to have nothing to do, but to "stand still, and see the salvation of God"; and found myself obliged and delighted to say, "Not unto us", not unto instruments and means, "but to thy name be glory". God appeared to work entirely alone, and I saw no room to attribute any part of this work to any created arm.'

Secondly, the revival was *rational in its nature*. Too frequently, religious awakenings have been attended with circumstances which have gone far toward discrediting them in the eyes of men. Even in the New England revival linked with the name of Jonathan Edwards, some were seized with violent bodily convulsions which gave it a repulsive appearance and afforded ample ammunition for enemies of the truth. The movement at Crossweeksung was happily free from such extremes. 'There has been', Brainerd remarked, 'no appearance of those convulsions, bodily agonies, frightful screamings, swoonings, and the like, which have been so much complained of in some places; although there have been some who, with the jailer, have been made to tremble under a sense of their sin and misery; numbers who have been made to cry out from a distressing view of their perishing state; and some, who have been for a time, in a great measure, deprived of their bodily strength, yet without any such convulsive appearances.' He also pointed out that on the very day of the great stir, August 8, the concern of the Indians was very rational and just, being based on a view of the wickedness of their hearts and actions, and a fear of the anger of God against them because of their sins. Only in a very few cases were they excited by such mental disorders as visions, trances, and imaginations. It was such doctrines as the depravity of man, the need of regeneration, and above all, 'Christ crucified' which aroused the feelings of the Indians.

Thirdly, the revival was very *practical in its outworkings*. In some modern movements, multitudes make a 'decision for Christ' but appear little influenced by their experience. Not so with these Indians. Page after page in Brainerd's Journal records the amazing change of manners that resulted from the outpouring of the Spirit of God. Upon their profession of faith, they immediately abandoned their pagan superstitions and idolatrous practices. Drunkenness, a sin which, as Brainerd said, 'easily besets them' became a thing virtually unknown in their midst. Those who before would not pay their debts and cared little for principles of justice were now honest and upright in all their business dealings. The divine laws regarding marriage, which before were unknown or ignored, were now studiously maintained. The Lord's day was carefully and seriously observed, and family prayer was set up in the homes. Among the converted people, an appearance of bitterness or censoriousness never arose, but Christian charity reigned in their hearts. Concerning this, Brainerd observed, 'Never did I see such an appearance of Christian love among any people in all my life. It was so remarkable, that one might well have cried with agreeable surprise, "Behold how they love one another".' Also, the converts eagerly desired to learn more about the Word of God. Once Brainerd recorded, 'My house being thronged with my people in the evening, I spent the time in religious exercises with them, till my nature was almost spent. They are so unwearied in religious exercises, and insatiable in their thirsting after Christian knowledge, that I can sometimes scarcely avoid labouring so as greatly to exhaust my strength and spirits.' If this was not a practical revival, what could deserve the name?

Lastly, the awakening was *permanent in its effects*. Brainerd laboured among the Indians in New Jersey for a year and a half after the revival broke out, and during this time the Indian community continued to grow and prosper. Eventually ill health forced him to leave them, but his brother John took his place and filled the post with distinction. Under John's care, Edwards reported after Brainerd's death, 'the mission continues much to flourish'.

IX. Cranberry (1746-47)

The latter half of the year 1745 and the beginning of 1746 was a period of blessing and triumph for David Brainerd. A work of God among the Indians which had long been his heart's desire, was now a reality. On March 24, 1746, he numbered over one hundred and forty souls who had gathered together as his 'stated hearers' since his first coming among them. Most of these had given evidence of true conversion and made up a Christian community known far and wide for their sincerity and devotion to Christ. Brainerd was now cast into a new role: that of a pastor, a position which involved many responsibilities and problems. He must have asked himself, or rather his Lord, many questions – how must he minister to the spiritual and temporal needs of his Indians? What must he teach them? What methods of instruction must he apply? How must he deal with the souls under conviction, and those who professed faith in Christ? How must he apply the principles of Christianity to his flock's economic, domestic, and social concerns? The Journal gives the answer to most of these questions. From it we learn the tremendously deep concern which Brainerd had for the eternal welfare of souls committed to his ministerial care.

The doctrinal content of Brainerd's preaching is given in an appendix to his Journal. He says that it was 'the principal scope and drift of all his discourses' to dwell on the being and perfections of God; the obligations mankind were under to love and honour Him; the sinful condition of men and their inability to save themselves; the insufficiency of external reformations or performances to bring them into the favour of God; the necessity of a Saviour; the freeness and riches of divine grace; and the sinners' duty to betake themselves for mercy to God through Christ. He laid great stress also on the fact that the Person and work of Christ was the dominant theme in all his preaching. The Christocentric nature of his public ministry is evident from the following quotation: 'I have often-times remarked with admiration, that whatsoever subject I have been treating upon, after having spent time sufficient to explain and illustrate the truths contained therein, I have been naturally and easily led to Christ as the substance of every subject. If I treated on the Being and glorious perfections of God, I was thence naturally led to discourse of Christ as the only "way to the Father". If I attempted to open the deplorable misery of our fallen state, it was natural from thence to show the necessity of Christ to undertake for us, to atone for our sins, and to redeem us from the power of them. If I taught the commands of God, and showed our violation of them, this brought me in the most easy and natural way to speak of and recommend the Lord Jesus Christ, as one who had "magnified the law", which we had broken, and who was "become the end of it for righteousness, to everyone that believes". Never did I find so much freedom and assistance in making all the various lines of my discourses meet together and centre in Christ, as I have frequently done among these Indians.'

After Brainerd's Indians had attained a considerable degree of understanding of the principles of Christianity, he decided that the best method of continuing their instruction would be by 'catechetical lectures'. The plan was to ask them questions pertaining to the Scriptures, receive their answers, and then enlarge upon the subject as he saw fit. He was surprised how readily and rationally they responded to the questions and how advanced they became in the knowledge of the Scriptures.* He gives several specimens of this method, of which the following is a sample:

Question: You see I have already shown you what good things Christ gives his people while they live, and when they come to die; now, will he raise their bodies, and the bodies of others, to life again at the last day?
Answer: Yes, they shall all be raised.

*It is amazing to note what Brainerd records concerning the eagerness of the Indians to learn, and their inquisitiveness about even the more mysterious doctrines of Scripture. He writes, 'Many of the doctrines which I have delivered, they have queried with me about, in order to gain further light and insight into them; particularly the doctrine of predestination; and have from time to time manifested a good understanding of them, by their answers to the questions proposed to them in my catechetical lectures.'

Question: Will their bodies ever die any more after they are raised to life?

Answer: No.

Question: Will God's children then be as happy as they can desire to be?

Answer: Yes.

Question: Will they never be weary of God and Christ, and the pleasures of heaven, so as we are weary of our friends and enjoyments here, after we have been pleased with them awhile?

Answer: No, never.

Question: Could God's people be happy if they knew God loved them, and yet felt at the same time that they could not love and honour Him?

Answer: No, no.

This method of teaching and examination Brainerd carried out successfully during his Indian pastorate.

In no way do we see the wisdom and thoroughness of Brainerd as a shepherd of souls better than in his dealings with the awakened and professed converts. Only those who gave manifest evidence of a work of grace were admitted to the ordinance of Baptism and into church membership. Recognizing the danger of counterfeit experiences, he made sure that those who made up the church had been impressed by the power of the truth upon their hearts, and had not merely been carried away by visions or trances. Not only was a thorough conviction for sin required of the converts, but also they had to give evidence that they had actually come to an assured faith in Christ and had experienced a sense of divine forgiveness. In the appendix to his Journal he writes, 'It must be noted, that I have baptized no adults, but such as appeared to have a work of special grace wrought in their hearts; I mean such as have had the experience not only of the awakening and humbling, but, in a judgment of charity, of the renewing and confirming influences of the divine Spirit. There are many others under solemn concern for their souls, who, I apprehend, are persons of sufficient knowledge, and visible seriousness, at present, to render them proper subjects of the ordinance of baptism. Yet since they give no comfortable evidence of a saving change, but only appear under convictions of their sin and misery ... I have thought proper hitherto to defer their baptism.' Recognizing the weakness of the Indians for strong drink, Brainerd feared to baptize some of his 'serious but not confident' hearers prematurely, lest they bring scandal to their profession by lapsing again into their former evil habits.

The spiritual interests of the Indians were by no means the only concern of their pastor. At the outset they were not only naturally very ignorant of the gospel of Christ and the principles of Christianity, but they knew practically nothing about the pecuniary responsibilities, domestic decencies, and social amenities which come with civilization. To the Indians Brainerd became not only a spiritual father but also a patron of culture and education and a friend who watched over their temporal interests at many points. He tells us he felt called upon to 'take care of all their secular affairs, as if they were a company of children; to ride about frequently in order to procure collections for the support of the school, and for their help and benefit in other respects; to hear and decide all the petty differences which arise among any of them; and to have the constant oversight and management of all their affairs of every kind'. He taught them the importance of faithfulness and industry in ordinary business, secured money to discharge their debts, and protected them when outsiders sought to drive them away from their lands by intimidation.

Early in the year 1746 Brainerd became increasingly aware that there were many disadvantages attached to residence at Crossweeksung as far as the Indian community was concerned. The land there was unsuitable for cultivation and the Indians themselves had no permanent homes, which hindered their instruction in the English tongue and prevented their attending public worship with regularity. He felt that if they could all settle in one place these problems would be partially solved. With this in view, a fertile plot of land a little more than fifteen miles north-east of Crossweeksung was chosen, and in March, 1746, the Indians began the work of clearance. This place was at Cranberry, New Jersey, where modern Cranbury is located today. In May, after the Indians had moved there permanently, a school was established for their education in the English language and a schoolmaster was hired. Four months later the Indians built Brainerd himself a small house at Cranberry where he continued his residence until his ministry among the Indians ceased in March, 1747.

X. The Susquehanna (1744–46)

Thus far we have sketched briefly the fortunes of Brainerd in the four Indian settlements where he took up temporary residence: Kaunaumeek, The Forks of the Delaware, Crossweeksung, and Cranberry. At the first and second, he met only limited success, at the third he was blessed with the amazing developments already described. During his stay at the Forks, Crossweeksung, and Cranberry, he made four trips further west to preach to Indians along the Susquehanna river which flows through the Allegheny Mountains in Central Pennsylvania. These trips form one of the most interesting though pathetic phases of his life.

On October 2, 1744, he began his first trip, accompanied by Moses Finda Fautaury his interpreter, two Indians from the Forks of the Delaware, and James Byram, a minister. They lodged that night at one of the last houses on the road, twenty-five miles from their starting point. Before them lay 'a hideous and howling wilderness'. The diary entry for the next day gives a fair sample of the hardships of the journey. 'We went on our way into the wilderness, and found the most difficult and dangerous travelling, by far, that ever any of us had seen. We had scarce any thing else but lofty mountains, deep valleys, and hideous rocks, to make our way through. . . . Near night, my beast that I rode upon, hung one of her legs in the rocks, and fell down under me; but through divine goodness I was not hurt. However, she broke her leg; and being in such a hideous place, and near thirty miles from any house, I saw nothing that could be done to preserve her life, so I was obliged to kill her, and prosecute my journey on foot. . . . Just at dark, we kindled a fire, cut up a few bushes, and made a shelter over our heads, to save us from the frost, which was very hard that night; and committing ourselves to God by prayer, we lay down on the ground and slept quietly.'

Four days after starting, the party reached a place called Opehol-haupung on the Susquehanna. Finding twelve Indian houses, Brainerd greeted the chief, informed him of his mission, and obtained his approval to his proposals. He preached that day and several times afterwards. The Indians seemed eager to listen to him but were just as eager to raise objections against his Christian gospel. This somewhat 'damped' his spirit. After three days he planned to leave the settlement and to leave the Indians free to engage in the hunting expedition which they had planned, but, to his surprise, they wanted to hear him preach again.

On October 9, Brainerd and his party left for the Forks of the Delaware. That night they rested in a 'shelter of bark' with a fire burning near them. 'In the night, the wolves howled around us', Brainerd recorded with astonishing serenity, 'but God preserved us.'

Jonathan Edwards sums up the second trip to the Susquehanna, in May of the following year, in his own succinct way. 'The next day, he set out on his journey to the Susquehanna, with his interpreter. He endured great hardships and fatigues in his way thither through a hideous wilderness; where, after having lodged one night in the open woods, he was overtaken with a north-easterly storm, in which he was almost ready to perish. Having no manner of shelter, and not being able to make a fire in so great a rain, he could have no comfort if he stopped; therefore he determined to go forward in hopes of meeting with some shelter, without which he thought it impossible to live the night through; but their horses – happening to eat poison, for the want of other food, at a place where they lodged the night before – were so sick, that they could neither ride nor lead them, but were obliged to drive them, and travel on foot; until, through the mercy of God, just at dusk, they came to a bark hut, where they lodged that night.

After he came to the Susquehanna, he travelled about a hundred miles on the river, and visited many towns and settlements of the Indians; saw some of seven or eight distinct tribes, and preached to different nations by different interpreters. He was sometimes much discouraged, and sunk in his spirits, through the opposition which appeared in the Indians to Christianity. At other times, he was encouraged by the disposition which some of these people manifested to hear, and willingness to be instructed. He here met with some who had formerly been his hearers at Kaunaumeek, and had removed hither; who saw and heard him again with great joy. He spent a fortnight among the Indians on this river, and passed through considerable labours and hardships, frequently lodging on the ground, and sometimes in the open air. At length he fell extremely ill, as he was riding in the wilderness, being seized with an ague, followed with a burning fever, and extreme pains in his head and bowels, attended with a great evacuation of blood; so that he thought he must have perished in the wilderness. But at last coming to an Indian trader's hut, he got leave to stay there; and though without physic or food proper for him, it pleased God, after about a week's distress, to relieve him so far that he was able to ride. He returned homewards from Juncauta, an island far down the river, where was a considerable number of Indians, who appeared more free from prejudices against Christianity than most of the other Indians. He arrived at the Forks of Delaware on Thursday, May 30, after having rode in this journey about three hundred and forty miles.'

When the revival came at Crossweeksung in August, 1745, Brainerd's hopes for success at the Forks of the Delaware and the Susquehanna were raised, in spite of the rather fruitless year and a half at the former, and two long, tedious, and essentially unproductive trips to the latter. For this reason, on August 27, he started again for the Forks, purposing to go from there to the Susquehanna. He went by Philadelphia where he obtained a recommendation from the governor of Pennsylvania to the chiefs of the Indians.

Brainerd's preaching had a much more favourable response this time at the Forks of the Delaware than at any time in the past.

On September 1, 1745, during the first preaching upon the journey, 'the word appeared to be attended with some power and caused some tears in the assembly'. Two days later, after more preaching, the Indians seemed greatly concerned. Some who before would sleep while he discoursed now were aroused from their lethargy. He asked one Indian who was weeping profusely why he now cried. He answered that 'when he thought how Christ was slain like a lamb and spilt his blood for sinners, he could not help crying when he was all alone', bursting again into tears when he had spoken. He enquired of another, 'Has Christ seemed to be near you of late as in time past?' She replied, 'Yes, He has been near to me, and at times when I have been praying alone, my heart loved to pray so, that I could not bear to leave the place, but wanted to stay and pray longer.' Brainerd rejoiced, for it seemed that the revival work of the Spirit had now spread to his former field of labour.

On September 9, he began the one hundred and twenty mile trip westwards to the Susquehanna river. Three days later he arrived at Shaumoking, his destination. Though kindly received by the Indians of three different tribes, speaking languages 'wholly unintelligible to each other', he was greatly disturbed by a heathenish dance and revel which he saw. The noise and disorder made him cry, 'Of a truth the dark corners of the earth are full of habitations of cruelty.' 'The Indians of the place', he lamented, 'are accounted the most drunken, mischievous, and ruffianly fellows of any in these parts; and Satan seems to have his seat in this town in an eminent manner.' He had ample opportunity in the next few days to learn how sadly accurate was their reputation. With sorrow he viewed their wild singing, howling, chanting, and dancing. Their dark savagery was encouraged by some white people near them who constantly sold them strong drink. Seeing that he was not accomplishing much with them, after a fortnight's stay, weak in body and dejected in mind, he started home again where the joys of Christian fellowship awaited him, and the door opened for him so wondrously by the Spirit of God.

XI. The Susquehanna Continued (1746)

There come times in the life of every man when he must make critical decisions upon which the whole course of his future life hinges, either for better or for worse. Such a time for David Brainerd was the summer of 1746. In His mercy, God had raised up a numerous and affectionate band of believing Indians at Crossweeksung. It seemed that now God might be leading him to settle among them and become their pastor permanently. After all, the long rides through the backwoods had almost wasted him. He was pale, thin, and weak. Whatever course he took, consumption, a disease which ran in his family, might overtake him, and certainly, without seasons of physical rest in a congenial, settled spot, he could not last long. Then too, how pleasant it would be for him to have the quiet confines of a home of his own, with friends all about him to bring comfort and cheer! By this time, also, he entertained the prospect of marriage with Jerusha, the second daughter of Jonathan Edwards, whose acquaintance he had made by his association with her father. Should he stay, or continue his lonely rides to the west to take the gospel to 'regions beyond'?

One day as he meditated on these things, thinking especially of the joy that he could have in a home and family life of his own, he made his decision. Let us listen as he records the fateful choice. It is couched in words charged with refined spiritual feelings, and brimming over with loyal attachment to the interests of the gospel: 'But now these thoughts (taking up permanent residence, etc.) seemed to be wholly dashed to pieces, not by necessity, but of choice; for it appeared to me that God's dealings towards me had fitted me for a life of solitariness and hardship, and that I had nothing to lose, nothing to do with earth, and consequently nothing to lose by a total renunciation of it. It appeared to me just right that I should be destitute of house and home, and many of the comforts of life, which I rejoiced to see others of God's people enjoy. At the same time, I saw so much of the excellency of Christ's kingdom and the infinite desirableness of its advancement in the world, that it swallowed up all my other thoughts, and made me willing, yea, even rejoice, to be made a pilgrim or hermit in the wilderness to my dying moment, if I might promote the blessed interest of the great Redeemer. If ever my soul presented itself to God for His service, without any reserve of any kind, it did so now. The language of my thoughts and disposition now was, "Here I am, Lord, send me; send me to the ends of the earth; send me to the rough, the savage Pagans of the wilderness; send me from all that is called comfort in earth, or earthly comfort; send me even to death itself, if it be but in Thy service, and to promote Thy kingdom." At the same time, I had as quick and lively a sense of the value of worldly comforts, as ever I had: but only saw them infinitely overmatched by the worth of Christ's kingdom, and the propagation of his blessed gospel. The quiet settlement, the certain place of abode, the tender friendship, which I thought I might be likely to enjoy in consequence of such circumstances, appeared as valuable to me, considered absolutely and in themselves, as ever before; but considered comparatively, they appeared nothing. Compared with the value and preciousness of an enlargement of Christ's kingdom, they vanished as stars before the rising sun. Sure I am that, although the comfortable accommodations of life appeared valuable and dear to me, yet I did surrender and resign myself, soul and body, to the service of God, and to the promotion of Christ's kingdom; though it should be in the loss of them all, I could not do any other, because I could not will or choose any other. I was constrained, and yet chose, to say, "Farewell, friends and earthly comforts, the dearest of them all, the very dearest, if the Lord calls for it: adieu, adieu; I will spend my life, to my latest moments, in caves and dens of the earth, if the kingdom of Christ may thereby be advanced".'

From that moment, there was little doubt as to what lay ahead for David Brainerd. His life would now, in the strictest sense of the word, be a living sacrifice, consumed upon the altar of love for the salvation of the Indians of the American wilderness.

Driven by a sort of cruel, self-immolating dedication, Brainerd made preparations on August 11, 1746, for his fourth trip to the west. It was to be his last. He and his people bowed in united prayer that the trip would be successful – that God would 'send His blessed Spirit with the word and set up His kingdom among the poor Indians in the wilderness'. Just before he left, he gave an exhortation on the latter part of the 72nd Psalm where it is promised that all nations would bless the Redeemer. 'My soul was refreshed,' he said, 'to think that this day, this blessed glorious season, should surely come, and, I trust, numbers of my dear people were also refreshed.'

On August 12, he left Cranberry with six Christian Indians from his congregation whom he had chosen to assist him in this endeavour. He decided not to make this trip by travelling directly to the Susquehanna over the huge mountains and 'hideous wilderness' which had made his former trips so difficult, but to go through Philadelphia and ascend the river to reach the Indian villages from the south. On August 18, he arrived at Paxton (now Paxtang) on the Susquehanna.

The record of what followed is the record of a daily fight with disease and infirmity. On August 20, after lying all night in a cold sweat, he awoke coughing blood. He was 'under great disorder and melancholy', but was encouraged at the thought that he might speedily be dismissed from earth with all its toils and sorrows. August 27, he lodged all night in a house filled with thick smoke, which almost choked him. At night he could not rest; in the morning he was troubled with pains in his head and neck, but a cold easterly storm and the raw air without drove him back into the smoky interior.

On the next day, he discoursed to the Indians, persuading them to turn to God. 'I scarce ever saw more clearly than this day,' he said, 'that it is God's work to convert souls and especially the poor Heathens. I knew I could not touch them; I saw I could only speak to dry bones, but could give them no sense of what I said. My eyes were up to God for help: I could say the work was His; and if done, the glory would be His.'

Five days later, while riding fifty miles north from Shaumoking, toward 'The Great Island' to visit some Indians there, he was very faint and feeble. 'I thought it would kill me,' he laments, 'to lie out in the open air.' Having no axe, he climbed into a pine tree and with his knife cut the branches to make a shelter from the dew; yet he was 'wringing wet' all night from sweat. In spite of the 'melancholy situation' he tried to think how much worse things could be. 'What if I were among enemies?' he thought.

Returning to Shaumoking in the night of September 4, he lay down in the woods to sleep without even fire to cook food, to keep him warm, and to ward off the wild beasts. 'Never was I more weak or worn out in all my life,' he said. After ten o'clock, however, some Indians came who wanted to hear him preach and who were able to minister to his needs.

Brainerd's ministry among the Indians of the Susquehanna region on this final visit there was not without some good effect, though not to the extent he had desired. He was frequently enabled to speak the word of God with power, and in many instances the truths he spoke made impressions on the hearers. 'Some seemed to cleave to us and to be well disposed to Christianity, but others mocked, shouted, and discouraged those who were friendly.' Whatever the outcome, Brainerd was sure that his efforts would not be in vain. 'Whether the issue of it (this trip to the Susquehanna) would be the setting up of Christ's kingdom there, or only the drawing of some few persons down to my congregation in New Jersey; or whether they were now only being prepared for some further attempts, that might be made among them, I did not determine; but I was persuaded, the journey would not be lost. Blessed be God, that I had any encouragement and hope.'

On September 9, he rode thirty miles down the river where he discoursed upon the 'life and power of religion', dealing with what were and what were not the evidences of true conversion. The Indians there were amazed to behold Brainerd's Indians giving thanks at a meal. They considered that to be a very great evidence of spirituality, but to their astonishment Brainerd insisted that neither public nor private prayers were infallible evidences of salvation. 'O the ignorance of the world!' he exclaimed. 'How are some empty outward forms, that may all be entirely selfish,

[65]

mistaken for true religion, infallible evidences of it! The Lord pity a deluded world!'

During this time, in his Journal, Brainerd constantly complains of hardship in travelling alone, lack of appetite, weakness, nocturnal sweats, and coughing of blood. He was a sick man – too sick for the long ride back to Cranberry. But on September 11 he 'rode homeward'.

XII. A Mission Report

On March 21, 1745, the Missionary Society of Scotland with which Brainerd was connected wrote a letter to their Correspondents in America in which they requested detailed information concerning the mission work among the Indians. They wished the missionaries to explain, among other things, the difficulties and obstacles they had encountered in their work and how they had gone about overcoming them. In June, 1746, Brainerd complied with this request and prepared a detailed report which not only gives an insight into his work among the Indians, but is a valuable source of information on Indian customs and religious beliefs as well.

1. Brainerd was reluctant to make mention of the difficulties attending his work lest he should seem to be complaining or holding himself up as an example of self-denial and constancy in confronting these obstacles, but he spelled out four principal problems he had to encounter in Indian evangelism. The first of these, and by far the most important, was 'The rooted aversion to Christianity which prevailed among the Indians'. On this matter Brainerd wrote, 'They are not only brutishly stupid and ignorant of divine things, but many of them are obstinately set against Christianity, and seem to abhor even the Christian name.'

In examining the aversion of the Indians to Christianity, Brainerd found that the immorality and vicious behaviour of many professed Christians was a prime factor. The Indians observed that many nominal Christians were guilty of wicked acts, and assumed that all white people were alike. When Brainerd spoke to them about Christianity they pointed to the scandalous practices of certain white men, which their own consciences condemned, which caused them to question the value of the religion of the whites. 'They have observed to me,' said Brainerd, 'that the white people lie, defraud, steal, and drink worse than the Indians; that they have taught the Indians these things, especially the latter of them; who before the coming of the English knew of no such thing as strong drink; that the English have by these means made them quarrel and kill one another; and in a word brought them to the practice of all those vices which now prevail among them.' 'Now,' they said, 'we are more wicked and miserable than when you Christian white men came among us.' This objection to Christianity, based on notorious facts, was not easy to answer. The missionary tried to show them that there was a difference between real Christians and merely nominal Christians, the ill examples they cited being of the latter sort. Be it remembered that Brainerd himself was about the only example of a true Christian they had seen.

Another source of their prejudice against Christ was their fear of being enslaved. Brainerd found the Indians to be extremely averse to a state of servitude and at the same time void of any concept of generosity or kindness. As a result they were very suspicious of the benevolent deeds of others, fearing that beneath the apparent goodness was a plot to take advantage of them and bring them into a bondage like that of the negroes. Thus when Brainerd recommended Christianity to them they replied that they could not believe that he really had their welfare at heart, for white men like him were wont to cheat them out of their lands and had driven them back to the mountains from their pleasant places by the sea. They interpreted all his kindness to them and the hardships he endured for them as a design to draw them together that they might be brought into captivity or fight in wars in behalf of their captors. 'He never would,' they reasoned, 'take all this pains to do us good; he must have some wicked design to hurt us some way or other.' When Brainerd assured them that he was not sent by those who stole their lands but by godly people at a great distance who wished to do them good, they replied, 'But why did not these good people send you to teach us before, while we had our lands down by the sea? If they had sent you then, we should likely have heard you and turned Christians.'

The Indians' prejudice against Christianity was also caused by their pagan religious beliefs. They did not believe in one supreme God but had a strange and confused notion of a plurality of invisible deities under a variety of forms and shapes to which they paid homage. After the white men came, they imagined that there were only three deities because they saw people of three different kinds of complexion: English, Negroes, and Indians. They also paid superstitious reverence to beasts, birds, fishes, and reptiles upon which they fancied invisible beings bestowed great powers. Brainerd once saw an Indian burn fine tobacco for incense in order to appease the wrath of a god who presided over rattlesnakes and was supposedly angered because one of them had been killed by a fellow-Indian.

The Redskins' views of a future state of existence were vague and uncertain. 'Many of them,' Brainerd wrote, 'imagine that the chichung, i.e. the shadow, or what survives the body, will at death go southward, and in an unknown but curious place will enjoy some kind of happiness such as hunting, feasting, dancing, and the like.' Some of the Indians had no concept of reward and punishment in a future life, though others conceived that 'bad folk' would be excluded from the good world where happy souls dwell.

The Indians frequently offered sacrifices by which they sought to appease the gods and persuade them to be good to them. Brainerd had seen such a sacrifice at Jancauta Island in the Susquehanna. He described it thus, 'In the evening they met together, nearly a hundred of them, and danced around a large fire, having prepared ten fat deer for the sacrifice. The fat of the inwards they burnt in the fire while they were dancing and sometimes raised the flame to a prodigious height; at the same time yelling and shouting in such a manner, that they might easily have been heard two miles or more. They continued their sacred dance nearly all night, after which they ate the flesh of the sacrifice and so retired each to his own lodging.'

Dreams were deemed very important by the Redskins because they thought that at such times the invisible powers gave them directions and instructions. Also they were very much attached to all sorts of fabulous traditions, received from their ancestors, and other superstitious notions. Some claimed to have had fantastic and weird experiences. One Indian professed to have been dead for four days during which time he would have been buried had it not been necessary for some of his relatives who lived at a great distance to be summoned. Before they arrived, he arose from the dead. During this time he claimed to have gone to the place where the sun rises. At a great height over this place he was, he said, admitted into a tremendous house several miles in length where he saw many things which Brainerd described as 'too tedious and ridiculous to mention'. A woman claimed to have been dead for several days in which she went southward and feasted and danced with happy spirits. Attachment to these imaginary experiences made the Indians not a little reluctant to embrace Christianity.

Brainerd was also hindered in his work by certain weird persons known as *powwows* (meaning conjurers or diviners) who were supposed to have 'the power of foretelling future events, recovering the sick, charming, enchanting, and poisoning others by their magic divinations'. Their spirit, in its various operations, seemed to be a Satanic imitation of the gift of prophecy which existed in the early church. Some, apparently, received this power even in infancy. Brainerd found that as a rule this spirit did not depend upon any act of volition or effort of its subject. It was supposed to be conferred upon little children by making them swallow a small live frog upon which certain superstitious ceremonies had been performed.

One of these powwows was converted under Brainerd's ministry, and he tried to find out from him something about the nature of his conjuration. To the missionary it was a veritable 'mystery of iniquity', quite unintelligible and certainly inexplicable. The powwow himself seemed not to understand his spirit of divination after it had left him. He did, however, relate the experience through which he got this power, which is curious indeed. He told Brainerd that he was once admitted into the presence of a great man in a world above at a vast distance from the earth. This man was 'clothed with the day, yea, with the brightest day he ever saw, a day of many years, yea of everlasting continuance'. The whole world seemed to be 'drawn upon him' so that the earth and all things could be seen in him. He told the Indian that he loved, pitied, and wanted to help him. By the side of this tremendous personage was his shadow or spirit which was as lovely as the man himself and filled all things. As if this were not preposterous enough, the powwow told Brainerd that this experience took place before he was born. He was convinced that this was the case, because this god-like man prophesied the circumstances of his birth, including the name of his mother, and also many things that would befall him during his life. All came about as predicted. The great one also told him that his shadow or spirit would accompany him down to earth and would be with him forever. This also, according to the Indian, proved to be the case. The shadow directed him in dreams as to where he should hunt, assuring him that if he did as instructed he would always be successful. The powwow always found the shadow's directions accurate and true. Such was the account of his experience, undoubtedly one of Satan's 'lying wonders' designed to hold him in the darkness of his pagan unbelief.

The Indians considered these powwows to be highly favoured of the gods and held them in great reverence. The fear that they might harm them in some way made them reluctant to become Christians.

2. The second thing which Brainerd lists as an outstanding difficulty in 'his attempts to Christianize the Indians' was that of conveying truths to the Indians' understandings. For example, he laboured under the disadvantage of not having an interpreter who had an understanding of and sympathy with the truths he was conveying. Due to his lack of spiritual perception, the interpreter regarded Brainerd's teachings as foolishness, and consequently he delivered them to the Indians in an indifferent and heartless manner. Sensing the attachment of the Indians to their super-

stitions, and thinking Brainerd's preaching to be futile, he often said, 'It signifies nothing for us to try, they will never turn.' To the missionary this was a great discouragement.

A major problem was posed by the Indian languages. Brainerd was forced to attempt to preach to Indians speaking a variety of dialects which appeared to be wholly unrelated. Uniformity in the Indian tongues would have greatly assisted his work, but this did not exist. Furthermore, as might have been expected, the Indian languages were very deficient in vocabulary. Brainerd said, 'There are no words in the Indian language to answer our English words, "Lord, Saviour, salvation, sinner, justice, condemnation, faith, repentance, justification, adoption, sanctification, grace, glory, heaven", with scores of the like importance.' He had to call regeneration 'the heart's being made good', and entering into glory was described as 'being made more happy'. He also complained, 'What renders it more difficult to convey divine truths to the understandings of these Indians, is that there seems to be no foundation in their minds to begin upon; I mean, no truths which may be taken for granted, as being already known while I am attempting to instil others.' He goes on to explain how he set about teaching the Indians the perfections of God, the difference between the soul and the body, the reality and nature of sin, and the necessity of Christ's work for salvation. It is clear that he showed considerable skill in adapting his presentation of the truths of Scripture to the mental capacities of the Indians.

3. The third problem which Brainerd faced in Indian evangelism was 'Their inconvenient situations, savage manners, and unhappy method of living'. He records: 'I have been often obliged to preach in their houses in cold and windy weather, when they have been full of smoke and cinders, as well as unspeakably filthy; which has many times thrown me into violent sick headaches. While I have been preaching, their children have frequently cried to such a degree that I could scarcely be heard, and their pagan mothers would take no manner of care to quiet them. At the same time, perhaps, some have been laughing and mocking at divine truths; other playing with their dogs, whittling sticks, and the like; and this, in many of them, not from spite and prejudice, but

for want of better manners.' Brainerd describes in some detail how their extreme poverty, lack of any sense of gratitude, indolence and sloth, and their tendency to wander to and fro, militated against their accepting Christianity. Concerning their indolence and slothfulness he says, 'They have been bred up in idleness, and know little about cultivating land, or indeed of engaging vigorously in any other business. . . . They have little or no ambition or resolution. Not one in a thousand of them has the spirit of a man.'

4. The last difficulty Brainerd mentions is the opposition he encountered from white men in his approaches to the Indians. He writes, 'Some in all parts of the country where I have preached to them, have taken pains industriously to bind them down in pagan darkness.' Brainerd's enemies resorted to any means – slander, intimidation, ridicule – in order to prejudice the Indians against Christianity and deter them from attending on his ministry. The Redskins were told that they were 'happy', 'good', and 'safe' enough already, and did not need to be troubled with Brainerd's teachings. The missionary himself was sometimes called a knave and a deceiver who only sought to impose on his obsequious hearers. He was even accused of designing to sell the Indians as slaves, than which nothing was more calculated to terrify them. Also certain traffickers in liquor sued the Indians and threatened them with imprisonment for debt after they embraced Christianity, the reason apparently being that 'the hope of future gain was lost'. Other lies were invented, as ridiculous as they were vicious. A report circulated that Brainerd was actually a Roman Catholic who was sent by some papists for the purpose of training the Indians in the business of cutting the throats of white men. Some actually went to the civil authorities, urging that the Indians only appeared decent, orderly, and friendly in order that they might deceive those whom they wished to murder. Thus opposition took various forms, but without success, for Brainerd was able to say, 'Through the mercy of God, they were never able by all their abominable insinuations, flouting jeers, and downright lies, to create in the Indians those jealousies with which they desired to possess them; and so were never suffered to hinder the work of grace among them.'

Such, then, were the major obstacles which Brainerd had to overcome in his work. They render the more remarkable his skill and patience as a witness for the truth among the Redskins, and the greatness and wonder of the work of God among them.

XIII. The Beginning of the End (1746–47)

Brainerd's Diary and Journal provide ample evidence that the bodily constitution of our missionary was unfitted to endure for long the hardships of his wilderness wanderings. He was now so weak that he was unable at times to perform his ordinary functions as a preacher. Long rides in inclement weather, poor food, and lack of rest 'weakened his strength in the way', and certainly 'shortened his days'. The end could not be far away.

On his way back from his last trip to the Susquehanna, he had been asked to preach at a colonial church, but had to refuse. He was brought so low that he could not even keep his Diary constantly now, a practice which he had continued without interruption for several years.

Yet despite his failing powers, he drove himself on, preaching and teaching his flock at Cranberry. Though sometimes scarcely able to stand, he discoursed regularly to the Indians, usually with the same remarkable effect that had been manifested in the past. A trip for rest back to New England, lasting from November, 1746, to the spring of the next year, helped him somewhat, but did not serve to arrest his illness. On March 18, he returned to 'his people' and called them together for singing and prayer. They showed great affection when they saw their pastor again, which he humbly hoped was 'more than natural'. But his emaciated appearance stirred them deeply. They had good reason to fear, for this was to be their last meeting.

On March 20, he left again for New Jersey, never to return to the scene of his missionary labours, though, as far as his strength allowed, he took part in various religious exercises and functions in the coming days. April 7, he performed the marriage ceremony at Newark for Jonathan Dickinson, an old friend and well known Calvinist preacher, and his spouse. April 9, he helped in an ordination, and on the 13th he helped to examine his own brother John, who five days later left to minister to the Indians in David's place. A week later he left New Jersey.

Occasionally there seemed promising signs of improved health, but on June 18, during a visit to Boston, Brainerd was brought 'to the gates of death' by a manifestation of the last stages of his illness. His physician surmised that ulcers had broken out in his lungs. For several weeks he was unable to speak or even whisper. During this time he walked, as it were, on the brink of death. Eternity seemed quite near. His feelings, while in this condition, are described in a very interesting letter to his brother Israel dated June 30: 'It is on the verge of Eternity I now address you. I am heartily sorry that I have so little strength to write what I long so much to communicate to you. But let me tell you, my brother, Eternity is another thing than we ordinarily take it to be in a healthful state. O, how vast and boundless! O, how fixed and unalterable! O, of what infinite importance is it that we be prepared for Eternity! I have been just a-dying, now for more than a week; and all around me have thought me so. I have had clear views of Eternity; have seen the blessedness of the godly, in some measure; and have longed to share their happy state, as well as been comfortably satisfied that through grace I shall do so. But O, what anguish is raised in my mind to think of an Eternity for those who are Christless, for those who are mistaken and who bring their false hopes to the grave with them! The sight was so dreadful I could by no means bear it; my thoughts recoiled, and I said, under a more affecting sense than ever before, "Who can dwell with everlasting burnings!" O, methought, could I now see my friends, that I might warn them to see to it that they lay their foundation for Eternity sure. And for you, my dear brother, I have been particularly concerned; and have wondered I so much neglected conversing with you about your spiritual state at our last meeting. O, my brother, let me then beseech you now to examine whether you are indeed a new creature, whether you have ever acted above self, whether the glory of God has ever been the sweetest and highest concern with you, whether you have ever been reconciled to all the perfections of God; in a word, whether God has been your portion, and holy conformity to him your chief delight. If you cannot answer positively, consider seriously the frequent breathings of your soul; but do not, however, put yourself off with a slight answer. If you have reason to think you are graceless, O, give yourself and the throne of grace no rest, till God arise and save. But if the case should be otherwise, bless God for His grace and press after holiness. My soul longs that you should be fitted for, and in due time go into, the work of the ministry. I cannot bear to think of your going into any other business in life. Do not be discouraged because you see your elder brothers in the ministry die early, one after another. I declare, now I am dying, I would not have spent my life otherwise for the whole world. O, my dear brother, flee fleshly lusts, and the enchanting amusements, as well as the corrupt doctrines of the present day; and strive to live to God.'

About the same time, Brainerd wrote to a young ministerial candidate: 'How amazing it is that the living, who know they must die, should, notwithstanding, "put far away the evil day", in a season of health and prosperity, and live at such an awful distance from a familiarity with the grave and the great concerns beyond it! Especially it may justly fill us with surprise that any whose minds have been divinely enlightened to behold the important things of eternity as they are, I say, that such should live in this manner. And yet, Sir, how frequently is this the case! How rare are the instances of those who live and act from day to day as on the verge of Eternity, striving to fill up all their remaining moments in the service and to the honour of their great Master! We insensibly trifle away time while we seem to have enough of it; and are so strangely amused as in a great measure to lose a sense of the holiness and blessed qualifications necessary to prepare us to be inhabitants of the heavenly paradise. But O, dear Sir, a dying bed, if we enjoy our reason clearly, will give another view of things. I have

[75]

now, for more than three weeks, lain under the greatest degree of weakness; the greater part of the time expecting daily and hourly to enter into the eternal world: sometimes have been so far gone, as to be wholly speechless for some hours together. O, of what vast importance has a holy spiritual life appeared to me to be at this season! I have longed to call upon all my friends to make it their business to live to God; and especially all that are designed for, or engaged in, the service of the sanctuary. O, dear Sir, do not think it enough to live at the rate of common Christians. Alas, to how little purpose do they often converse, when they meet together! The visits, even of those who are called Christians indeed, are frequently extremely barren; and conscience cannot but condemn us for the misimprovement of time while we have been conversant with them. But the way to enjoy the divine presence and to be fitted for distinguishing service for God, is to live a life of great devotion and constant self-dedication to Him; observing the motions and dispositions of our own hearts, whence we may learn the corruptions that lodge there and our constant need of help from God for the performance of the least duty. And O, dear Sir, let me beseech you frequently to attend to the great and precious duties of secret fasting and prayer.

'I have a secret thought, from some things I have observed, that God may perhaps design you for some singular service in the world. O then labour to be prepared and qualified to do much for God. Read Mr. Edwards' *Treatise on the Religious Affections* again and again, and labour to distinguish clearly upon experiences and affections in religion, that you may make a difference between the gold and the shining dross. I say, labour here, if ever you would be a useful minister of Christ; for nothing has put such a stop to the work of God in the late day as the false religion and the wild affections which attend it. Suffer me, therefore, finally to entreat you earnestly to "give yourself to prayer, to reading and meditation" on divine truths; strive to penetrate to the bottom of them, and never be content with a superficial knowledge. By this means, your thoughts will gradually grow weighty and judicious; and you hereby will be possessed of a valuable treasure, out of which you may produce "things new and old", to the glory of God.'

Lengthy portions of these letters have been transcribed because they are replete with sound counsel, and reveal much of the spiritual depth of the experience of their author.

While at Boston, Brainerd was busy, though practically an invalid. For one thing, he entertained many visitors, some 'of considerable note and character'. A group of wealthy Bostonians who conversed with him were so impressed with his success as a missionary that they contributed large sums to buy Bibles for his congregation at Cranberry and donated funds for further work among the Redskins in general. He also collected and revised several papers of the New England Puritan, Thomas Shepard, which were soon to be printed; and, at the request of the Society which had employed him, he approved some missionaries to be sent to the Indians. But the end drew rapidly nearer.

XIV. His Last Days and Death (1747)

Brainerd's last days, July to October, 1747, were spent at Northampton, Massachusetts, in the home of Jonathan Edwards, the celebrated Puritan theologian, preacher, and philosopher. It was fitting that Edwards should provide an asylum for the dying missionary, for he and Brainerd had been associated closely for several years. The elder had been a spiritual father to the younger; in fact any one who is well acquainted with Edwards' views on theology and Christian experience will easily discern that Brainerd was almost his replica.

From his childhood Brainerd had known something of Jonathan Edwards. When the future missionary was but ten years old, Edwards became pastor of the Congregational church at Northampton, and by the time Brainerd himself entered the ministry, Edwards was known far and wide for his power as a preacher and writer. For profundity, accuracy of thought, extent of Biblical knowledge, and depth of spiritual insight, he had no equal in the colonies. He was recognized even in Europe as no ordinary thinker. Edwards was not just a metaphysician, however, but a shepherd of souls as well. It was under his ministry that the famous revival broke out in which scores of people were caused to walk in newness of life. His essay on the awakening, which was read on both sides of the Atlantic, was sufficient in itself to earn him a place among the leading divines of his day.

When Edwards' writings first began to circulate, Brainerd was one of his steady readers. He found himself swept along irresistibly by the logic of the Northampton pastor. He saw that Edwards was right in saying that God was absolutely sovereign in all realms and perfectly just in sending men to hell for their sins. Though his heart at first rebelled against such teaching, after he was converted Brainerd assented to it with all his heart.

Brainerd's first opportunities of seeing and hearing Edwards came while the former was a student at Yale. Edwards was greatly interested in the progress of that institution, for not only was he one of its graduates but he had married Sarah Pierrepont, daughter of James Pierrepont who was one of the founders of Yale. He made frequent trips to New Haven to attend special functions of the college and to speak to the students. Thus Brainerd had numerous opportunities to hear and admire the famous New England divine.

As previously stated, the first meeting between Brainerd and Edwards came about at New Haven in 1743 where they had both come to attend the Yale baccalaureate service of that year. It did not take long for them to realize that they had much in common. Brainerd had often revelled in the preaching of Edwards and had long since become a sharer of his theological outlook. Edwards was greatly impressed with the personal devotion, spiritual understanding, and humility of the 'student in disgrace'. After their first meeting, Brainerd and Edwards saw much of each other.

Their association takes on a very tender aspect at this point, for it was through Brainerd's friendship with Edwards that he came to know Jerusha, the second daughter of his spiritual model. The story of the love affair between David and Jerusha would make an interesting book in itself; here the salient facts only can be mentioned.

Although the information we have about Jerusha is quite meagre, we are able to deduce from the few references to her in Brainerd's Diary and her father's writings, that she was an extra-ordinary young woman. Her father said of her, 'She had not seen one minute for several years wherein she desired to live one minute longer, for the sake of any other good in life but doing good, living to God, and doing what might be for his glory.' She apparently was of much the same temperament as Brainerd himself: solemn, humble, and self-denying. Obviously, no one could have been better qualified to make a wife for David Brainerd, had God so designed it.

Brainerd actually says very little in his Diary, at least the part of it that has come down to us, about his love for Jerusha, but his feelings are apparent from many incidental details. He carried on correspondence with her during the time of his mission work among the Indians, and took many trips to Northampton, which were certainly not merely for the purpose of fellowship with Mr. Edwards. Sometimes she accompanied him when he went from place to place in New England filling his preaching appointments, and she was by his side constantly during his last stay at Boston. Jerusha found great satisfaction in helping to care for one whom she regarded as an 'eminent servant of Christ'. Brainerd's strong attachment to her is reflected in one of his more amorous comments: 'It is a little piece of heaven to be in her presence.' This was not merely the love of a man for a woman, however, but the affection of one saint for another who shared his joys, sorrows, and sympathies to a remarkable degree.

We can well imagine what strong feelings Edwards himself must have had for Brainerd. If Edwards was to Brainerd the personal embodiment of spiritual greatness and doctrinal sound-ness, Brainerd must have seemed in Edwards' eyes the living image of all he felt a Christian should be. The missionary seemed to embody all the qualities which he had extolled in his great classic on *The Religious Affections*, a book which Brainerd cherished and often recommended to others. But Brainerd's interest in Jerusha, and Jerusha's in her David, certainly en-shrined him forever in Edwards' heart.

But life for Brainerd was more than Jerusha. In the twilight of his days, he was careful to improve his time and engage in profitable pursuits. When too ill to preach he wrote a preface to the diary of Thomas Shepard and also corrected his own private writings. Even when his pen was at rest his mind was active. He spent much time in reflecting upon the character of his past ministry and the nature of true religion. Edwards says that he spoke much of the prosperity of Zion, a theme upon which he delighted to dwell. 'His mind seemed to be carried forth with earnest concern about it, and intense desires that religion might speedily and abundantly revive and flourish.'

On September 17, there were unmistakable signs that death was approaching. 'Oh, the glorious time is now coming', he said. 'I have longed to serve God perfectly; now God will gratify those desires!' As his departure hastened, he continued to speak cheerfully of it as 'that glorious day'. But his desire to leave the world was not merely to quit a life of pain; he wanted to be where he could fully honour the Lord. 'My heaven is to please God, and glorify Him, and to give all to Him, and to be wholly devoted to His glory: that is the heaven I long for; that is my religion, and that is my happiness, and always was ever since I suppose I had any true religion; and all those that are of that religion shall meet me in heaven. I do not go to heaven to be advanced, but to give honour to God. It is no matter where I shall be stationed in heaven, whether I have a high or low seat there; but to love, and please, and glorify God is all. Had I a thousand souls, if they were worth any thing, I would give them all to God; but I have nothing to give, when all is done. ... It is impossible for any rational creature to be happy without acting all for God; God Himself could not make him happy any other way. I long to be in heaven, praising and glorifying God with the holy angels; all my desire is to glorify God.' After a few moments spent in uttering such expressions as these, he said, 'This is the last sermon I shall ever preach.' A week later, in great pain, he cried, 'Come, Lord Jesus. O, why is his chariot so long in coming?'

During these closing days, he was constantly waited on by Jerusha. The following touching scene is recorded by Edwards:

'On the morning of the next day, being Lord's day, October 4, as my daughter Jerusha, who chiefly attended him, came into the room, he looked on her very pleasantly and said, "Dear Jerusha, are you willing to part with me? I am quite willing to part with you . . . though if I thought I should not see you, and be happy with you in another world, I could not bear to part with you. But we shall spend a happy eternity together." That evening a friend came into his room with a Bible in her hand. When he saw it, he said, "O that dear book! that lovely book! I shall soon see it opened! the mysteries that are in it and the mysteries of God's providence will be all unfolded."'

On October 8, the pain in his chest was almost unbearable. The greater part of the day his reason seemed to leave him, a symptom unknown before. His physical distress increased late in the night to an even greater degree, but his mind became more composed. As the day was breaking on the morning of Friday the 9th, his weary soul was released from its shattered tabernacle to be forever with the Lord.

The following Monday at the funeral service held in the Northampton church, eight of the neighbouring ministers, many 'well-to-do' persons, and a great throng of people heard Jonathan Edwards deliver a solemn message. His subject – 'Christians when absent from the body are present with the Lord.'

Among the mourners that day was Jerusha, firm to the end in her love. But her days of mourning were not to be long, for the following February, at the tender age of eighteen, she also died, apparently from consumption, which she had contracted during the nineteen weeks she ministered to her lover. She was buried beside him in the churchyard at Northampton.

Thus ended the lives of David Brainerd, missionary and saint extraordinary, and his devoted Jerusha. 'Lovely and pleasant were they in their lives, and in their death they were not divided.'

The visitor to the Yale University campus of today will find an interesting tribute to David Brainerd. On one of the men's dormitories, the inscription, 'David Brainerd, Class of 1743' appears. This structure was built by the University in honour of a man whom it sent forth in disgrace from its halls two hundred years ago. Not only so, but, as the engraving indicates, Yale actually officially includes Brainerd today in its roll of graduates. The University, as one has put it, 'has confessed her errors and paid tribute to the greatness of the man's total career'. Quite fittingly, the institution which dealt to Brainerd his most humiliating setback now honours him in one of its memorial inscriptions.

But in reality, Brainerd survives today, not so much in inscriptions of stone, but in the living hearts of those who still find his life and ministry a challenge and inspiration. In fact, wherever men today mourn over sin, watch and wait and weep over perishing souls, and above all, bow in rapture before the 'God of unspeakable glory', there Brainerd's spirit, or better, the Spirit of his Master lives; for such devotion is generated and sustained by the living Christ Himself, who yet directs His distracted and suffering but resolute church to ultimate triumph.

XV. An Evaluation of Brainerd's Life and Character

We have studiously sought to avoid making this biography of Brainerd a mere series of dates, places, and statistics, for however much details may elucidate the life of an individual and make interesting reading, they usually do not reveal – they sometimes actually conceal – the dynamic of an individual's personality. The essential and most striking traits of Brainerd's character have already appeared in this biography in the extensive quotations from his Diary, Journal, and letters. It only remains to give a concise evaluation of Brainerd as a Christian, a religious teacher, and especially as a missionary. This will be done under three heads: his personal character, his doctrinal views, and his contribution to Christian missions.

A. HIS PERSONAL CHARACTER

Naturally enough biographers commonly tend to extol the virtues of their subjects while carefully concealing the faults, or at least magnifying the one while ignoring, minimizing, or even extenuating the other. It is also easy to become guilty of 'glorying in man' and using exaggerated language in praising mere creatures of the dust. But with due regard to the limitations imposed upon us by truth and sober thinking, it is not too much to claim that certain of the most beautiful traits of Christian character were displayed in an extraordinary degree in the life of David Brainerd. It is doubtful if there remains upon record in modern times any man who exhibited more fully in his life and experience the power of true Christianity than he. If love to Christ, humility, patience in trial, tenderness toward all mankind, contempt for earthly pleasures and comforts, fervency in prayer, and diligence in the work of the Lord are indicative of an advanced state of spirituality, then this was the case with David Brainerd, for he exhibited these qualities in abundant measure. His greatness does not lie in his eloquence as an orator, his profundity as a scholar, or his brilliance as a leader, for in none of these fields did he particularly excel, and that for a very simple reason: he never strove to do so. Though equipped with an unusually clear mind and an exceptional ability to express himself, and though possessing general talents sufficient to gain the admiration of his fellows had he so willed it, he ever sought to achieve excellence in the noble and needful but not so illustrious field of practical Christian endeavour. He chose to disdain even the opportunity of acquiring fame as a great thinker, theologian, or leader of a party, and made it his business to learn the ways and workings of the human heart in its relation to God. In this he met with amazing success.

It is fully recognized that while Brainerd was an unusually humble, devout, and zealous man, he was, after all, a man. One fault Edwards himself acknowledged and lamented – our missionary's excessive tendency to melancholy. The pessimistic outlook and the despair of life which came over him frequently seems unhealthy from both a physical and a spiritual viewpoint. In this respect, David Livingstone who, when leaving his homeland to go to dark and dangerous Africa said that he was more prone to levity than despondency, excelled him.

But if Brainerd's scale of emotion descended low, it also reached a height few Christians experience in this world. As his writings frequently reveal, at times he seemed to be in such transports of spiritual delight that all earth faded about him. Indeed, it is probable that his very proneness to melancholy, which was, after all, a part of his mental constitution, was closely connected with deep spiritual feelings; for not only is it a simple matter of experience that highly sensitive minds, more than others, are capable of great grief as well as of great joy, but those acquainted with the Word of God know that Christ has chosen His holy ones in the 'furnace of affliction' for their spiritual refinement. Seekers for pearls must dive deep in the ocean. Miners find the choicest jewels far below the surface of the ground, where gigantic pressures transform carbon into priceless diamonds. This has its counterpart in the spiritual realm. It is in dark deep valleys that the Lord makes Himself precious to His people and works rare graces in their hearts.

Undoubtedly Brainerd had his faults, but where can we go, outside the New Testament, to find his equal as an example of self-sacrifice and suffering for the sake of Christ and His gospel? Where such gentle devotion, such meek forbearance, such agonizing intercession, such tireless toil, such passionate pursuit of holiness, such patient, persistent preaching – all amid gigantic obstacles and terrific tribulations? Who today would, like Brainerd, be able to bid farewell to all earthly comforts and be willing to spend his life in the 'caves and dens of the earth' that Christ's kingdom might be advanced? Who would resign himself to seeing his body racked with pain and wasted away with disease in order to obtain one goal – the glory of God in the salvation of souls? The grace of God alone can enable a Brainerd cheerfully to forsake all selfish interests and follow the Lamb 'even unto death'.

B. HIS DOCTRINAL VIEWS

Many Christians today would be very enthusiastic in celebrating Brainerd's practical piety, but it is more than likely that few would rise to sing his praises as a doctrinal divine, for some of the theological tenets which Brainerd and most of his contemporaries held dearest are thrown out by modern evangelicals. Brainerd belonged to the class of men in centuries past known as Puritans. The name derives its significance from the movement in England in the 17th century which sought to cast out the Arminianism and looseness so rife in the State church. In their homeland, such outstanding men as John Owen, Stephen Charnock, Thomas Manton, and Samuel Rutherford spread their deep and profound piety among the people. Others like John Cotton, Thomas Hooker, and Thomas Shepard left their homes in England and emigrated to the new world, where they endeavoured to set up a pure church and a society rooted in the fear of God.

The type of doctrine they held – that known as Calvinistic – would be looked at askance by the majority of professed Christians today. Almost to a man, the Puritans were strong advocates of the doctrines named after the man who, though by no means the first, has long been regarded as their most distinguished advocate – the Genevan theologian, John Calvin. Brainerd and Edwards, born as they were after the Puritan period closed, nevertheless inherited its rich tradition, including its Calvinism. In fact, as appears in the preceding narrative, Brainerd believed firmly in divine sovereignty even before he was converted. As he went forth into the wilderness to preach to the Indians, he did so, fully believing that those would certainly be saved whom God had chosen unto salvation. For that reason he ever judged that success in his work depended solely on the good pleasure and power of God. Closely associated with his Calvinistic convictions was his belief that God had called him not to be successful but faithful. Typical is this entry in his Diary (under date February 3, 1745): 'I felt peace in my own soul and was satisfied, that if not one of the Indians should be profited by my preaching, but should all be damned, yet I should be accepted and rewarded as faithful; for I am persuaded, God enabled me to be so.'

It is also worthy of note that Brainerd's Calvinism was not contradictory to, but in fact included in its very essence, the necessity and importance of the earnest and faithful use of means. Certainly God had ordained all things according to the counsel of His own will, as far as Brainerd was concerned, but it was through diligence in prayer and a faithful witness borne to men that God accomplished His purposes in the salvation of sinners. A belief that his diligence was the ordained means of gathering in the elect of God caused Brainerd to toil and spend himself with a zeal and dedication that is almost unbelievable. Also, his confidence that God's purposes would most assuredly be accomplished and that Christ did not die in vain, accounts for the patience and perseverance he showed amid habitually discouraging circumstances.

But if Brainerd's Calvinism made him zealous and patient, it also produced a saneness and sobriety in his evangelistic efforts among the Indians. Since the glory of God even more than the good of man was, after all, his main concern, Brainerd never used any unscriptural methods to excite the Indians, and he never lowered his doctrinal or practical standards in order to multiply empty professions. It is true that he toiled between two and three years before gaining a single convert, but when his success came, it was not wood, hay, and stubble but the manifest work of God.

Again, Brainerd, in keeping with all the Puritans, saw no inconsistency between the doctrine of divine sovereignty and the free preaching of the gospel to all. It is doubtful if any Arminian ever lived who pleaded more passionately with men to turn to God than did Brainerd. When he preached he put the responsibility for sin squarely upon the hearers, and insisted continually that their guilt was greatly aggravated by 'rejecting the offers of mercy'. Neither he nor Edwards had any sympathy for the unscriptural notion that gospel invitations and commands were to be addressed only to certain classes of hearers, a view which stultifies evangelistic effort and turns the eyes of men inward rather than to Christ.

While Brainerd held firmly to the doctrines which today might receive the label of 'conservative', 'fundamentalist', or 'evangelical', he can best be described as a Puritanic Calvinist. His Calvinism was strict and unswerving but it was not a dead intellectualism, accompanied by spiritual barrenness and indifference. It made him careful and strict in daily living and warm in missionary effort.

The Christian world finds the personal godliness of Brainerd inspiring and his doctrinal views interesting, but it is as a missionary that he has found his niche in the history of the church. After all, it was to mission work among the Indians that he devoted his life: he never sought any other distinction.

His work was limited in time – the actual missionary service was concentrated into four short years. It was limited in its geographical outreach – not for Brainerd the task of bringing an entire continent, or even an extensive State, under the sound of the Gospel. Yet in its intensity and degree of spiritual power, Brainerd's brief period of ministry will bear comparison with the careers of men of greater name and wider, though not greater, achievement.

Who, after reading the well-established facts, can deny that Brainerd was dedicated to the Lord to a degree which should make the great mass of Christians blushingly ashamed of their comparative coldness of heart, and their unfeeling indifference to the claims of the kingdom of God? Brainerd's example reveals the vast majority of professed believers as little better than renegades towards the sacred cause of Christ. Which of us dare for one moment claim to have been exercised in soul to one tenth the extent that is made public by the self-revelation of our missionary in his Diary and Journal? Clinging as we do so tenaciously to all the comforts and amenities of our boasted civilization, as if we could not live apart from them, which of us, after reading Brainerd's writings, dare claim to be at best more than a pale shadow of this son of Connecticut, or rather, this child of the living God? As we view his willingness to endure all things for the elect's sake among the Indian tribes, we feel challenged by his example and rebuked for our own slothfulness. As we feel his heart-beat of devotion to Christ, we come under divine constraint to utter a prayer to God that a portion of his heavenly spirit may fall on us.

Brainerd's example of selfless devotion is such that it might seem to put all other missionaries to a perpetual reproach. We know that this is not so. Wisdom is justified of all her children.

But, comparisons apart, by any Christian criterion, David Brainerd is a missionary star of the first magnitude. The light that streams from his life and labours has flooded, not only the Church of God in America, but the Church in all the continents, and many have found in its warming rays a new urge to labour for the Lord.

It is for this reason that we remember Brainerd today. He stands out not so much because of the good he did among his beloved Indians, but because of the inspiration he has given to untold multitudes of others, and especially missionaries, who have, through reading, felt the impact of his faith. Only a few hundred were brought to Christ as a direct result of his preaching, but no one can fully calculate how many hearts have been set aflame with love to souls and have devoted themselves to a life of self-sacrifice for the glory of God by the example he set.

When Brainerd died, he left his Diary, Journal, and private correspondence in the hands of Jonathan Edwards who immediately realized their autobiographical value. He began at once to prepare them for publication, with his own remarks scattered throughout the Diary and in footnotes. *The Memoirs of the Rev. David Brainerd* soon came off the press and was hailed far and near as a classic. Since its first publication in 1749, it has gone through numerous editions, the most recent being in the Wycliffe series by the Moody Press of the United States. Our main interest now is the impact this volume had on the generations of readers from Edwards' day until the present. In this connection, a discussion appearing in the December, 1961, edition of *The Journal of the* (American) *Presbyterian Historical Society* is useful. It says, 'William Carey, the first missionary of the great movement of modern Protestant missions, read the life of Brainerd and held him, along with the Apostle Paul and John Eliot, in the highest esteem. In the operation of the Serampore mission, Ward, Marshman, and Carey all affirmed a covenant three times a year which included the following statement: "Let us often look at Brainerd, . . . in the woods of America pouring out his very soul before God for the people. Prayer, secret, fervent, expectant, lies at the root of all personal godliness. A competent knowledge of the languages where a missionary lives, a mild and winning temper, and a heart given up to God – these are the attainments which more than all other gifts, will fit us to become God's instruments in the great work of redemption."

'Thomas Coke, the early Methodist missionary leader, was also influenced by Brainerd. Robert Morrison, missionary to China, acknowledged in his diary the high position of Paul, Brainerd, and Eliot as missionaries. Another early great missionary, Henry Martyn, traces his first inspiration and renewed consecration to David Brainerd among others. In the United States, Edwards' publication of the Memoirs of the Rev. David Brainerd affected Samuel Mills who was influential in the beginnings of the American Protestant missionary movement.'

To this impressive list might be added the name of Robert M'Cheyne, who cherished the life of Brainerd and sought to emulate him. In his diary he writes, 'Life of David Brainerd. Most wonderful man! What conflicts, what depressions, desertions, strength, advancement, victories within thy torn bosom! I cannot express what I think when I think of thee. Tonight, more set upon missionary enterprise than ever.' (M'Cheyne's *Works*, Volume I, p. 20.)

It may be conjectured that multitudes of Christian missionaries whose names are forgotten by all but the Lord, have found inspiration in Brainerd's pages, and not a few may, under God, have been actually induced by them to count not their lives dear unto themselves, that they might preach among the heathen the unsearchable riches of Christ. Whatever be the case, the history of missionary enterprise cannot do other than place David Brainerd in the very front rank of missionary pioneers.

Let us never forget, however, that the cause that inspired Brainerd still moves the hearts of men, and the God who conquered him is still in the business of saving souls. Even yet, over two hundred years after American Indians heard the gospel for the first time through the preaching of Connecticut's greatest son, the fields are white unto harvest. Even today, in a world priding itself on its enlightenment, culture, and progress, 'The heathen in his blindness, bows down to wood and stone', and needy souls all over the world cry out, 'Come over and help us.' Perhaps God will call someone in our own age to leave home, friends, and earthly comforts, to bear His Evangel to the 'regions beyond'. Maybe some will have the vision and devotion, even now, sincerely to pray – with the lives of men like Brainerd before them:

'They climbed the steep ascent of heaven thro' peril, toil, and pain:
O God, to us may grace be given to follow in their train.'

Bibliography

Day, Richard Ellsworth, *Flagellant on Horseback*. Philadelphia: The Judson Press, 1950.

Dwight, Sereno Edwards, *Memoirs of Rev. David Brainerd*. New Haven: S. Converse, 1822.

Edwards, President, *The Works of*, with a Memoir of His life, Vol. I. New York: G. & C. Carvill, 1830.

Edwards, President, *The Works of*, containing Memoirs of the Rev. David Brainerd, Vol. X. New York: G. & C. Carvill, 1830.

Howard, Phillip E., Jr., *The Life and Diary of David Brainerd*, Newly Edited and with a Biographical Sketch of President Edwards. Moody Press, 1949.

Norris, Rev. William H., *The Life of the Rev. David Brainerd*, abridged from Authentic Sources. New York: Carlton & Phillips, 1853.

Pearce, Winifred M., *David Brainerd*. London: Oliphants Ltd., 1957.

Presbyterian Historical Society, *Journal of*, Vol. 38. Lancaster Pa. and Philadelphia, Pa. Published by the Department of History of the United Presbyterian Church in the USA, 1960.

Sherwood, J. M., *Memoirs of Rev. David Brainerd*, Missionary to the Indians of North America; Based on the life of Brainerd prepared by Jonathan Edwards, D.D., and afterwards revised and enlarged by Sereno E. Dwight, D.D., New York: Funk & Wagnalls, 1884.

Smith, Oswald J., Litt. D., *David Brainerd, His Message for Today*, Foreword by A. J. Gordon. London, Edinburgh: Marshall, Morgan & Scott, 1949.

Styles, John, *The Life of David Brainerd*. Boston, 1821.

Wesley, John A. M., *An Extract of the Life of the Late Rev. David Brainerd*. London: 1800.

Wynbeek, David, *Beloved Yankee*, A Biography of David Brainerd. Grand Rapids, Michigan: Wm. B. Eerdmans Publishing Co., 1961.

GREATHEART OF CHINA

A brief life of
WILLIAM CHALMERS BURNS, M.A.,
Scottish Evangelist and Revival Leader,
and Early Missionary to China

by

R. STRANG MILLER, B.A., LL.M., B.D.

I. A Chosen Vessel

William Chalmers Burns was born in a Scottish manse, and enjoyed the moral momentum of a godly ancestry. His father, William Hamilton Burns, after training for the ministry of the Church of Scotland at the University of Edinburgh, was ordained and inducted as assistant and successor to the elderly minister of the parish of Dun, County of Angus, in 1800, at the age of twenty-one. Six years later W. H. Burns married Elizabeth Chalmers of Aberdeen, seven of their ten children being born at Dun, and the three youngest at Kilsyth, whither their father was translated in 1821, on a presentation from the Crown.

John, the eldest son, died in his second year; James became founder of the publishing house of Burns & Oates, London; Margaret married George Moody, writer, Paisley (brother of the Rev. A. Moody Stuart of St. Luke's, Edinburgh); Jane married the Rev. Charles Stewart, Free Church minister at Fort William, Argyll; William Chalmers, the fifth child and third son, is the subject of this brief life; Islay also entered the ministry, and became Professor of Divinity in the Glasgow College of the Free Church of Scotland; Charlotte married Miller Berrie, a Dundee merchant; Elizabeth married the Rev. Thomas Bain, Free Church minister at Coupar-Angus; Walter went into business in Belfast as a music publisher; while the youngest child, also named John, died in his third year.*

Thus shadows fell on the brightest hours of this devout Scots family; but joy abounded, and true happiness predominated. The father was said to be 'gentle, reverent, gracious, full of kind thoughts, devout affections, and fresh and genial sympathies, serious without moroseness, cheerful, and even sometimes gay without lightness'; while the mother is described as 'active, buoyant, all life and motion, the glad sunshine and bright angel of

*Fasti Ecclesiae Scoticanae, Vol. III, p. 480.

the house'. Well could the future missionary say with the Psalmist, 'The lines are fallen unto me in pleasant places; yea, I have a goodly heritage' (Ps. 16. 6).

William was born in the manse of Dun on April 1, 1815; and was six years old when the family removed to Kilsyth, a town twelve miles east of Glasgow. Here he attended the parish school, whose headmaster was the Rev. Alexander Salmon, later of Sydney, Australia, and 'a teacher of rare intelligence and skill'. The boy worked well, and took a good place in all his classes; but he was especially fond of sport and recreation, and loved to ramble in the fields and woods. Outside school, he showed little interest in books – with two notable exceptions: *The Pilgrim's Progress*, which he eagerly devoured while recovering from an accident, and the *Life of Sir William Wallace*, the great Scottish hero.

In addition to the Sabbath services, the father's direct influence on his sons included a half-hour session of private reading with them in the study before breakfast in the morning, and the regular Sabbath evening hour of catechizing and prayer.

Possibly because most of his fellow-pupils contemplated such a calling, William too at first thought of taking up farming. But a maternal uncle from Aberdeen, on a visit to the Kilsyth manse, recognized in the twelve-year-old boy a 'lad o' pairts', and persuaded the parents to let him take their son back to the Aberdeen Grammar School for a year. There young Burns came under the spell of the Rector, Dr. James Melvin, a brilliant classics scholar, and finished the year as one of his best pupils.

He then entered the University of Aberdeen, taking fifth place in the entrance list of bursars or open scholars of Marischal College, out of a field of more than a hundred competitors. In his two sessions there, he was well placed in all his classes. Then in 1831 he returned home, having decided now to follow in his uncle's steps, and qualify for the profession of law. This was a great disappointment to his father, who had hoped for a son to succeed him in the ministry, and it was only with reluctance that he gave his consent. In reaching this decision, the lad was moved entirely by worldly considerations, remarking quite frankly that he 'saw lawyers rich and with fine houses!'

With this prospect in view, William then went to Edinburgh, where he entered the office of his father's brother, Alexander Burns W.S.,* with the intention of becoming an articled clerk. But providentially, before the articles were completed and signed, something happened which gave a new purpose and direction to his life. His intimation of this change was quite dramatic. Appearing unexpectedly at the Kilsyth manse one evening, looking more serious than usual, he enquired: 'What would you think, Mamma, if I should be a minister after all?' What had led to this momentous decision, and to his walking thirty-six miles from Edinburgh to announce it?

'The first touch of serious thought' detected by his brother, was when William, probably just home from Aberdeen and before proceeding to Edinburgh, overheard his father's voice in prayer late at night, and remarked in a whisper: 'There can be no doubt where *his* heart is, and where he is going.' Islay adds, 'It was not long before the great, decisive change took place, and may possibly have been the first living seed of grace that sunk into his heart.'

On a visit to Edinburgh ten years later, Burns could recall the very room, at 41 York Place, 'where, when reading Pike's *Early Piety* on a Sabbath afternoon, I think about the middle of December, 1831, an arrow from the quiver of the King of Zion was shot by his Almighty sovereign hand through my heart, though it was hard enough to resist all inferior means of salvation.' He also revisited his former lodgings at 69 Broughton Place, 'where my earliest days as a child of grace were spent, and where first the Spirit of God shone with full light upon the glory of Jesus as a Saviour for such as I was. This was, I think, about the 7th of January, 1832'.

'The means by which my change of heart was brought about were these, I think – Mr. Bruce's preaching, which engaged me much, and the fear of sudden death from the approach of cholera, were preparatory. A letter from my sisters at home, in which they spoke in a single sentence of going as pilgrims to Zion, and leaving me behind, proved a word in season and touched my natural

*'W.S.': Writer to the Signet, the Scottish term for a solicitor or attorney ('Signet' refers to the smaller seal of the reigning Sovereign.)

feelings very deeply.' Thus 'the way was prepared, but as yet I am fully conscious that my heart was spiritually dead.

'However the set time came. I sat down, with solemn impressions arising from the causes now mentioned, to read a part of Pike's *Early Piety*, which my dear father had given me at leaving home; (ah! little did he know what use God was to make of it, little did the author of that solemn treatise know one of the purposes for which he wrote it!); and in one moment, while gazing on a solemn passage in it, my inmost soul was in one instant pierced as with a dart. God had apprehended me.'

'From the first moment of this wonderful experience, I had the inspiring hope of being saved by a sovereign and infinitely gracious God; and in the same instant almost I felt that I *must* leave my present occupation, and devote myself to Jesus in the ministry of that glorious gospel by which I had been saved.' It was now his uncle's turn to acquiesce reluctantly in his decision to transfer from Law to Divinity. Burns then returned home for the summer; and, towards the end of 1832, took up residence again at Aberdeen, but now with a view to preparing himself for the ministry of the Church of Scotland.

Those who had known him during his previous residence at the University were quick to notice 'a visibly heightened tone of earnestness and energy in all his work, due to the higher motives and principles which now inspired him. A true Christian, he became more than ever an earnest student'. That session he took first place in the Senior Mathematics class; and in his fourth and last session at Aberdeen, he tied with another for the Mathematics scholarship, 'then and for long afterwards the highest attainable distinction in the University'.

Graduating as Master of Arts in 1834, Burns then elected to take his Divinity course at the University of Glasgow. One might have expected that the growing reputation of Dr. Thomas Chalmers would have drawn him to Edinburgh; but perhaps Glasgow was chosen as being nearer to the family home at Kilsyth. His fellow-students there included James Hamilton, later renowned minister of the Gospel in London, and William Arnot, soon to achieve fame as a Bible expositor, with whom 'he spent many hallowed hours of sweet communion in conference and in prayer'.

He was diligent in study, submitting 'a long series of prize essays on Old Testament subjects for the Hebrew class', winning a medal for Hellenistic Greek, and even finding time to study French. He was also a foundation member of the Glasgow University *Students' Missionary Society*, in which he became an influential leader, and through which he heard the call to foreign service, when Dr. James Kalley spoke of his own call to China. In the event, considerations of health prevented the Doctor from going overseas; but Burns was to prove in due course a worthy substitute.

During his last two sessions in Glasgow, Burns derived great profit and inspiration from regular attendance upon the ministry of the Rev. John Duncan at Milton Street Church. Dr. Duncan was to become the Church of Scotland's first missionary to the Jews at Budapest, Hungary, and then, after the Disruption, the first Professor of Oriental Languages in the New College, Edinburgh. Nicknamed 'Rabbi' Duncan, and known to posterity as 'the Scottish Pascal', he was undoubtedly a spiritual genius, whose literary remains are a rare treasure; and one can well imagine the benefit Burns would derive from his ministry. Indeed it seemed to him that every Sabbath spent in Milton church was like a day on Patmos, and every sermon heard there like the opening of the gate of heaven.

As the end of his course of training came in sight, Burns solemnly reflected that 'I am approaching, as you know, an era of my history, if we except the time of conversion, the most important that can occur to a human being in this world – soon must I offer myself, miserable as I am, to the Church of God as a candidate for the work of an evangelist; and still more, that Church must decide, so great is the honour I have in prospect, whether in this land or among the perishing heathen it shall be my lot to preach to sinners the unsearchable riches of Christ crucified'.

During these critical weeks of decision, his mother went into Glasgow one day to transact some business, and was passing through the Argyle Arcade when she saw her son suddenly appear round a corner and walk slowly towards her. He was deep in thought, and did not notice her till she came up and spoke to him. 'Oh mother!', he exclaimed, 'I did not see you; for when walking along Argyle Street just now, I was so overcome with the sight of the countless crowds of immortal beings eagerly hasting hither and thither, but all posting onwards towards the eternal world, that I could bear it no longer, and turned in here to seek relief in quiet thought.'

His course of study completed, and trials for license satisfactorily sustained, William Chalmers Burns, M.A., was licensed to preach the gospel as a probationer for the ministry, by the Church of Scotland Presbytery of Glasgow, on March 27, 1839. What should he now do? In an interesting memorandum prepared later, he narrates the way by which God led him to and beyond this point.

'At Glasgow University, during the winter 1837–38, I was led, from my connection with the College Missionary Association, to feel so deeply my personal responsibility in regard to the spread of the gospel among the heathen, that after much prayer and many solemn exercises of soul, I took the solemn step of writing to my father, to request that, if he thought good, he should communicate with Dr. Gordon, the convener of our India Committee, and let him know that, should the Church deem me qualified, I would be ready to go as a missionary to Hindustan. He did this, and the Committee having given me encouragement in the matter, I looked upon myself as publicly devoted to the missionary field. In my own soul, and in all my public duties connected with missionary meetings, etc., etc., I felt from that time forward a greatly enlarged measure of the presence and blessing of God, tending to confirm me more deeply in my cherished hope and purpose.

'This was the last Session which I needed to spend at College to complete my curriculum; but, partly because I found myself profitably engaged in study, and still more, I believe, because I waited in expectation of a call to the missionary field, I remained at College during the following winter, and in the spring of 1839 a proposal was made by the Colonial Committee that I should go out for a season to fill a charge at St. John's, New Brunswick, and proceed direct from America to India when the India Committee should require me. It was expected that the India Committee would accede to this proposal but they refused, wishing that their agents should be free to go when wanted, and so the matter ended.

'This was at the very time when Mr. M'Cheyne, about to set out for Palestine, wrote, asking me to take his place at Dundee. I found myself unexpectedly free to do this, and being speedily licensed I entered on my duties in that memorable field. This was at the beginning of April. In the month of June or July I received the call that I had long looked for, being asked by the India Committee to go to Poona in the Presidency of Bombay. My engagement at Dundee stood in the way of my at once complying, and another call which the Jewish Committee gave me to go to Aden and Arabia increased the difficulty.

'While asking guidance in regard to my duty, I went to the Communion at Kilsyth in July, when the Lord began to employ me in a way so remarkable for the awakening of sinners, that in returning to Dundee, and finding myself in the midst of a great spiritual awakening, I was obliged to make known to both Committees that, while my views regarding missionary work remained unchanged, yet I found that I must for the time remain where I was, and fulfil the work which God was laying upon me with a mighty hand.'

By this unusual chain of circumstances, the fulfilment of the vow of William Burns to serve God in the foreign field, was deferred for nine years – deferred but not defeated. The intervening period was crowded with useful and extraordinary labours; and when the call came afresh, it found this chosen vessel ready to respond immediately, 'Here am I, send me'. But whereas the immediate field would have been India, or Arabia, or European Jewry, the ultimate field was to be China, the world's largest mission field, then slowly and reluctantly opening to foreign influence and witness.

II. Times of Refreshing

Burns began his ministry in the parish church of St. Peter's, Dundee, as stated supply for the seraphic Robert Murray M'Cheyne (then on a visit to Palestine with the Church of Scotland's Mission of Inquiry to the Jews*), in April, 1839. The text of his first sermon was Romans 12. 1, which aptly epitomized both the ministry then commencing, and his whole subsequent career.

It was no light thing thus to take the place and fill the pulpit of one of the most gifted and successful evangelical ministers of that or any age in Scotland. Yet the young licentiate acquitted himself well, and had hardly entered on his work when his power as a preacher began to be felt. Crowds continued to flock to the church, and the people hung on his words, his popularity proving an embarrassment to himself. 'Discovered through grace', he writes, 'an awful hungering after applause from man.' And again, 'I had an affecting disclosure to myself of the pride and vanity of my heart, which praise of late has awfully stirred up; none but an omnipotent and infinitely gracious Saviour will suit my case.'

He was diligent in study, mentioning incidentally the benefit derived from reading 'Fleming's remarkable and precious *Fulfilling of the Scripture* regarding the strength afforded to God's saints under trials and for difficult duties. Praise the Lord! But O for a revival of that experimental, deep-laid religion which Fleming valued and exemplifies so fully in his pages!' His life was also steeped in devotion. 'Yesterday spent the morning in prayer. Walked, and read Boston's life – a precious monument to the praise of grace – noble standard of ministerial character.' He prayed, 'O that the Lord would give me the skill of a Brainerd or a Dickson, for my present difficult and most precious duties!'

---

*The Narrative of this Mission, which runs to 555 octavo pages, was first published in 1843. It is intensely interesting.

When obliged to defer a candidate for church membership, he wrote: 'Oh what need of the powerful presence of the Holy Ghost, without whom a free Saviour will, and must be, a Saviour despised and rejected of men. How hard it is to unite in just proportions the humbling doctrine of man's inability to come to Christ without regeneration, and the free gospel offer which is the moral means employed by God in conversion!'

Thus the first few months passed. Yet he was not satisfied, and later wrote that 'during the first four months of my ministry, which were spent at Dundee, I enjoyed much of the Lord's presence in my own soul, and laid in large stores of divine knowledge in preparing from week to week for my pulpit services in St. Peter's Church. But though I endeavoured to speak the truth fully, and to press it earnestly on the souls of the people, there was still a defect in my preaching at that time which I have since learned to correct, viz. that, partly from unbelieving doubts regarding the truth in all its infinite magnitude, and partly from a tendency to shrink back from speaking in such a way as visibly and generally to alarm the people, I never came, as it were, to throw down the gauntlet to the enemy by the unreserved declaration and urgent application of the divine testimony regarding the state of fallen man and the necessity for an unreserved surrender to the Lord Jesus in all his offices in order that he may be saved'.

'During the last three Sabbaths that I was at Dundee, before coming to Kilsyth, I was led in a great measure to preach without writing, not because I neglected to study, but in order that I might study and pray for a longer time; and in preaching on the subjects which I had thus prepared, I was more than usually sensible of the divine support. The people also seemed to feel more deeply solemnized, and I was told of some who were shedding silent tears under the Word of the Lord.' Another circumstance 'accompanied with a blessing from Jehovah to my soul', was the death in the Lord of his brother-in-law, George Moody. At the funeral at Paisley, Burns wrote, 'I had a glorious anticipation of the Second Coming of the Lord, when He would himself raise up in glory everlasting that dear body which He had appointed us to bury in its corruption and decay.'

In ways like these this chosen vessel was prepared for the conspicuous service he was to render at the Kilsyth Communion season. The place too had been prepared. It had shared with Cambuslang, almost a century before, in the gracious awakening under the ministry of James Robe in 1742–43. And it had long enjoyed the faithful ministry of Burns' father, whose attention had been drawn increasingly to that previous revival, and to the need for a fresh outpouring of the Spirit of God. 'Finally, on a Sabbath afternoon in August, 1838, standing on the grave of his revered predecessor, Mr. Robe, on the anniversary of his death, and taking as his text the words inscribed in Hebrew letters on his tomb, Isaiah 26. 19, he pled before a vast assemblage of his people, in behalf of Christ and the new birth unto eternal life, in tones of unaccustomed earnestness, and which stirred the hearts of many in a manner never to be forgotten.'

The following August, 1839, Burns joined his father for the Kilsyth Communion, being delayed en route by the funeral at Paisley, but arriving in time to preach on the Friday evening. He also spoke briefly at the third Table service on the Sabbath, and preached again that evening; 'but, as far as I can recollect, without remarkable assistance or remarkable effects. At the close, however, I felt such a yearning of heart over the poor people among whom I had spent so many of my youthful years in sin, that I intimated I would again address them before bidding them farewell – it might be never to meet again on earth. This meeting was fixed for Tuesday at 10 a.m., as I intended that day to leave Kilsyth on my return to Dundee.

'I can hardly recall the feelings with which I went to preach on Tuesday morning – a morning fixed from all eternity in Jehovah's counsels as an era in the history of redemption.' But, 'though I cannot speak with precision of the frame of soul in which I went to the Lord's work on that memorable day, yet I remember in general that I had an intense longing for the conversion of souls and the glory of Emmanuel, that I mourned under a sense of the awful state of sinners without Christ, their guilt in rejecting him as freely offered to their acceptance, my own total inability to help them by anything that I could do, and my complete unfitness and unworthiness to be an instrument in the hands of the Holy Ghost in saving their souls; while at the same time my eyes were fixed on the Lord as the God of salvation with a sweet hope of his glorious appearing.'

In the event 'the morning proved very unfavourable for our assembling in the open air, and this seems to have been a wise providential arrangement; for while, on the one hand, it was necessary that our meeting should be intimated for the open air, in order to collect the great multitude; on the other hand, it was very needful, in order to the right management of so glorious a work as that which followed, that we should be assembled within doors. At 10 o'clock I went down to the middle of the town, and with some others drove up before us some stragglers who were remaining behind the crowd. When I entered the pulpit, I saw before me an immense multitude from the town and neighbour-hood filling the seats, stairs, passages and porches, all in their ordinary clothes, and including many of the most abandoned of our population'.

Burns read Acts 2, and preached on Psalm 110. 3, 'Thy people shall be willing in the day of thy power'. In applying the text, he was led 'to allude to some of the most remarkable outpourings of the Spirit that have been granted to the Church, beginning from the day of Pentecost; and in surveying this galaxy of Divine wonders, I had come to notice the glorious revelation of Jehovah's right hand which was given at the Kirk of Shotts in 1630, while John Livingstone was preaching from Ezekiel 36. 26f., when it pleased the Sovereign God of grace to make bare his holy arm in the midst of us, and to perform a work in many souls resembling that of which I had been speaking, in majesty and glory!

'In referring to this wonderful work of the Spirit, I mentioned the fact that when Mr. Livingstone was on the point of closing his discourse a few drops of rain began to fall, and that when the people began to put on their coverings, he asked them if they had any shelter from the drops of Divine wrath, and was thus led to enlarge for nearly another hour in exhorting them to flee to Christ, with so much of the power of God, that about five hundred persons were converted. And just when I was speaking of the occasion and the nature of this wonderful address, I felt my own soul moved in a manner so remarkable that I was led, like Mr. Livingstone, to plead with the unconverted before me *instantly* to close with God's offers of mercy, and continued to do so until the power of the Lord's Spirit became so mighty upon their souls as to carry all before it, like the rushing mighty wind of Pentecost!

'During the whole of the time that I was speaking, the people listened with the most riveted and solemn attention, and with many silent tears and inward groanings of the spirit; but at the last their feelings became too strong for all ordinary restraints, and broke forth simultaneously in weeping and wailing, tears and groans, intermingled with shouts of joy and praise from some of the people of God. The appearance of a great part of the people from the pulpit gave me an awfully vivid picture of the state of the ungodly in the day of Christ's coming to judgment. Some were screaming out in agony; others, and among these strong men, fell to the ground as if they had been dead; and such was the general commotion, that after repeating for some time the most free and urgent invitations of the Lord to sinners (as Isaiah 55, Rev. 22. 17), I was obliged to give out a psalm, which was soon joined in by a considerable number, our voices being mingled with the mourning groans of many prisoners sighing for deliverance.' The meeting concluded at 3 p.m., having lasted five hours.

Two moments in that memorable gathering deeply impressed the preacher's brother, Islay. The one was when, as William steadily warmed to his theme, 'appeal followed appeal in ever-increasing fervour and terrible energy, till at last, as he reached the climax of his argument, and vehemently urged his hearers to fight the battle that they might win the eternal prize, the words, *No Cross, no Crown*, pealed from his lips, not so much like a sentence of ordinary speech, as a shout in the thick of battle!' The other 'moment of intense and uncontrollable emotion' was when, in 'urging sinners to an immediate closing with Christ in the offers of his grace', Burns used the illustration of a life-boat going to the relief of a doomed vessel. He graphically pictured 'the crouching, trembling throng clinging to the gunwale'; and 'as he saw them still hesitating and wasting in fatal inaction the last moments of opportunity, he cried aloud, as one might do from the summit of a neighbouring headland on the shore, "Are you in? Are you in? Flee for refuge to lay hold of the hope set before you! Now or never!" ' At the time, the preacher was twenty-four years of age.

Burns had to return to Dundee a day or two later; but the movement so remarkably begun, continued to grow in depth and solidity over the ensuing weeks, and towards the end of September he came back to Kilsyth for a second Communion season which the new birth of so many souls had rendered necessary. Arriving at noon on Saturday, he found himself due to speak at an afternoon service, and 'accordingly preached to about a thousand from Rom. 10. 4, with much assistance'. Next morning, he preached at the tent 'for about two hours from Isaiah 54. 5, to a congregation which, according to a calculation founded on the extent of the ground which it occupied, is thought to have been little short of ten thousand'. After another large and lengthy open air gathering in the evening, at which he preached, Burns suggested a further gathering in the church for prayer. The bell was rung about 10 p.m., and the church soon filled. 'We separated from this most precious meeting, in which not a few were awakened, at 3 a.m. of Monday, and after leaving the church, Mr. Somerville and I were forced to remain in the session-house with the distressed, instructing and praying till between 5 and 6 o'clock, when we went home to rest.'

Burns preached again that Monday afternoon, when many ministers were present; and, at the close of the evening service, he suggested that the unconverted should come forward to the front seats, to be addressed and prayed for. 'In this work I was assisted, I think, as much as ever before in my life, having a degree of tenderness and affection which my hard, hard heart is rarely privileged to feel, and in prayer I was favoured with peculiar nearness to God, insomuch that at one time I felt as if really in contact with the Divine presence, and could hardly go on; while at the same blessed season there seemed to be a general and sweet melting of heart among the audience, and many of the unconverted were weeping bitterly aloud, though I spoke throughout with perfect calmness and solemnity. We separated between 1 and 2 o'clock from this the last, and I think, without doubt, the most eminently blessed part of the whole communion season, at least in as far as I was a witness to it.'

Meantime there were showers of blessing at Dundee, and these continued throughout Burns' ministry there. In his admirable life of M'Cheyne, Andrew Bonar notes that 'for some time before, Mr. Burns had seen symptoms of deeper attention than usual, and real anxiety in some that had hitherto been careless. But it was after his return from Kilsyth that the people began to melt before the Lord. On Thursday, the second day after his return, at the close of the usual evening prayer meeting in St. Peter's, and when the minds of many were deeply solemnized by the tidings which had reached them, he spoke a few words about what had for some days detained him from them, and invited those to remain who felt the need of an outpouring of the Spirit to convert them. About a hundred remained; and at the conclusion of a solemn address to these anxious souls, suddenly the power of God seemed to descend, and all were bathed in tears.

'At a similar meeting, next evening, in the church, there was much melting of heart and intense desire after the Beloved of the Father; and on adjoining to the vestry the arm of the Lord was revealed. No sooner was the vestry door opened to admit those who might feel anxious to converse, than a vast number pressed in with awful eagerness. It was like a pent-up flood breaking forth; tears were streaming from the eyes of many, and some fell on the ground, groaning and weeping, and crying for mercy. Onward from that evening meetings were held every day for many weeks; and the extraordinary nature of the work justified and called for extraordinary services. The whole town was moved.'

At the height of the movement, a 'day of fasting, humiliation and prayer' was intimated for 'the fair-day', 'by the recommendation of the Session'. On returning home from a meeting late the previous evening, Burns 'found a letter from the magistrates interdicting the preaching in the meadows for Tuesday, which did not surprise me, but led me to meditate solemnly on that approaching conflict with the world and Satan in which many will probably be called to die for the name of Jesus. O Lord, may Jesus Christ be magnified in me, whether by life or by death!' The Ten Years' Conflict between Moderates and Evangelicals in the Church of Scotland was rapidly reaching its climax, and such clashes with the civil authority were becoming unhappily a commonplace. Burns, however, wisely took evading action. 'I immediately was led to see the propriety of exchanging the meadows for St. Peter's Churchyard, and accordingly next day, at the hour appointed, Mr. Baxter, Mr. Miller and myself, after intimating the will of the magistrates in the Meadows, walked accompanied by a great number, from thence to the churchyard, where many were already assembled.' But, perhaps because of the general excitement, Burns on this occasion had 'no enlargement, and after speaking about the usual time under great conscious desertion of the Spirit, I came to a close'.

But this was unusual; and the evangelist now began a fresh volume of his journal, which he headed: 'A record of the Lord's marvellous doings for me and many other sinners at Dundee, 1839.' Amongst the many ministers who came to observe this work of the Lord, was 'a reverend-looking oldish man', who proved to be 'Caesar Malan from Geneva', and who 'was desirous to preach this evening, which I intimated with joy to the people as they were dispersing'. Malan preached on John 14. 27; and 'his great design appeared to be to press on believers, "in the name of Jesus", the duty of believing that they *are* saved. His teaching seemed to me to differ from that which is common among our best ministers, not in holding that assurance is of the essence of faith, which he seemed plainly not to do; nor in anything at variance with particular redemption, which he seemed also to hold distinctly, speaking always of Jesus dying for "his beloved church", etc.; but in pressing us very specially to believe in the name of Jesus as the Son of God with adoration and love, and again pressing all who do so to believe that they *are* saved, because God says so, not seeming to notice or to suppose the case of those who do not know whether they believe or not'.

If the Scot was thus uncertain of his Swiss visitor and his emphasis, Malan for his part was critical of Burns and his methods. 'He seems', wrote the latter, 'to fear all excitement in divine worship, going to the very opposite extreme from the Methodists, saying as he did to me, that this leads men away from the simple testimony of God; and he told me he thought I had far too much when he heard me speak a few words and pray in the afternoon. I cannot, however, agree with him altogether, and I think many facts in regard to the preaching which has been most honoured in this land prove that that which is accompanied with the deepest impression of the truth on the speaker's soul, and consequently most affects the hearers, is in general most blessed for leading men to flee from the wrath to come.'

And so the Dundee revival went on, reaching its climax at the October Communion season, in 'a kind of spring-tide flood', 'when the late much esteemed and highly gifted Mr. Bonar of Larbert, assisted by Messrs. Bonar of Kelso, McDonald of Blairgowrie, and Flyter of Alness, dispensed the living bread to a vast concourse of hungering souls, "many of whom seemed burning with desire after nearness to Jesus". On the evening of the day three several congregations were assembled – one vast assemblage in the church, and two lesser ones formed out of its overflow in the adjoining school-rooms, and were addressed respectively by Mr. Bonar of Kelso, Mr. Bonar of Larbert, and Mr. Burns.'

At length M'Cheyne returned from his fact-finding tour, and Burns' term of supply at St. Peter's came to an end. The prospect of separation from a flock to which he had become deeply attached, affected him as much as it did the people. On Thursday evening, November 23, he writes, 'I met Mr. M'Cheyne at his own home at half past six, and had a sweet season of prayer with him before the hour of the evening meeting. We went both into the pulpit; and after he had sung and prayed shortly, I conducted the remaining services, speaking from II Samuel 23. 1–5, and concluding at ten. We went to his house together and conversed a considerable time about many things connected with the work of God, and his and my own future plans and prospects.'

III.   Labours More Abundant

During his seven or eight months at Dundee in 1839, Burns found
time to respond to calls to minister briefly in a number of other
Scottish cities and towns. Thus we find him preaching, as a rule
'with much assistance', to 'densely crowded' audiences, at
Paisley, Kirkintilloch, Denny, Edinburgh and St. Andrews, the
meetings at the two last-named places being attended by 'the
genteel society of Edinburgh', and 'the elite of the town, including
Sir David Brewster'. The return of M'Cheyne to Dundee freed
him for regular evangelistic activity of this nature. Limitations of
space preclude mention of all the places he visited, and all the
meetings he addressed, in a land which he found 'ripe for the
harvest'. But space must be found for some record of his extended
and effective visits to Perth and Aberdeen.

After a brief, earlier visit, the Perth meetings began on the last
Sabbath of 1839. For the forenoon service, the East Church was
full, with 'the gay people of Perth, and the magistrates present'.
At St. Leonard's in the afternoon, there was a 'great crowd', and
the 'solemnity deep', his subject being conversion. Inquirers were
invited to meet at 7 p.m., and again at 1 o'clock on Monday
afternoon. One hundred and fifty attended the former gathering,
when 'the Lord was very near', and from two to three hundred
were present on the Monday for 'a solemn season' from 1 to 4 p.m.
On Monday evening there was 'an immensely crowded audience
in the Gaelic Church', when Burns felt 'much aided'; and on
Tuesday there were meetings at 1 p.m. ('a few hundred present'),
7 o'clock (a 'dense crowd'), and '10 o'clock in St. Leonard's
Church, to bring in the New Year ... We separated about 1
o'clock on the New Year's morning; a sweet season. I never
brought in the New Year so sweetly before'.

And so on, from day to day and night to night, for nearly four
months. Thus on the first Sabbath evening in January, 1840, he
preached 'in Dr. Findlay's immense church, from II Cor. 5. 21;

very much aided in exposition and application; densely crowded; thousands went away, I am told, without getting in'. On Sabbath evening, February 9, 'the crowd was so great seeking to get into St. Leonard's Church, that it was supposed there were more collected in the street an hour before the time than would have several times filled the church. The press was so great when the doors were opened, that several persons were somewhat injured.' On Sabbath, March 22, he 'rose this morning strong in body, but with much conscious deadness of soul, and awfully assaulted, as I *often* am, by doubts regarding every truth of God in his Word'. As usual, however, he got through, and 'saw the tears starting from the eyes of some men advanced in years, and felt that the Lord was indeed present. The meeting lasted three hours and a half'.

Just before leaving Perth, Burns completed the twenty-fifth year of his life, and the first of his ministry as a preacher of the everlasting gospel. The occasion was marked by a fresh outpouring of the Spirit. His own report is: 'I went to the church (St. Leonard's) at six with clear direction to Deut. 32. 35 as my subject. The church was as usual a solid mass of living beings.' He availed himself of many hints in Jonathan Edwards' famous sermon on 'Sinners in the hands of an angry God'; and the message 'appeared to be accompanied with an extraordinary measure of the Holy Ghost, and the feeling of the hearers became so intense that when one man in the gallery passage audibly exclaimed, "Lord Jesus, come and save me", the great mass of the congregation gave audible expression to their emotion in a universal wailing'. 'When the impression became so deep and overpowering, many that did not like, or did not understand, such a glorious manifestation of the divine power, were offended, and one man came up the stair of the pulpit and asked me to dismiss the people!' 'This glorious night seemed to me at the time, and appears from all I have since heard, to have been perhaps the most wonderful that I have ever seen, with the exception perhaps of the first Tuesday at Kilsyth.' 'This is the last Sabbath of the first year of my ministry as an ambassador of Christ! To the praise and glory of infinite, eternal, free and sovereign mercy and grace. Praise the Lord!'

One of his hearers recalled that 'the first part of his discourse always embodied a mass of telling doctrine, holding up the divine law right in face of the sinner's conscience. The appeals in the latter part were irresistibly winning, brimming over with the freely offered love of Jesus'. 'His theology was unbiased, and swung like a pendulum across the truth of God, avoiding all limited, classified, partial, and one-sided expressions of it. His training of young converts was thus invaluable to them. "No cross, no crown", was the term of enlistment. "Suffering is the law of the kingdom". "The greater your sacrifices for Christ, the more of his joy will fill your heart". "Forsake the glass, the dance and the song, if you would drink of the rivers of his pleasures, if you would leap for joy on the shores of Emmanuel's land, if you would take up the unending hallelujah".' Another memorable saying of his was, 'The longing of my heart would be to go once all round the world before I die, and preach one gospel invitation in the ear of every creature.'

His next major mission was in Aberdeen, where the record paralleled that of Kilsyth, Dundee and Perth. 'Sermons to densely crowded audiences in three several churches on each Lord's day; prayer meetings in the morning and afternoon, and a public address in the evening of each week-day, with generally an additional hour of counsel, instruction and prayer, for those whose intense anxiety still detained them after the long service was over, with words by the wayside and conferences with inquirers and young disciples at all other available hours, constituted the daily history of his work . . . for weeks together.'

Not content with speaking only in churches, Burns also engaged in open-air preaching – as on April 26. 'In the evening, I preached in Castle Street to an immense audience, chiefly men, on the willingness of Jesus to save the chief of sinners, from the "thief on the cross". I felt more of the divine presence than on any former occasion in Aberdeen, and laboured to pull sinners out of the fire. The impression was very deep; many weeping, some screaming, and one or two quite overpowered.' He adds that 'none of the ministers were in favour of the street-preaching but Mr. Parker. He and his session all went to Castle Street', where the meetings touched some of the 'poorest and vilest of the people in that degraded district'. In addition to such open-air gatherings, he gained an entrance to the Barracks, where many of the soldiers heard him gladly.

This Aberdeen ministry was then interrupted, while the popular evangelist fulfilled other pressing engagements. But five months later he was back in the Granite City; and then 'for two months together, on week-days and Sabbath-days, the attendance at the meetings continued unabated, and the number of inquirers increased'. A notable occasion was November 22, when Burns 'preached for Mr. Foote in the East Church at 6 o'clock: the church was choked as soon as it opened. There could not be fewer than 2,500, a great number of whom were men . . . At 8 o'clock, I had to divide the subject in order to allow those to retire who needed. As many nearly came in as went out, and we continued till 9. I saw no *men* go away'. The meeting next evening lasted from 8 'until 11.30 p.m., and hardly one even of the scoffers went away; many, even gentlemen, remained riveted to the spot, evidently having a witness in their consciences to the truth. There were some avowed infidels present! Glory to the Lord!'

Again there were times of refreshing and revival, and again the enemy raged. A caustic account of the meetings appeared in the *Aberdeen Herald* newspaper, and the Church of Scotland Presbytery of Aberdeen felt itself under an obligation to investigate the matter, and appointed a Committee of Inquiry under the convenership of the Rev. William Pirie (later Professor of Divinity in the University of Aberdeen). Burns willingly appeared before the Committee, and was given a very fair hearing. He was closely questioned regarding his statement at a meeting in Bonaccord Church on November 23, that 'this is the outpouring of the Spirit', and also in connection with the more extreme manifestations of excitement alleged to have taken place. On the latter point, he said: 'I certainly did see, and expect to see in such cases, much weeping, some audibly praying to God for mercy, and occasionally also individuals crying aloud as if pierced to the heart. I don't remember that any one fell down or fell into convulsions on the night referred to, although I have occasionally seen such cases, both in Aberdeen and in other places, and among these, strong men in the prime of life.'

On the former head, Burns testified that 'the full and complete evidence of the Holy Spirit's work, whether in the case of a people or of an individual, is to be drawn from the manner in which they are affected under the preaching of the gospel, taken in connection with the truths by which they are so affected, and the effects which are afterwards habitually manifested in their temper of soul and outward conversation . . . I am, however, fully convinced that a minister of God, if experimentally acquainted with the saving work of God on his own soul, and especially if he has had opportunity of witnessing the work of the Holy Spirit on a large scale, may be warranted, in remarkable cases, to conclude that God's Spirit is at work among a people, before time has fully proved the work by its permanent effects . . . I conceive, for instance, that the Apostles must have been convinced that the Holy Ghost was remarkably outpoured on the day of Pentecost, when they saw the mighty power of the gospel on the souls of thousands. I have no doubt that Mr. Livingstone, and other ministers and people of God, were convinced, at the Kirk of Shotts, of the same things, without needing to wait until the permanent fruits of the work were developed. I could myself have no more doubt of this than of any Scripture truth, on that memorable day when the work of the Lord began in so glorious a manner at Kilsyth . . . In the meeting referred to, in Bonaccord Church, on Monday November 23, 1840, I could have no doubt, from the nature of the truth spoken, the manner in which I felt supported of God's Spirit in speaking it, and the evident effect produced by it on the minds of many of the audience, and, more or less, on the minds of almost all, that the Holy Ghost was then exerting his gracious power among us'.

It was to its credit that the Presbytery, on hearing the report of its Committee, completely exonerated Burns, and warmly commended him for his fruitful labours at Aberdeen and throughout Scotland. The fathers and brethren noted that the evidence 'amply bears out the fact that an extensive and delightful work of revival has commenced, and is in hopeful progress in various districts of

Scotland – the origin of which, instrumentally, is to be traced to a more widely diffused spirit of prayer on the part of ministers and people, and to the simple, earnest, and affectionate preaching of the gospel of the grace of God'. It was further observed, that many of the districts thus favoured were 'locally far distant from others'; that the movement had been 'attended with few of those evils which have generally more or less characterized seasons of great religious excitement'; that 'a very considerable number of persons, chiefly in early life', had been influenced in Aberdeen; 'and that the labours of Mr. W. C. Burns, preacher of the gospel, are peculiarly discernible in connection with these results.'

The Presbytery of Aberdeen felt obliged therefore 'to recommend to all ministers, preachers, and elders within their bounds, in their respective spheres, to labour more and more diligently and prayerfully, in the use of all scriptural means, to promote the cause of vital religion, which needs so much to be revived among us; and they would also exhort and entreat all the private members of the Church to study to grow in grace, to abound in all the fruits of righteousness, and to plead more earnestly with the great Head of the Church that He would pour out of his Spirit more plentifully upon us, and bless his appointed ordinances, that the wilderness may become a fruitful field, and the fruitful field be counted for a forest'. Truly the nation was in hopeful case when a responsible court of the National Church could thus go on record.

Burns' next main field of labour was Newcastle, in the north of England, which he found a tough nut to crack. To his friend John Milne, of St. Leonard's, Perth, he wrote urgently: 'I ask it as a favour, and plead for it, that you will lay before your people the case of Newcastle, an iron-walled citadel of Satan. Almighty power, and that alone, can make a breach and plant the banner of salvation in the Lamb on its proud ramparts.' 'The Scotch Church is low here,' and he added, 'very apathetic. The sleep of death is on the city.'

This graveyard peace was shattered when Burns, incensed by 'the announcement of a Sabbath pleasure trip of a more than usually offensive kind', denounced it in a terrible placard, which he signed with his own name and posted up in every street and open place in Newcastle. It fell like a bomb-shell in the midst of the community, startled the ears of friends and foes, and drew general attention to the preacher and his message. A solemn tract on the sins of the city and the impending judgments of God was at the same time prepared and sown broadcast among the people. The newspapers too, both local and metropolitan, took up the matter, bitterly denounced his proceedings, and thus still more loudly rang the bell of alarm in the ears of a community from whom he only desired a hearing.

This sensation also passed, and Burns almost despaired of making any lasting impact, when a break-through was effected in open-air preaching. Rather reluctantly he went to the cattle-show, and announced a meeting for the Cloth Market that evening. An immense crowd gathered, and attempts were made to silence him, first by legal action, and then by physical violence. 'Once a stone was thrown, again a quantity of manure, which bespattered my clothes. Gradually, however, the crowd was quietened; and until 10 o'clock, when we parted, there was the greatest solemnity, and a deep impression; and though I was frequently interrupted with questions, they all tended to bring out in a marvellous way the truth of God, so that they who put them were silenced and the people rejoiced. In fact, during the closing stages, the singing was truly sublime; and the whole scene, when contrasted with what it had lately been, was fitted to deepen the impression of the Word in the hand of the Spirit.'

One interjector wanted to know, 'How are you supported?' This Burns found 'a matter of general wonder. I answered him that I never needed to ask a penny from any one, but that even since I came here £10 had been sent to me unasked, and partly without a name! They seemed confounded.' His brother adds: 'It may be right to state here once for all, that from the time of his leaving Dundee until his departure for China, he relied wholly on such support as was spontaneously sent to him by those who desired to further his special work. The result was that while his own immediate wants were amply supplied, he seldom lacked sufficient also to contribute liberally in behalf of Christ's cause and Christ's poor.' Burns himself wrote in his journal: 'Oh Lord, deliver me from covetousness, and enable me with overflowing gratitude and joy to give all that I don't require to promote the extension of thy blessed kingdom in this poor ruined world!'

The following Sabbath evening, at a vast open-air gathering, the evangelist says: 'I also found myself in an agony to compel sinners to come to Jesus *now*, and not even the next hour, which I felt was not man's but God's. Indeed, I felt so much that I could almost have torn the pulpit to pieces, and the audience seemed to sympathize throughout. Oh, it was a glorious, an awfully glorious scene! The fleecy clouds were showing here and there bright stars, and the harvest moon was diffusing a sombre, peaceful light upon the quiet world around us . . . I trust that some were saved, I have no doubt that God was with us of a truth. At a quarter to nine we closed; and as we had remained so long in the open air (since 5 p.m.), I thought it better not to meet in the church as we intended, but to retire direct to our closets. After I had been a few minutes in the house, two friends came to me from the church, and told me that it was nearly full with a congregation entirely different from what I had had in the open air, and that they had been waiting for me since 7 o'clock!' Burns hurried to the church, therefore; and noted that 'we came out after a solemn meeting at a quarter to ten.'

After preaching in other centres in the north of England, including Sunderland, where he spoke to 'a dense and hungry audience, who seemed to open the mouth wide for the blessing', he returned to Scotland and settled for a time to a regular parish ministry.

IV.   Having Then Gifts Differing

The Rev. A. Moody Stuart, of St. Luke's Church, Edinburgh, on account of an affection of the throat, was advised to spend the winter of 1841–42 in Madeira, a popular health resort in the

Canary Islands; and the Rev. William C. Burns was asked to take his place in the pulpit and parish. The latter began this new phase of his ministry on November 14, preaching in the forenoon from II Corinthians 4. 1–6 ('Therefore seeing we have this ministry, as we have received mercy, we faint not . . .').

'The work of this winter', we are told, 'forms a unique chapter in his life. A special interest attaches to it. He had to become both pastor and evangelist. True to the motto of his family, *Ever ready*, he soon showed that he could be both. He at once began a course of lectures on the Sabbath forenoon upon the Epistle to the Romans, and another course at the Thursday prayer meeting upon the Epistle of James. On Monday evening he taught two classes: a female class for expounding the miracles, and a young men's class at a later hour, where he took up the parables of Christ. Every Saturday afternoon he conducted a class for children. Two courses of lectures, three classes, sermons upon the Sabbath afternoon suggested by the special circumstances of the times or of the congregation: here was sufficient work for an ordinary man. But he was no ordinary man. He was always longing to be on full work again. The College session had begun. He taught a Greek class in his lodgings. The College Missionary Association met every Saturday morning for prayer and the reading of essays upon topics connected with foreign missions. He attended these meetings, and by the blessing of God infused his own fire into the hearts of the students.' And so on!

Not surprisingly, 'a large number of students attended his ministry – not only divinity students, but gownsmen of all stages with their pale, eager faces . . . He invited them to his lodgings; he sympathized with their difficulties; he guided those who were groping in the dark and seeking the way to Zion. Those who had the rare privilege of meeting him in private, and seeing his close walk with God, were at no loss to understand the power which attended his public ministrations. With him the winning of souls was a passion; calm, but intense, consuming . . . He cast his net into all waters. He wished to get access to the soldiers in the castle. He visited the barracks, distributed tracts, and invited them to his open-air services in the High Street. He frequently visited the

Shelter, the Gaol, the Bridewell, the Magdalene Asylum, the Orphan Hospital, the Dean Bank Institution, etc., and preached to the inmates ... From the very refuse of society he gathered jewels for Emmanuel's crown. Very touching to see him', as this observer had, 'giving tracts and speaking tender words to the fallen.'

'In the midst of his abundant labours in Edinburgh, the Lord opened a wide door for him in Leith. From January to March he preached on Wednesday and frequently on Sabbath evening in North Leith, South Leith, and the Mariners' Church, to densely crowded, and (to use a favourite word of his own) "hungry" audiences ... It seemed as if the ever-memorable scenes of Kilsyth, Dundee and Perth were to be repeated in Leith. So widespread was the impression, that a gay lady in Leith said the people were all going mad. In his young communicants' class he soon gathered in abundant fruits of his labours in Leith – sheaves of joy. To use his own words, "The Lord gave him spring, summer and harvest, that winter in Leith."

'About the middle of March, in consequence of the resolution of the directors of the Edinburgh and Glasgow Railway to run trains upon the Sabbath, he bade the people of Leith farewell for a season, in order that he might give his whole heart to the work in Edinburgh ... It was on Sabbath the 13th of March (1842) that the first Sabbath train was run between Edinburgh and Glasgow. Mr. Burns' spirit was stirred to its depths in connection with this question ... He regarded the Sabbath as the palladium of Scottish Christianity. In name of the Session of St. Luke's, he wrote a remonstrance to the shareholders ... He attended the two great meetings held in the Hopetoun Rooms and in the West Church by the friends of the Sabbath to oppose the opening of the railway; and spoke with great thankfulness of the powerful speeches of Drs. Cunningham, Candlish and C. J. Brown, and Messrs. D. T. K. Drummond and Makgill Crichton, in favour of the entire sanctification of the Lord's day. He preached for several Sabbaths upon the subject, and discussed it in all its aspects.'

Indeed, Burns further 'intimated that he would preach at the railway station every Sabbath at seven in the morning and at six in the evening – the hours at which the trains were advertised to start. True to his word, he was at the railway station at 7 o'clock on the following Sabbath morning. He spoke of it as "a momentous day in the history of Scotland". A great crowd assembled, and joined with deep solemnity in the service. It was after nine before they dispersed, some of them in tears. He conducted the ordinary services in St. Luke's, at eleven and two, with unusual tenderness and power, as if the morning service had only put a keener edge upon his spirit; and was at the railway station again at six, surrounded by a dense concourse of several thousands ... Like a soldier mounting the breach, or leading a forlorn hope, he stood upon a large stone, and sang the psalm:

> "Horror took hold on me, because
> Ill men thy law forsake ...."

and preached one of his most characteristic sermons to a deeply impressed audience. He continued till 9 o'clock in the evening, having been about nine hours engaged altogether. For the next three months, his usual Sabbath work was four services – two at the railway station and two in St. Luke's ...; and yet he used to say that he was as fresh on Monday as on Saturday ... His brethren in Edinburgh were full of joy at his lion-like courage and noble testimony; and only wished that they had bodily strength to stand by his side'.

Despite these manifold labours, 'his soul, like Gideon's fleece, was drenched with dew, and his preaching was never marked by greater depth, variety and freshness. It was the culminating point of his work in Edinburgh. The church was overflowing. The Word was sharper than a two-edged sword. There was a Bethel-like fear over the congregation. Every head was bowed. It was felt that "the living God was in the place". Some who had entertained prejudices against the preacher were ashamed when they found that solidity and impressiveness were the leading characteristics of his teaching. At the spring Communion two hundred joined from other congregations!' Mentioning also 'four evangelistic tours which he made in the midst of his Edinburgh work', the tribute concludes: 'One recalls it with amazement. Here was a man who crowded the work of years into months – of months into weeks – of weeks into days. The work of many a lifetime was compressed into this single winter in Edinburgh.'

But a period was set to these times of refreshing. On May 18, 1843, the long-standing tension within the Church of Scotland was resolved, with the epic event of the Disruption, and the formation of the Free Church of Scotland. 'With the movement which led to that remarkable revolution, and with the principles which lay at the foundation of it, he most thoroughly sympathized; and when the critical day of exodus arrived, we find him hurrying away from the busy scenes of his evangelistic work in Fife, that he might witness that signal and illustrious act of faith, and share the inspiration and the triumph of that solemn hour.' His own journal entry reads: 'Tuesday, to Edinburgh, per steam(er), through a great storm on the way to the Assembly. Thursday, I was honoured to join in the solemn procession of ministers, etc., from St. Andrew's Church to the Free Assembly Hall, Canonmills, walking between my father on the one side, and Uncle George of Tweedsmuir on the other. This was a scene of which I know not what to say! The opening of the Free Assembly was graciously solemn. Surely the Lord was there.'

This astonishing exodus left the General Assembly of the Established Church of Scotland with a mere 'rump' of about one hundred members to transact its business; while, when the lists were made up, it was found that no fewer than 474 ministers (out of a total of 1,203) had adhered to the Free Church of Scotland, and signed the Deed of Demission, surrendering churches, manses, livings and stipends, 'for conscience' sake' – or, as it was often put, for 'the Crown Rights of the Redeemer'. A noble sacrifice! Lord Cockburn wrote: 'It is the most honourable feat for Scotland that its whole history supplies.' And his colleague, Lord Jeffrey, when informed of the event, exclaimed: 'I'm proud of my country; there is not another country upon earth where such a deed could have been done.' And it produced, in its first generation, a Church which has been described as representing Presbyterianism at its best.

But the ensuing months of ecclesiastical re-organization and reconstruction did not prove conducive to the prosecution of Burns' peculiar work as an evangelist; and he was led to see that, meantime, at least in Scotland, the propitious season for such activity had passed. This did not, however, lead him to desist from such work, but to look further afield for fresh openings. Accordingly, after assisting his esteemed friend, Professor John Duncan, by conducting a Hebrew class for him in the New College, Edinburgh, during that first winter (1843–44), he crossed the Irish Channel, and on April 6, found himself under the hospitable roof of the Rev. Dr. W. B. Kirkpatrick, one of the ministers of St. Mary's Abbey Church. To Islay Burns, Dr. Kirkpatrick wrote: 'I had seen your brother in Perth, and had invited him to my house in Dublin. He accepted my invitation; and after he had finished his immediate engagements in Scotland, he suddenly appeared at my door, with a small bundle in his hand, containing the whole of his travelling apparatus. His principal object in coming to Dublin was to find opportunities, if possible, of making known to Roman Catholics the message of the gospel.'

Selecting a suitable site in front of the Custom-house, Burns 'took his position evening after evening, and amidst innumerable annoyances and interruptions he sought to bring before his ignorant and prejudiced hearers the word of eternal life. It requires no small amount of courage, and tact, and temper, as everyone knows who has made the trial, to address an unsympathetic or hostile Irish mob. Mr. Burns was exposed to many opprobrious salutations, derisive questionings, vehement denials of the statements which he made; sometimes the uproar was so loud and long-continued that he was obliged to desist altogether; often his clothes were torn; not seldom the chair on which he stood was broken; but he never was impatient, nor ever for a moment lost his self-command. Amidst the most noisy and turbulent scenes, his countenance was beaming with joy, insomuch that some of his persecutors were constrained to say, "He is a good man; we cannot make him angry."

'The ringleaders of the mob occasionally joined hands, and rushed down upon him for the purpose of driving him from the chair, or of throwing him down upon the street; but he was

[123]

always protected from the danger of these assaults by a bodyguard of three young men, members of my congregation, who were never absent from these meetings; and who, standing behind him, caught him in their arms till the wave had passed by and spent its force; and then, having set him on the chair again, he proceeded in his address with as much quietude of manner as if no interruption had taken place!

'One Sabbath morning, his audience at the custom-house were more quiet than usual. His subject was Regeneration, "Except a man be born again", etc. At the close of his sermon a man who had been listening attentively said, "Well, sir, if what you have said be true, you had much need to come from Scotland to tell it to us, for we never heard of this doctrine before." After Mr. Burns left Dublin, several Roman Catholics came to inquire about him, speaking respectfully of his labours, and of the loving and genial spirit in which they were conducted.'

While frankly disappointed that Burns' ministry was no more effective in his own congregation, Dr. Kilpatrick was impressed with his prayers, which 'were very striking – distinguished by deep acquaintance with Scripture, by intense fervour, and by strong faith. He truly pleaded with God, and occasionally seemed to get near access to his presence.' The Doctor was also impressed with the fact that his visitor 'was bent earnestly and ever on the salvation of souls. This grand concern occupied and absorbed his daily prayers, his social converse, his public addresses, the whole course of his thoughts, the whole business of his life. Why are there not more of us like him?'

Returning to Scotland in May, 1844, Burns engaged in evangelistic work there for another three months, mainly in Paisley, Port Glasgow and Renfrew, before responding to a pressing invitation to visit Canada. He embarked at Greenock on August 10 in the brig *Mary* (Captain Kelso), being generously given a free passage. The seven weeks' voyage proved quite a rest-cure; and he reached Montreal in September much refreshed in body, mind and spirit. He was given a warm welcome by many friends in the 71st and 93rd Regiments of the British Army, who had been influenced by his ministry in Dundee and Aberdeen.

A brief outline only of his two years' ministry in the rising Dominion can here be given. He preached regularly to the troops in Montreal, and often in the open air at the '*Place d'Armes*, in the centre of the city, in front of the great Romish cathedral', where he was usually accorded a warm reception! Then he moved out through the Provinces of Ontario and Quebec. He brushed up his French in order to reach that section of the population with the gospel, and was described in one place as 'the best priest we ever heard speaking!' He also worked up his Gaelic, and delighted Highland settlers with his presentation of the good news in their mother tongue. At Toronto he spoke to students for the Presbyterian ministry; in Amherstburgh, near the American border, his audience included former negro slaves; while at Sarnia he spoke, through an interpreter, to a gathering of Red Indians.

At length, in the late summer of 1846, Burns sailed for home, reaching Glasgow again in the brig *Mary*, on September 15.

V.   The Regions Beyond

For a time Burns remained uncertain about the sphere of his future ministry. 'I sailed from Canada', he wrote, 'having a deep impression that I should find no special work to do in Scotland that would detain me there longer than a few months, but feeling quite uncertain what should be my ultimate destination.' With his command of French, he was quickly invited by his Church to undertake work in Paris; but 'did not see any prospect of doing much there during a brief visit, and I could not but reflect that at my period of life it must be now decided whether I was to preach from place to place to the end, or go to a heathen field, as originally destined.' He re-visited some of the scenes of his former fruitful labours, but now felt no leading to engage in such a ministry again, though pressed with invitations to speak.

'About the end of the year', he goes on, 'I arrived at the clear decision that I was not at liberty to labour any longer as hitherto without ascertaining whether our Missionary Committee would still desire me to fulfil my original intention. I accordingly called on Dr. Candlish, who readily agreed to place the matter before the Committee. The reaction, strangely enough, was that though no one would object to my going if I wished to do so, yet as the Indian stations were all occupied, there was no special opening for me. At this very time, and while they were actually conversing on the matter, a letter came to the Convener of the Foreign Mission Committee, Dr. James Buchanan, from James Hamilton of Regent Square, London, (Convener of the English Presbyterian Church Missionary Committee), making earnest inquiry whether Dr. Buchanan could point out any minister or preacher in Scotland who might be suitable to go as their first missionary to China, seeing they had contemplated this mission for more than two years, but had as yet been disappointed in finding suitable agents.'

Feeling that the coincidence was providential, Dr. Buchanan wrote to Mr. Hamilton, mentioning several possible names, including that of William Burns. In February, 1847, Burns received an enquiry from James Hamilton as to his availability for such a work. He replied, pleading for time for 'prayer and consideration, as well as for conference with the servants of God around me.' 'On receipt of my letter, their Missionary Committee instructed Mr. Hamilton to send me an express and earnest call to become their Church's first missionary to China.' It was a momentous decision for anyone to make, and Burns continued for nearly two months in an agony of indecision. At length light came.

Returning from a preaching tour of Bute and Arran, he says, 'On Tuesday, April 9th, I met in Glasgow James Denniston, returned from Jamaica, and on his way, if God will, to Constantinople as a missionary to the Jews. Thus, after so long an interval, we met again in the place where nine years before, at the University, he had given himself to the Lord to go to the circumcision, and I to go to the Gentiles. Having been so long engaged in other work, we had now the near prospect of entering on the fields in regard to which the vows of God were upon us. It was a confirming interview. To sovereign grace be the praise – the endless, unutterable praise!'

Thence he proceeded to Edinburgh, where so wise a counsellor as Dr. John Duncan strongly urged him to go, saying, 'Take care of His cause, and he will take care of your interests; look after His glory, and he will look after your comfort'. 'The impression of my duty', he admits, 'now became so strong that I felt I could no longer hesitate about signifying my willingness to go, and on Monday I wrote to that effect. I saw that I would dishonour my profession of the gospel, and thus wound the honour of Jesus, if I seemed to linger any longer.' Light evidently came to him the previous day, while preaching for Moody Stuart in St. Luke's, from the text John 12. 36 ('Walk while ye have the light'). A hearer says, 'His heart was enlarged towards the heathen; his prayers were full of pleadings on their behalf. Next morning he came to breakfast, and to our utter amazement told us he no longer saw his way to refuse the call.'

But now there was another difficulty in the way! The very day that Burns wrote accepting the appointment to China, the Committee met in London to hear the report of one of its members, Mr. Hugh Matheson, who had been on a business trip to the Far East, in the course of which he made enquiries on the spot, and brought back an adverse report. It was alleged, that the language presented a formidable barrier, that the country was still largely closed to the gospel, and that the supply of missionaries in the circumstances was adequate. Influenced by this report, the Committee resolved to recommend to Synod that the decision to enter China be reversed, and that work be undertaken instead in Central India.

Burns was not at all impressed with this change of front, remarking: 'That's the very thing that makes my call clear to go!' 'When I heard of this decision', he says further, 'I did not feel any sympathy with their proposal to draw back, and fearing lest they might do so, and thus dishonour the command and promise of the exalted Jesus, I was the more pressed in spirit to go forward, that such a consequence might be avoided. I accordingly resolved to go up to Sunderland on the 20th, and meet the Synod on the matter.'

On 'Tuesday morning the 20th April, at 9 o'clock the Committee met in Sunderland. After much consultation the brethren came to one mind, that we must not abandon China – the Church was committed to it – and Mr. Hamilton was instructed to draw up an entirely different report. No communication had been received from Mr. Burns; but the Church resolved that its duty was to keep by China, and to prosecute the missionary work there, as had been resolved upon two years before. Mr. Burns arrived in Sunderland the next day. His mind was unchanged. China was still his field, whether the Presbyterian Church abandoned it or no; and he was not a little amazed when he heard of the proceedings in Committee the previous day.

'The new report was read in Synod; Mr. Hamilton spoke and others followed. Mr. Welsh was asked to pray for guidance in the matter, and Mr. Burns was then invited to address the brethren. He did so; giving an account of his early life – his dedication to the missionary work – his arrest in Scotland, when the Lord gave testimony to the Word of his grace, and the reasons for the resolution now formed. The people were much affected, as was the speaker; he was obliged frequently to pause, and at last to stop altogether. A meeting for conference was shortly afterwards summoned, at which he fully opened up his wishes in the matter, especially as regarded ordination. He wished to go forth only as an evangelist, not to administer sacraments; "Christ sent me not to baptize, but to preach the gospel". Acts 13 was read; Mr. P. L. Miller prayed; and after much discussion it was resolved that he should be ordained the next day at 10 o'clock, and proceed to China forthwith.' For, when asked, in the course of the discussion, how soon he could be ready to enter on his work, Burns had replied with prompt decision, 'Tomorrow!'*

The ordination service was arranged by the Presbytery of Newcastle, the only Presbytery of the denomination in England, within whose bounds Burns had previously laboured. From this

*Burns' biographer records that a phrase learned in his early classical studies remained with him through life – *miles expeditus*, a soldier without baggage or heavy armour, unencumbered and so always ready for march or battle.

Presbytery, Robert Morrison, the pioneer Protestant missionary to China, had gone forth forty years earlier, his father being an elder of High Bridge Church, Newcastle. It was fitting also, that the sermon should be preached at Burns' ordination, by his cousin, William Chalmers, who had been born at Malacca, the centre of the early Chinese mission under Dr. Milne, and who later became a Professor in the English Presbyterian College at London. The questions were put, ordination prayer offered, and charge given, by Dr. Paterson, 'with extreme simplicity and apostolic fervour, 'Go forth then in His strength', he urged. 'Remember that God hath given the heathen to His Son for an inheritance. Remember that Jesus hath promised to be with you alway, even unto the end of the world.'

Burns left Sunderland the same afternoon for Newcastle, where he preached that evening in Groat Market Chapel. His companion says, 'I joined him there at 10 o'clock. A considerable number were waiting to bid him farewell . . . The next morning at 5 o'clock, I heard his heavy foot pass my door in time for the train to London, on his way to China as the first missionary of the Presbyterian Church in England.' Burns adds, 'I hoped to have gone off at once through France, and to have been in China in July by the Steam communication lately established. This was over-ruled, however, on the ground that I would reach the field at a trying season, and by a trying route; and so it was resolved that I should wait for this present vessel (the *Mary Bannatyne*), and in the interval visit the churches in this Synod. I have been accordingly in most of them – Liverpool, Manchester, Birmingham, Brighton, London, etc., and see much cause to adore the wisdom and grace of God in this delay.'

In fact Burns was on the point of entering the Scotch Church, Woolwich, to conduct a service on June 8, 'when an express from London reached him, conveying the information that a favourable wind had sprung up and carried the ship by a rapid run to Portsmouth, and that not an hour was to be lost if he wished to join her before she sailed.' He hurried to the railway station, but the last train for the day had already left. However, the first train next morning got him to his destination in good time, the ship being not due to sail till the evening. The last hours were spent in his cabin with his brother Islay, 'in reading the sacred Word, and in pouring out our hearts in prayer'. When the time came to part, William said: 'Oh, is it not blessed, is it not wondrous grace, to be separated in this way, separated for such a cause and for such a work!' He was last seen holding up his Bible, 'as if to say that there was the only thing worth living for in all the world.' Islay's own feeling was that 'I had parted not from a brother only, but from one far above me, a true and eminent saint of God.'

As the *Mary Bannatyne* slipped out of harbour on the evening of June 9, Burns wrote: 'I have now entered on a new sphere of duty and trial, I mean on board ship. Much fidelity and wisdom are needed to be a witness for the Lord in such circumstances . . . May all that sail with us be given to Jesus . . . I rejoice to go. I feel that I am where it is the Lord's gracious will that I should be . . . All the ends of the earth shall yet remember and turn to the Lord; and all the kindreds of the people shall do homage unto him; for the kingdom is the Lord's, and he is the governor among the nations.' A fortnight later he wrote: 'For a week after we set sail we were detained by contrary and, in general, stormy winds at the mouth of the British (English) Channel, but since that time the weather has been delightful, and we have been wafted speedily on our way, so that tomorrow morning, if the wind continues favourable, we shall pass by Madeira. During the first few days I was rather sick, but I have been able from the beginning to do a little at my Chinese studies, and during the last few days my progress has been, I think, encouraging. We have had public worship every evening in the public cabin, and today I succeeded in getting it begun also in the morning.'

After seven weeks on board, he wrote: 'I have suffered a good deal, and still suffer almost daily, from nausea, which abridges my ability for close application to study. I am, however, able to do a little from day to day in acquiring the Chinese, and occasionally I make more rapid advances. The work is pleasant and profitable from the Bible being my text-book, and in consideration of the momentous end which I have in view. Morrison was enabled to accomplish a great work in preparing such a version of the New

Testament as that which it is my privilege to study. I have felt much interested by his *Memoirs,* which I am again reading. He was a spiritual man as well as a man of strong natural parts, and was thus both naturally and by grace qualified for the work of translation.' Burns was now able to have worship with the seamen twice a week in the forecastle. They had just 'passed Trinidad,* a very picturesque island, uninhabited except by a few goats and swine. It stands quite alone in the midst of this vast ocean'.

Just over a week later, on August 5, at 4.30 a.m., 'Thomas McLeod, an apprentice in the ship, fell overboard and was drowned. They tried to render him assistance, but all was vain, as it was dark and rainy, and the wind was changing at the time. He was aged about seventeen, a native of Rothesay, and the son of a widow. The evening before last I had worship in the steerage or half-deck with him and some of the other men, and was led to speak specially of the danger of sudden death to which they were exposed. He seemed attentive, and answered me the question in the Shorter Catechism, "What is Prayer?" I had also conversed and prayed with him previously when sick . . . We are now about 1,600 miles from the Cape of Good Hope . . . I go on pretty regularly with my Chinese, and find it gradually become more familiar, although it is evident from the nature of the language that it must require long practice to render it at all natural to a European mind and tongue. I occupy myself much in translating the English New Testament into Chinese, and comparing these rude attempts with Morrison's version. This I find an admirable method of mastering the substance of the language, although the peculiar Chinese manner of thought and expression can only be fully attained from studying native authors. This I am also practising to a certain extent.'

On August 24, 'it blew almost a hurricane from the north-west. I was standing on the poop when a lofty wave broke over the vessel. By its force and the rolling of the vessel I was lifted from the deck, but having a firm hold I was mercifully preserved. My watch was filled with salt water, and the chain snapped. How in a moment

*Not Trinidad off the coast of Venezuela, but an island in the South Atlantic, 900 miles East of Rio de Janeiro.

might the pulse of life have been thus arrested! One of my daily duties is to teach Dr. Morrison's little daughter to read. She had just got the alphabet, but is now making encouraging progress – an interesting child.'

October 3 found them at the entrance to the Java Sea. The weather that Sabbath morning was thick; but 'at 10 a.m. the curtain was uplifted, and opposite my cabin window appeared the high land of Sumatra at the mouth of Sunda Straits. On Tuesday morning we were within ten miles of Anjer, sailing slowly over a glassy sea covered with the canoes of the Javanese and Malays fishing, or bringing off provisions to offer for sale.' Next Monday Burns was struck with the appearance on the quarter-deck, of 'an old gray-haired man, unlike any person I had before seen'. He proved to be a Chinese, and 'was the first of that great nation that I had seen in person. I exchanged with him a few words in English, which he spoke very well, and when he learned that I knew a little of Chinese, he took out a paper (a receipt for goods that had been bought from him), written in English and Chinese, to see if I knew the characters. I recognized some of them, and found that I had got the correct pronunciation. I went on deck soon after with a part of the Chinese Scriptures (New Testament), that I might show it to him, but he was just leaving the vessel, and our intercourse ended. I had at least mentioned to him the name of Jesus.'

Burns now found language study difficult 'on account of the heat, which has been very great and oppressive'. But he could rejoice that, by October 25, we 'are now about 700 miles only from our destination'. The near prospect of missionary work led him to spend a Sabbath, apart from necessary public duties, in his cabin in prayer and fasting, when he 'feasted in the Lord's presence, and upon his truth and grace', and 'enjoyed more than usual liberty and depth both in confessing sin and in pleading for grace to myself and others'. He adds, 'I have often found of late the chapters in Mr. M'Cheyne's Calendar for the daily reading of the Scriptures exceedingly suitable to my wants. His *Memoir and Remains* also I find now more valuable than ever. I am reading also again, and with new interest as we approach the scene of his labours, the memoirs of Dr. Morrison, the Chinese missionary. The earlier part of these memoirs especially contains a precious development of his very genuine and eminent spiritual character ... Oh for grace to follow in this respect in his footsteps. Dr. Milne was a precious man of God, and his Chinese tracts – some of which I have – seem to be of much value. In these, his works, I doubt not, will follow him. His life by Philip has too much of Dr. Philip and too little of Dr. Milne to possess all the interest and importance which might belong to such a work.'

A fortnight later, when they were 'close to the coast of Luzon, a large island belonging to the Spaniards, in which Manila is the chief port, it began to blow a gale, which continued to increase during the whole of Sabbath, and since this morning has been so very severe that some part of the main-mast has been blown away, and until this moment (8.30 p.m.) we are running under bare poles, i.e. unable to carry the smallest sail, at the mercy of the winds and waves, or more truly at the mercy of that living God "who bringeth the wind out of his treasures".' During the night, happily, 'the storm abated', and the light of Tuesday 'revealed the land very near – about twelve or fifteen miles off. Had the storm overtaken us fifteen hours sooner, our peril must have been imminent, as we were then within six or eight miles of the shore'.

Eventually, after a voyage of just over five months, on which 'The Lord hath been gracious and true, we had favourable winds, and anchored in Hong Kong Bay at midnight on Saturday the 13th November, 1847'. After landing he wrote: 'Our deliverance from the perils of the deep appears now the greater, since we have heard within the last few days that the *Anne and Jane* from London, with which we were in company in the Java Sea, was on the 8th (November) driven on shore near Manila and totally lost. All, however, were saved except one of the crew and a passenger ... Another vessel also narrowly escaped, getting into Manila with the loss of all her masts.'

VI. The Land of Sinim

China, which many scholars identify with the Biblical 'Sinim', was and is the most populous nation in the world. Long resistant to foreign influence, it had only recently, and partially, opened to the Gospel of Christ. Robert Morrison, a Presbyterian from Newcastle, pioneered the modern missionary movement to China's millions, landing at Macao on September 4, 1807. Though circumscribed in his movements, and able after twenty-five years to report only ten baptized believers, this sturdy agent of the London Missionary Society accomplished much for the cause of God and truth. His particular legacies to posterity were, his compilation of a *Dictionary of Chinese*, the fruit of ten years' laborious toil, and his translation (with the help of William Milne, from Aberdeenshire) of the whole Bible into Chinese.

Morrison died in 1834. Eight years later, by the Treaty of Nanking (1842), the ports of Canton, Amoy, Foochow, Ning-po and Shanghai were opened to foreign residents and trade. At the same time Hong Kong was ceded to Great Britain. These developments were naturally welcomed by the Missionary leaders of the day, and representatives of the principal American and British Societies were soon on the field. By 1847, when Burns reached China, the Protestant missionary strength there had passed the fifty mark.

Landing at Hong Kong on November 15, Burns was most gratified at 'meeting a very kind and Christian welcome from the friends of the gospel here, and finding such doors of useful labour immediately opened to me, as confirm me in the soundness of those convictions of duty which brought me here. I am most comfortably boarded with a Mr. and Mrs. Power, close to the Mission premises of the London Society. Mr. Stevenson has been prevented from coming out to minister to the Presbyterians here, and this gives me a greater hold of my own countrymen, to whom I have opportunity of preaching once every Lord's day in the

London Society's chapel. My progress in Chinese is slow compared with my desires; but still I hope encouraging, considered in the view of the difficulties of this very peculiar and hard language.'

On December 27 Burns wrote: 'Among our own countrymen last Lord's day was interesting, as that on which for the first time a congregation met here in connection with the Presbyterian Church.' While not his first priority, this ministry continued during the year or more of his regular residence in Hong Kong. But his first concern was for the nationals of the country. To master their language as quickly as possible, he attended the daily Chinese service at the mission house, and gave English lessons to two lads, who 'repaid him with their Chinese, which he endeavoured to speak with them as best he could; sometimes succeeding in being understood, and sometimes provoking a smile only'. Yet there was progress, and he found it 'encouraging even already to be able to point even in a few expressions to the Lamb of God who taketh away the sin of the world – to that Root of Jesse to whom the Gentiles are to seek, and find his rest to be glorious.'

In fact, during December he was entrusted with a special responsibility. 'Dr. Morrison (whose little daughter I still give a lesson to, and with whose Chinese comprador* I read the Scriptures in English and Chinese) asked me to go and visit in prison three Chinese criminals under sentence of death for murder, and who were in deep distress and anxious to be visited by the ministers of Christ. Unable to do much, I felt called to do what I could; and . . . had almost daily opportunities of meeting these poor men. I generally went alone, but at other times in company with the Chinese preacher Chin-seen. They were very anxious to hear of the way of salvation through Jesus, and evidently strove to understand my broken Chinese. Although unable to say much to them I made them read with me Christian books, and on several occasions I even joined with them in prayer, through the medium of their own tongue . . . I felt encouraged, and enjoyed, I think, something of the power of grace in praying with and for them.'

Burns' next step was to remove to the Chinese quarter, so that

*A word of Portuguese origin, meaning (in China) a chief native servant in a European business house.

he might more completely identify himself with his adopted people. From his new lodgings, at the corner of Aberdeen Street and Queen's Road, he wrote on February 29, 1848: 'During these two months mercy has abounded towards me . . . Early in January I began to feel my need of having the assistance of some native of this province to read with me, in order that I might get acquainted with the colloquial dialect, and acquire as far as possible the right mode of intoning each word – a point of the greatest importance in order to effective speaking, and one of the greatest difficulty. The Lord has graciously, I trust, guided me in this. A brother missionary spoke of my want to Mr. Gutzlaff, who kindly furnished me with a teacher, a young man from Canton city, whom I have found very suitable. He came to me on January 25. After a week or two I found it would be desirable, in order to give full employment to my teacher, and also to open up my way into Chinese society, that I should get him if possible to open a small Chinese school; and I thought it would be well if I could get a house having accommodation for this purpose, and where I might myself live with none but Chinese around me, and so be obliged to speak the language at all times. It is in this view that I have taken the house in which I now am. I entered it a week ago, and found myself alone, with none but my two Chinese servants, to whom, however, I had been providentially directed, and whom I found willing from the first day to come and worship with me.'

His teacher joined him, and a month later Burns wrote: 'I was uncertain whether he would succeed in getting a school formed on the principles of the gospel. In this, however, I have been encouraged beyond my expectation. He got a few boys to come from a little distance of his own acquaintance, and as soon as he opened the school others came from the neighbourhood of their own accord; so that for the last fortnight he has had regularly from twelve to fifteen scholars. Were we to make any effort I believe we could get more; but in the first instance I want to go on gradually until the character of the school becomes fixed on right principles . . . Three of the boys stay with us in the house, and all of them come regularly to worship in the morning, when we have a little meeting of seventeen or eighteen persons in all. The school is of course shut up on Sabbath, but the last two Sabbaths most of the boys have been with us most of the day learning a Christian book, and have also attended Chinese worship of their own accord at the chapel of the London Society, where a native at present officiates ... The Chinese are diligent in learning after their own manner ... They are an intelligent and interesting race, and when the gospel takes hold of them in elevating and saving power, they will be interesting in another manner.'

1848, his first full year on the field, thus passed in steady preparation and quiet usefulness; but always the teeming millions of mainland China were in his mind's eye, and he longed to preach the Word to them. In a letter home, he remarked: 'You desired that three doors might be opened to me – the door of entrance into the language, the door of access into the country, and the door of admittance for the Lord's truth into men's hearts. The first of these has been opened in an encouraging degree already; and it now remains to seek by prayer and actual trial that the other two doors may be opened also.' Accordingly, on January 28, 1849, Burns intimated the discontinuance of his English services, as no successor was in sight; and next day announced 'that the school, which is at present interrupted by the Chinese New Year, will not be again re-opened': his purpose being to go 'forth into the field at large in order at once to attain in a proper manner the spoken language, and to spread abroad the gospel of salvation among these unsaved millions ... I need not add that in these circumstances I shall have special need of special prayer to be made in my behalf, and in behalf of the people among whom I may be led from time to time. China is not only forbidden ground to a foreigner, but it is a land of idols and a land without a Sabbath. How great then must be that power which can alone open up my way and make it successful!'

From 'Shap-pat-hoeung (Eighteen Villages)' he wrote on February 26: 'I am now no more among our countrymen, but am dwelling among this heathen people – alone, were it not for the presence of a covenant God and Saviour ... I left Hong Kong on Wednesday the 7th (instant) for the opposite continent of China, and have been, since that time, going from place to place with my

Chinese assistants and one servant, much as I used to do in Scotland in days that are past. In some places I have spent only one day; in others I have remained for a longer time, the population being large and the door open. As yet I have been furthered and prospered far beyond what I looked for; and although the difficulties are many, even of an outward kind, yet I do not despond in looking to the future. One of our difficulties arises from the constant fear the people are in of robbers, who suppose, though in my case without cause, that foreigners have much money with them; and again in places where there are mandarins a foreigner is likely to be dislodged at once. This was my experience at first setting out; for I had spent only one night at Kowloon, opposite to Hong Kong, when I was warned to remove, and so had to retreat for the time ... But with all this I have hitherto had great liberty of access to the population, and as far as I have been able to declare my message I have found attentive, and in some cases earnestly attentive hearers.'

After a spell back at base, he was out again, and wrote from 'the village of Pan-seen, to the north of Hong Kong about eighty-five miles', on April 16: 'Since coming back I have visited four villages of 1,000 to 1,500 inhabitants each, remaining generally for a few days, and embracing such opportunities as are given me, both in going out among the people, and in the visits which many pay to us, to make known something of the gospel message. We were some time ago invited to come to the village where we now are; and not only do we here enjoy the fullest external liberty to speak to the people, but there are some who receive us with much cordiality, and seem to manifest some interest in our message. One man in particular who this evening worshipped with us seems as if his mind were opening to the truth. But ah, when I speak thus you must not judge of such a case as if it were similar to those which we remember at Kilsyth, Dundee and Perth, in days that are past! ... In other days it has been my solemn privilege to enter into the labours of others, and it may be that here I am to labour where others are to reap.'

Following a third tour of the mainland villages, Burns wrote from Hong Kong on June 21: 'I went on the last occasion more to the westward . . . and there we found the people everywhere so averse to the presence of a foreigner, that after sleeping nine successive nights on the water in going from place to place, and not being allowed to lodge on shore, I returned here, where I have again resumed my quiet studies, and where I enjoy opportunities of doing what I can amongst this people, not only in speaking to the patients in the hospital, but in visiting others in the neighbourhood. The season also at present, both from great rain and great heat, is not so favourable for that mode of life which I have been following for some previous months on the opposite continent . . . Perhaps you are by this time aware that Dr. James Young, a much valued friend here, offered himself some time ago to the Presbyterian Church in England as a missionary. The last mail has brought to him the intimation of his offer of service being accepted; but where and how we may be located and employed on these shores is not yet fully determined; nor can Dr. Young leave his present employment until the close of the present year.

'It was a great mercy that in my last journey as well as in the two previous ones I was preserved from every danger, although surrounded with perils seen and unseen. The night before I landed here we were not, I suppose, above half a mile from a Macao passage-boat when it was attacked by pirates and robbed with the loss of some lives. The firing was so loud that, in the darkness, we supposed it must be some English war-steamer in pursuit of pirates.' He adds, 'The person who has charge of the Chinese hospital where I am now lodged is a converted Jew, Dr. Hirschberg, connected with the London Missionary Society. I have long enjoyed his friendship, and now for a season I am very favourably situated in lodging with him, both for learning the language and for speaking a little among the patients who come seeking cure to their bodily diseases.'

On a fourth tour inland from Hong Kong in November, Burns encountered even greater difficulties than previously, being relieved by robbers of all his personal effects, and returning only with the clothes he was wearing. This clearly indicated a closed door in that direction meantime; and the question was, Which way should he now turn? The Home Committee favoured Amoy as a permanent sphere of work, and Dr. Young heartily concurred. Burns for his part felt strongly the call of Canton, strategic centre of South China, only ninety miles from Kowloon, whose dialect he had been strenuously endeavouring to master.

To Canton therefore he went, sailing from Hong Kong on the last day of February, 1850. It proved a hard field. The only accommodation he could get was 'the expiring lease of a lodging, from a fellow-missionary about to return to Scotland'. There was ample scope for proclaiming the everlasting gospel, and he seldom lacked hearers; but the message did not seem to reach the heart, few coming back of their own accord or troubling to enquire further. Burns was even tempted to doubt whether the Chinese in their present state were capable of deep spiritual impressions. Yet he went on patiently sowing in hope; and when urged to desist and remove to Amoy, he pleaded for 'this very important station – a station so difficult and important, that I believe no agent who is in any degree suited for it, and who has a heart to love and labour for its proud and suspicious people should be encouraged to leave it'.

'Last Tuesday evening', he could add, 'when looking on an assembly of from fifty to sixty engaged listeners, while a native was addressing them before I did so, my heart said, "How can I leave these dear and precious souls for whom there are so few to care?" I can now tell them of the way of life with some measure of clearness and acceptance, and so long as God gives me standing ground to gather and address them, I must go on to do so, leaving the issues in his own hand, with whom it is to bless and save! Help us to maintain the combat in this great heathen city, until its gates are opened to the King of glory! Brethren, pray for us that the word of the Lord may have free course and be glorified!'

But the door soon closed. His lease expired; he received notice to quit; and all efforts to secure other suitable premises failed. The closing of this door, taken in conjunction with the wide open door of opportunity at Amoy, seemed decisive as to the path of duty; and, after a residence of sixteen months, Burns left Canton by sea in June, 1851.

VII.   First-Fruits of the Land

Shortly after reaching Amoy, a populous port and island four hundred miles north-east of Hong Kong, Burns wrote home on July 15, 1851: 'As you see from the date I am now at Amoy, having left Canton only a few days after I last wrote you, and having been here already ten days. My expectations of getting the house I had in view at Canton were completely disappointed, and my way seemed hedged up to come here. I embarked accordingly at Whampoa in the English barque *Herald* for Amoy on the evening of June 26th, and after spending the Sabbath and Monday at Hong Kong by the way, we reached here on the forenoon of July 5th. The passage was a delightful one, and very refreshing to the bodily frame after sixteen months in Canton. The days I spent in Hong Kong were pleasant. I had two opportunities of preaching in Chinese, and stayed with my old friend Dr. Hirschberg.'

'I have found a very kind Christian welcome among the missionary brethren, English and American, here, and my expectations are more than exceeded in all I have seen as yet of Amoy as a place and as a missionary station. I stayed for three nights with Mr. and Mrs. Stronach of the London Missionary Society, members of old in the Albany Street Congregational Church, Edinburgh; and I am now very much to my mind lodged in the middle of the Chinese population, in a little room connected with the school which was made over to Dr. Young by an American missionary on his removal here a year ago. Thus settled down amid Chinese voices, and with a Christian native servant (who prays with me; I cannot yet pray with him in his own dialect), and a Chinese teacher who comes daily, I am endeavouring to exchange my Canton for the Amoy Chinese. To speak this new dialect publicly and well may require a good deal of time; but even already I can make myself easily understood about common things, and am able to follow a good deal of what I hear in

Chinese preaching. Dr. and Mrs. Young are well, and seem to be getting on well, through the divine blessing and guidance. I feel it a great privilege to be connected with him as well as with the other missionary brethren here, who all go on in much harmony, and not without tokens of divine encouragement. The people here present a striking contrast to the people of Canton in their feelings and deportment towards foreigners. Here all is quiet and friendly, and although there is here also a great apathy on the subject of the gospel, yet a good many seem to listen with attention, and the missionaries have inquirers who come to be taught.'

Early in the new year (February 7, 1852), he could report: 'I am now engaged a good deal in the work of spreading the gospel among this people, being in the gracious arrangements of God's providence favoured with the co-operation of professing Christians, both indoors and in the open air. One of these baptized since I came here by the American missionaries aids me regularly, and others from time to time. We have meetings in the chapel of Tai-Hang, where Dr. Young resides, but get greater numbers in the open air when giving addresses in the open places of the city. During this week I also went to the neighbouring country among the villages, spending a night in one of these in the house of my servant, and preaching the Word with my companions . . . in six different villages. The work increases in interest and hopefulness. "Thy kingdom come!" '

The next report reads: 'On Tuesday the 24th February I again set out to visit some villages on the island of Amoy, and returned in much mercy on Tuesday the 2nd (March), being absent seven nights . . . We had large audiences everywhere. We generally addressed five or six meetings in the course of the day, and in all must have made known something of the truth to at least two or three thousand people . . . The people were everywhere friendly and attentive. We distributed a large number of tracts and hand-bill copies of the Ten Commandments. May the seed of the Word sown spring and bear fruit to the glory of God and the salvation of souls!'

On a third tour, beginning March 16, Burns crossed over to the mainland, and in a week made a circuit of thirty villages, sowing in all of them the good seed of the kingdom. The welcome was uniformly friendly, and the audiences large and often attentive, hospitality being provided freely wherever they went. He was so thrilled at the scope and prospects of the work, and so convinced of the need of more labourers to reap the whitening harvest, that he enthusiastically wrote home donating a year's salary (£250) for the furtherance of the work! Reporting this generous gesture, the Convener, James Hamilton, remarked: 'Surely that field is ripe unto harvest, when the reaper sends home his own wages to fetch out another labourer!'

Other useful work also occupied his mind and pen. Thus, on March 12, 1853, Burns noted in his journal: 'In the great mercy and by the gracious and constant aid of the Lord and Saviour, I was enabled on the 10th to complete the last revised copy of Bunyan's *Pilgrim* (First Part) in Chinese, which has occupied us from June 1st, 1852, until now, with the exception of a month at the end of last summer, when through feverish sickness I was obliged to lay it aside. The whole has been looked over by Messrs. Doty and A. Stronach with their teachers, and the work has been benefited by a number of their suggestions. One hour after finishing the last sheet in the form in which it will be printed, I received from Shanghai a copy of the *Pilgrim* in Chinese, printed two years ago by Mr. Muirhead of the London Society, chiefly for the use of pupils. It is not, however, a continuous translation of the whole.'

This literary venture was a real labour of love to Burns, and he was fascinated to observe the effect of the immortal dreamer's work on the Chinese mind. 'Thus when occupied with the inimitable portraiture of *Ignorance*, the Chinese teacher who was working with him, and who was then only half a Christian, was greatly taken with the flippant and copious talker, whose fluent tongue and knowledge of all subjects, physical and metaphysical, human and divine, positively enchanted him, and drew forth audible expressions of admiration and delight as he proceeded with his task; and it was only when the character had fully developed itself and the glittering tinsel fell off from the base metal beneath, that noisy approbation gave place to a silent thoughtfulness which showed that the master had achieved his object.' Burns was also working thus early on a collection of hymns for Chinese worship, which became very popular, not least with the children, and went through many editions.*

Just after completing the translation of Bunyan's work, the missionary was out in the field again, this time visiting the great prefectural city of Chang-chow. On May 16, 1853, he reported: 'Last month I had the privilege of paying a visit to Chang-chow-foo, a large city in this neighbourhood, at the distance of about forty English miles. We left Amoy on the morning of April 13, and returned here on the 26th, being absent about a fortnight, nine days of which were spent at Chang-chow, preaching to large and very interesting audiences both inside and outside the city. A week or two before our going, two native Christians, of the American Mission here, had visited Chang-chow, and preached to crowds for a number of days with much encouragement; and as they were purposing to go again, at the earnest desire especially of one of them, it was arranged that I should also go, although there was some reason to fear that, unless God should graciously open our way, there might be some unwillingness on the part of the authorities to allow a foreigner to pay more than a brief visit, or to preach at large to the people. To avoid difficulty as far as possible, it was arranged that we should live on the river, in the boat which carried us there, going on shore only to preach.

'On our arrival we immediately went on shore, and being at once surrounded by many people, we had a fine opportunity, within a few steps of our boat, of preaching the Word of life fully and without hindrance. We continued thus to preach on the bank of the river for three days, going upwards from our boat in the morning, and downwards in the afternoon, and addressing large companies for three or four hours at a time, until we had exhausted all the suitable stations near the river. We then went inwards, but still outside the walls, and at the very first station at which we preached, a man came forward and pressed us to go further on, and preach again opposite his house. This man the following morning came and was with us at worship in our boat; and when it

*In the rendering of Western hymn-tunes, the Chinese tendency to ignore semi-tones imparted a 'character quite peculiar' to the singing.

[144]

began to rain, and our boat was more uncomfortable, the same individual opened his house to us, and here we stayed (making the man a small remuneration) for five days; and going on from this as our headquarters, still inwards, we enjoyed the fullest liberty, both within and without the city, of preaching to large and very much engaged audiences. I do not think, upon the whole, that I have spent so interesting a season, or enjoyed so fine an opportunity of preaching the Word of life since I came to China, as during these nine days.'

The opening months of 1854 brought even greater encouragement. On May 8 Burns wrote: 'It is exactly four months since I first set out this season on a missionary tour; and you are already aware that God so remarkably opened the door in the place to which we first went, that we found it our clear duty to remain at that place as our headquarters for a longer period than we had intended – visiting the numerous villages and market-towns within our reach, while we carried on regular services at *Pechuia*, our central station. The work there was so interesting that we felt it could not be abandoned, but as we were anxious to extend our efforts to one or two central positions farther inland, it was necessary that other agents should take our place in order to leave us free to go forward. Accordingly, when, two months ago, I returned from Amoy to Pechuia, an addition was made to the number of native assistants, and leaving two of these to occupy Pechuia, I proceeded on the 9th of March farther inland, in company with the two native Christian companions with whom I had originally set out on the 9th of January from Amoy . . . We were almost everywhere favourably received, and our message listened to with attention, although there were no cases, as at Pechuia, of persons coming out and declaring themselves on the side of the gospel. While at Bay-pay, we heard it reported that at Pechuia one family had publicly destroyed their idols and ancestral tablets (the latter the dearest objects of Chinese idolatry), and that another man had closed his shop on the Lord's day, refusing admittance to a person who wished to trade with him.'

Returning to Pechuia, Burns says, 'we found to our delight that the work there had made decided progress in our absence. The two native Christians (members of the American Mission Church at Amoy), whom we had left in charge, seem to have been much aided in teaching the people. The preaching room had been crowded every night to a late hour by from forty to sixty persons, and those who had from the beginning shown an attachment to the truth had evidently advanced in knowledge and earnestness of spirit, and resolved to obey the gospel at the risk of much reproach and opposition. In our absence the station had also had the benefit of a short visit from Mr. Doty of the American Mission. After returning from our inland tour, we continued our meetings at Pechuia with much encouragement, several members of the native church in Amoy having successively come out of their own accord to aid in the work. During the last two or three weeks, however, the aspect of things at Pechuia has been considerably changed; for while those on the side of the gospel seem to go on in a way that fills our hearts with thankfulness and our mouths with praise, a disposition has been shown on the part of others to interrupt our meetings, which has obliged us at night to hold them upstairs, and more privately. The state of the weather also at this rainy season has prevented us from doing so much as before among adjacent villages. When I left Pechuia last Monday, it seemed that, including young and old, there might be about twenty persons who have declared themselves on the side of the gospel, but some of these are children, and two or three are women whom we have not seen – mothers who have received the truth from their sons or husbands. Among the number of those who are attached to the gospel are two whole families of six members each.'

While Burns was thus rejoicing over scenes which 'call to mind former days of the Lord's power in my native land', and feeling 'as much at home here as I would wish to do on this side of the Jordan', a distressing event took place within the Mission circle, in the untimely and unexpected death of Dr. James Young's wife, late in 1853. The Doctor bore up bravely, but it was soon evident that he had received such a shock as to necessitate immediate furlough. Companionship on the long trip home was also essential, and it was happily and quickly agreed that Burns should accompany him; a Chinese Christian nurse, Boo-a, going as well, to care for Dr. Young's child. They were in Scotland for some months; and Boo-a's attendance at church was always a matter of great interest to the congregation. A special interest attached to the crowded meeting in Free St. Luke's, Edinburgh, where Burns interviewed her in face of the congregation, translating her answers into English.

In addition he visited many other congregations to whom he was previously well known, thus quickening Scottish interest in the China Mission, and strengthening the recently formed Auxiliary of the English Presbyterian Mission. Friends were quick to notice his changed appearance and more mellow outlook, observing in him 'less of the Baptist, more of the Christ'. He was greatly interested in his nieces and nephews, jotting down their names that he might remember them all in prayer. But all along, his heart was in China. 'He talked of Chinese scenes, sang Chinese hymns, recited chapters of the Chinese Scriptures and Psalms far into the night, and abounded in details of Chinese life such as he rarely found time to mention in his letters home.'

One day he received a letter from the little church at Pechuia, over which he pored with intense delight. It ran as follows:

'Given to be inspected by Mr. Burns and all the disciples.

'We, who have received the grace of Jesus Christ, send a letter to pastor William Burns. We wish that God our Father and the Lord Jesus Christ may give to all the holy disciples in the Church grace and peace. Now we wish you to know that you are to pray to God for us; for you came to our market town, and unfolded the gracious command of God, causing us to obtain the grace of God. Now, as we have a number of things to say, we must send this communication. We wish you deeply to thank God for us, that in the seventh month and thirteenth day, pastor Johnston established a free school here; there are twelve attending it. Formerly, in the third month, a man, whose name is *Chun-sim*, belonging to the village of *Chieng-choan*, heard you preaching in the village of *Hui-tsau*. Many thanks to the Holy Spirit who opened his blinded heart, so that in the seventh month he sent a communication to the church at Amoy, praying the brethren to go to the village. They went and spoke for several days, and all the villagers with delighted heart listened. Also in the town of *Chioh-bey*, the Holy Spirit is powerfully working; the people generally desire to hear the gospel. The brethren and missionaries have gone together several times; and now, in the village of *Ka-lang*, there are two men, *Ch'eng-soan* and *Sui-mui*, who are joining heart with the brethren in prayer.

'Teacher! we, in this place, with united heart, pray, and bitterly (earnestly) beg of God to give you a level plain (prosperous journey) to go home, and beg of God again to give you a level plain (good journey) quickly to come. Teacher! you know that our faith is thin (weak) and in danger. Many thanks to our Lord and God, who defends us as the apple of the eye. Teacher! from the time that we parted with you in the seventh month, we have been meditating on our Lord Jesus' love to sinners, in giving up His life for them; also thinking of your benevolence and good conduct, your faith in the Lord, and compassion for us. We have heard the gospel but a few months; our faith is not yet firm. Teacher! you know that we are like sheep that have lost their shepherd, or an infant that has lost its milk. Many thanks to the Holy Spirit, our Lord, morning and evening, comforts our hearts [and gives us] peace. And in the seventh month, the 24th day, the brethren with united heart prayed, and shedding tears, bitterly begged of God again to send a number of pastors, quickly to come, again to teach the gospel. We wish that God our Father may grant this prayer, which is exactly that which the heart desires.'

The prayer of the infant church was speedily granted, for the death of his esteemed friend and colleague Dr. Young, at Mussel-burgh on February 11, 1855, cleared the way. Thus his first and only furlough ended within a month. As he boarded the train for London he was overheard to exclaim with satisfaction: 'Now for China!' When he embarked in the *Challenger* on March 9, he was accompanied by a new recruit, the Rev. Carstairs Douglas, M.A., a graduate of the University of Glasgow and New College,

Edinburgh, who had been ordained and set apart for work in China, by the Free Church Presbytery of Glasgow a few weeks earlier.

VIII. Instant, In Season, Out of Season

On reaching the field, the seasoned missionary's first task was to attempt to make contact with the Taeping* rebels at Nanking, it being freely rumoured that Christian influences were at work among them. 'It was about the beginning of August, 1855, ten days after reaching Shanghai from England, that, in company with a Chinese servant . . . I set out in a *woo-sung* boat to try whether the way were open to reach the insurgent camp.' They were able to proceed a considerable distance up-river, but were turned back – doubtless providentially – a little short of their objective. On the return journey, however, they had splendid opportunities to distribute Christian literature. 'The sight of this poor people, so eager to get our books, but alas! so little able to understand them, was fitted to affect the heart.' The applicants at one place included 'several Buddhist priests'.

For the next six months, with Shanghai as centre, Burns engaged in a water-borne ministry, along the rivers and canals of the surrounding 'garden of China'. Thus on December 13 he reported: 'I write these lines on board a river-boat, which has been my principal habitation during the past three months, and in which I returned to this place on Monday last, after an absence in the surrounding country of twenty-six days. I was accompanied by a native professing Christian, received into the visible church during the present year, and now employed to circulate the Scriptures in connection with the *Million Testament Scheme.*' The

*The Taeping rebellion aimed at the overthrow of the Chinese Manchu Emperor. It broke out in 1850. After 2 years its leader had occupied most of South China. However, as Shanghai was threatened, the English and French assisted the Emperor to defeat the rebels. It was in this campaign that General Gordon ('Chinese Gordon') led his Ever-Victorious Army.

places visited included Fung-king (Maple-tree creek), 'where a foreigner had hardly been seen, and where the interest felt in our message was rather greater than usual'; Tung-keang, where 'we found but little encouragement, and the rabble were even inclined to use us a little unceremoniously'; and Min-hang, where 'we had usually large and attentive audiences . . . with whom at the close I felt at liberty to join in public prayer to the living and true God in the name of Jesus'.

The next report is of special interest, with its mention of Burns' first meeting with Dr. J. Hudson Taylor, founder of the China Inland Mission, who had reached the field less than two years earlier, and on whom Burns at this stage had a profound influence. Under date January 26, 1856, the latter says: 'It is now forty-one days since I left Shanghai on this last occasion. An excellent young English missionary, Mr. Taylor, of the Chinese Evangelisation Society, has been my companion during these weeks – he in his boat, and I in mine – and we have experienced much mercy, and on some occasions considerable assistance in our work.' But if Taylor was indebted to Burns now and later, Burns was indebted to Taylor. 'Four weeks ago, on the 29th of December, I put on the Chinese dress, which I am now wearing. Mr. Taylor had made this change a few months before, and I found that he was in consequence so much less incommoded in preaching, etc., by the crowd, that I concluded that it was my duty to follow his example.'

But the Shanghai field was comparatively well served by missionaries. So when Captain Bowers, the Christian master of the *Geelong*, mentioned the need of Swatow, a rising commercial centre to the east of Canton province, and offered a free passage thither, Burns felt a clear call from God to pioneer a new field. Taylor accompanied him, and, 'after a favourable passage of six days', they reached their destination on March 12. Burns adds, 'We were very averse to the thought of being located even temporarily on the island, on which some of our countrymen have, by compact with the local magistrates, taken up their headquarters, but were anxious, if possible, to find a location in the Chinese town of Swatow, which is on a promontory of the mainland, five English miles further up, at the mouth of the river Han. We were apprehensive lest we should not be permitted thus to locate our-selves; but ... two days after our arrival we were, to our own surprise and joy, enabled to take possession of the lodging which we have since been occupying unmolested. Our lodging is not indeed large, being only a small upper flat of a house occupied below as a shop; but it is sufficient for our present wants, and we are the more thankful for it as of vacant houses here there are almost none.'

The foreign shipping at Double Island offered scope for work, the services on March 30 being attended by the captains and crews of a dozen or more ships, among whom were 'an unusual number of Scotchmen'. Burns 'felt it a great privilege to be allowed to preach the gospel in a place where it has been, as far as we know, seldom before proclaimed.' But the evangelisation of the Chinese was their first and paramount concern; and he goes on: 'Mr. Taylor and myself came here quite undecided whether we should be able to attempt more than simply to make a running visit for the purpose of Scripture and tract distribution to the open parts of the country; but now that we see more fully the importance of this region as a vast and unoccupied scene for missionary labour, we are anxious, before going further, to prepare ourselves for the purpose of teaching the people orally by acquiring some knowledge of their dialect. This is a comparatively easy work in my case, the dialect spoken here being ... very similar to that spoken in Amoy.'

From 'Nan-ying, ten miles from Swatow', Burns wrote on July 16: 'During the last fortnight I have been moving from place to place, making known the gospel message and distributing tracts, etc., in company with two professing Christians, natives of this district, who came up from Hong Kong fully a month ago, sent by Mr. Johnson, an American missionary, to co-operate with us. Previously to their coming, I had been out on a missionary tour accompanied by a servant only. Mr. Taylor having occupied himself in learning the dialect of this district since our arrival at Swatow, left us a fortnight ago for Shanghai, intending, if the Lord will, to return in the course of a month or two, and bringing with him his medical apparatus, use his knowledge of medicine for the purpose of opening a door for more regular missionary operations among the people. Had we obtained a place suitable for indoor preaching at Swatow, I would not have ventured at this hot season to go about in the country. Difficulties, however, have been thrown in the way of our obtaining such a place, and so no other course has been left open but the one we are now following. We have met as yet with but little decided encouragement, but still something is done to spread an incipient knowledge of the truth, and in a field which has been so little cultivated we must not be discouraged if we meet not with immediate success.'

Some of the particular difficulties are then mentioned. 'The people in this district are, I think, if possible, more blind and hardened in idolatry and sin than in any place (if we except Canton) where I have formerly laboured. Although society presents here the usual features of Chinese civilization, it is coupled with a barbarity in certain circumstances which I have seen or heard of nowhere else in China. The fishermen, boatmen, and people working in the fields, pursue their work in summer in a state of savage nudity; and within the last twenty years I am credibly informed, persons taken prisoners in the clan feuds have not only been cut to pieces, but their hearts boiled and eaten by their enemies. Such is heathenism in this part of civilized China. The ravages of opium we meet with here on every hand, and the deterioration of the morals of the people generally I cannot but ascribe, in great part, to the use of this ensnaring and destructive drug. When will measures be taken by those in power to lay an arrest on the opium traffic, which is inflicting such an indescribable injury on this people . . .? How blinded by the love of money are they who seek to enrich themselves by the gains of such a traffic!'

In a postscript Burns adds: 'About 2 o'clock a.m., or past midnight, July 18th, 1856. We have just been visited by robbers, who have taken all but the clothes we wear, without however doing us any injury. This is a new call to pity, and to pray for this poor people, sunk so low in darkness and sin . . . We are preserved in much peace, and have just been joining in praise and prayer for this poor people.' In his next letter, dated 'Canton, October 10th', he gives the sequel: 'When I last wrote you in the middle of July, I and my companions had just been robbed in our lodgings at a village about sixteen miles from Swatow. The following day one of my companions returned to Swatow with my letters, and to obtain a fresh supply of books and money, while my other Christian companion and I went forward, as we had intended, to the town of Tang-leng, about six miles further on. We were without money, but God provided support for us in a way that was new to me. The people who took our books gladly contributed small sums of cash for our support, and the first day we thus collected enough to keep us for two days; a countryman also, going the same road, volunteered to carry our bag of books for us; it was heavy for our shoulders, but easy for his, and he said he would want no money, but only a book. Thus the Lord helped us in going forward on his work, instead of turning back to Swatow for help.'

They were 'very well received' at Tang-leng, where they found 'two native Christians, converted in connection with the American Baptist Mission in Siam', witnessing faithfully. Heavy and continuous rain, however, detained them there for some weeks; and on August 18 they set out on the return journey to Swatow. 'Our course by water leading us to within five or six miles of the Chaon-chow-foo (chief city of the Chaon-chow department), we agreed to pay it a visit; but fearing lest we should give offence to the authorities, we determined, instead of living on shore, to make the boat which conveyed us there our headquarters while we remained. On Tuesday the 19th we went on shore, and were particularly well received by the people. The demand for our books among persons able to read them, was unusually great. In the meantime, however, an alarming report of the presence of a foreigner outside the city having been carried to the authorities, we were in the evening suddenly arrested in our boat, and, with all our books, etc., taken prisoners into the city. The same night we were examined publicly by the district magistrate, and after the interval of a day we were examined anew by a deputy (I suppose) of Che-foo, or chief magistrate of the department'.

It was evidently on the latter occasion that 'the magistrate required him to go down on both knees to be examined, as is the practice in China. Mr. Burns very firmly but respectfully refused, saying that he would go down on one knee, as he would do to his sovereign, Queen Victoria; but that he would only go down on both knees to the King of kings. The magistrate was struck by this answer, solemnly and respectfully uttered, and allowed the missionary to be examined on one knee'. 'On these occasions', Burns says, 'my companions and myself had valuable opportunities of making known something of the gospel, and of the character and objects of Christ's disciples in China; and as there was a great demand for our books, the work of many days seemed to be crowded into one or two. The magistrates examined us with great mildness and deliberation, seeming anxious to obtain information rather than to find fault.'

They were at first minded to release him on security, but then decided that, having arrested a foreigner, their proper course was to hand him over to his consul at Canton, whither he was sent by river-boat on August 30. The trip took a month. 'I was provided with a servant, and with whatever food I wished, at the expense of the government; and had I been well, and had had with me a good supply of Christian books, I might have enjoyed the journey much.' But as it was, his supply of books was almost exhausted, while 'a slight cold which I had caught before coming to the city had, through excitement, etc., taken the form of an intermittent fever, with chills (ague), which, violent at first, continued more or less during all my journey'. Hence he was much relieved when Canton was reached, and he was taken straight to the office of the British Consul.

He there learnt that 'the Consul has had a communication from the Governor-general about the case. I did not see it, but the Consul informed me that it was conceived in a mild strain, much more so than he had expected, and I am thus wonderfully preserved and freed from the infliction of any punishment or penalty'. The document which the Consul did not show to Burns is full of interest, as it gives a view of the missionary as seen through official eyes. It runs as follows:

'Yeh, High Imperial Commissioner, Governor-General of the two Kwang Provinces, etc., addresses this declaration to

H. S. Parkes, Esq., Her Britannic Majesty's Consul at Canton.

'I have before me an official report from Wang-ching, Chief Magistrate of the district of Hae-yang, in the department of Chaon-chow, which contains the following statements: –

"It being the duty of your subordinate to act with Le-seuen-fang, the major commanding at this city, in the inspection of the defences of the place, we suddenly observed, whilst engaged in this service, three persons seated in a boat on the river whose appearance had something in it that was unusual. We found in their boat, and took possession of, seven volumes of foreign books, and three sheet tracts; but these were the only things they had with them. On examining the men themselves, we observed that they all of them had shaven heads, and wore their hair plaited in a queue, and were dressed in Chinese costume. The face of one of them, however, had rather a strange look; his speech in respect to tone and mode of expression being not very similar to that of the Chinese.

"We, therefore, interrogated him carefully, whereupon he stated to us that his true name was Pin-wei-lin (William Burns); that he was an Englishman, aged 42 years, and, as a teacher of the religion of Jesus, had been for some time past engaged in exhorting his fellow-men to do good deeds. In 1847 he left his native land and travelled to China, and took up his residence first at Victoria, where he lived two years, and afterwards in the foreign factories at Canton, where he remained for more than one. Subsequently, he visited Shanghai, Amoy, and other places, and there spent several years; wherever he went he made himself acquainted with the languages of the Chinese, and by this means he delivered his exhortation to the people, and explained to them the books of Jesus, but without receiving from any one the least remuneration. In 1854 he embarked in a steamer from Amoy, on a visit to his native home, and in December, 1855, joined himself to one of his countrymen, surnamed Tae, who was going to Shanghai to trade.

" 'I accompanied him thither', said Burns, 'in his vessel;

but from Shanghai Tae returned home again, whilst I remained there and engaged myself in the distribution of Christian books. In the sixth month of the present year, I left Shanghai, and took passage in a foreign sailing vessel to Swatow, in the district of Chinghae. There I fell in on the 12th day of the 7th month with Le-a-yuen and Chin-a-seun, the two Chinese who have now been seized with me. I called upon them to be my guides, and we proceeded in company to Yen-fan, and from thence came on to this city, where we had it in contemplation to distribute some of our books. Scarcely, however, had we arrived at the river's bank on the 19th day of the 7th month, when to our surprise we found ourselves under surveillance, and deprived of our liberty. We entertained, however, no other views or intentions than those which we have stated, and declare that these statements are strictly true'."

'Such is the account given by the missionary, William Burns, who, together with his seven volumes of foreign books and his three sheet tracts, was given over into the charge of an officer, and brought in custody to this office.

'Having examined the above report, I have to observe thereon that the inland river of the city of Chaon-chow is not one of the ports open to commerce; and it has never on that account been frequented by foreigners. I cannot but look upon it, therefore, as exceedingly improper that William Burns (admitting him to be an Englishman) should change his own dress, shave his head, and assuming the costume of the Chinese, penetrate into the interior in so irregular a manner. And although, when closely examined by the magistrate, he firmly maintained that religious teaching and the distribution of books formed his sole object and occupation, it may certainly be asked, why does William Burns leave Shanghai and come to Chaon-chow, just at a time when Kiang-nan and the other provinces are the scene of hostilities? Or, can it be that a person, dressed in the garb and speaking the language of China, is really an Englishman, or may he not be falsely assuming that character to further some mischievous ends?

'I have directed Heu, the assistant Nan-hae magistrate, to hand him over to the consul of the said nation, in order that he may ascertain the truth respecting him, and keep him under restraint; and I hereby, by means of this declaration, make known to him the above particulars.

'William Burns, seven volumes of foreign books, and three tracts, accompany this declaration.

'*Heenfung*, 6th year, 9th month, 2nd day (September 30, 1856).'

In view of this lenient treatment, and being now 'graciously restored' to health again, Burns planned to return again to Swatow and resume work there; but 'was met by a message from the British plenipotentiary (Dr. Bowring), conveyed to me by the Consul, to the effect that, "after the representations of the Imperial Commissioner, he should deem it imprudent and improper that I should return to the district from which I have been sent".' This left him with no choice but to remain meantime in Canton, helping the American and English missionaries there, while awaiting word of Hudson Taylor's movements. The latter did not return to Swatow, and early in 1858 Burns learnt with surprise 'that my friend and former fellow-labourer here, Mr. J. H. Taylor, has just been married at Ningpo to a daughter of a late missionary, Mr. Samuel Dyer.'

Burns himself was, however, soon back in Swatow, initially with a view to inquiring after his Chinese companions on the recent evangelistic tour, who were still in prison. He was distressed to learn that they had been cruelly treated, but rejoiced to know that they had stood firm and witnessed a good confession; and it was as a result of his representations that, after four months' captivity, they were released. Meanwhile he received a warm welcome at the Treaty Port, 'enjoying favour in the sight of rich and poor, the rulers and the ruled', and being able at last to effect a permanent settlement. His influence for good was greatly widened when he enlisted the services of Dr. De la Porte, a Wesleyan, who was practising his profession among the foreign shipping at Double Island. Very willingly the Doctor came up twice a week, Burns acting as his interpreter, while two native evangelists preached to the forty or fifty patients who might be treated each time.

Unfortunately Britain was now at war with China;* and, through Lord Panmure, Burns was offered a chaplaincy to the British Forces in the area, with the rank and allowances of a major. He respectfully but firmly declined the appointment, principally on the ground that it would inevitably prejudice his subsequent relations with the Chinese. About this time also he met Lord Elgin, en route to Peking on an important mission. 'Lord Elgin in his way to the north called in at Swatow, about a month ago. I was invited to breakfast with him, on board H.M.S. *Furious*, and had a full opportunity of expressing to him my convictions and feelings on various points – the coolie trade, opium, etc. He made particular inquiries in regard to the progress of the missionary work among this people, and also heard in detail the facts connected with my arrest, etc., in 1856.' They later had correspondence when Lord Elgin was Viceroy of India.

In February 1858 Burns wrote from Double Island, where he was enjoying a temporary change of occupation, repairing and improving Dr. De la Porte's house. It spoke well for his workmanship that, in a violent typhoon which shortly swept the area, wrecking the entire shipping fleet in port, and levelling most of the houses on the island, this was the only one in the vicinity which withstood the blast! A cholera epidemic also raged for several months while Burns was at Swatow; and he thought it 'melancholy to see the means to which the people resort in order to free themselves from this dreadful visitation of God's hand'; noting also that 'not one word is heard of the need of repentance, or of turning from any of the sins in which this people are lying, and in which they seem to go on with as unblushing boldness as before. How true that darkness covereth the earth and gross darkness the people! What need that He should arise and shine who is the Light of the world!'

*This (the second) war between Britain and China (1857–8) was occasioned by disputes over Chinese treatment of the *Arrow*, a Chinese vessel registered at Hong-Kong and flying the British flag, but alleged by the Chinese authorities to be sheltering a notorious pirate. British forces burned down the Emperor's Summer Palace at Pekin before the Chinese Government finally submitted to British demands. Lord Palmerston was the British Prime Minister at the time.

The departure of Dr. De la Porte for England in June was shortly followed by Burns' own departure from Swatow. When he handed over the work to a younger missionary, the Rev. George Smith, he could not point to a single decided convert. But he had thoroughly broken up the soil; and a rich harvest was in due course to be reaped.

IX. Not in Vain in the Lord

Burns left Swatow by sea in October, 1858, and a few days later was at Amoy. Here, where signal triumphs of grace had previously been witnessed, tares had appeared among the wheat. The return of Burns was therefore timely. On February 22, 1859, he wrote: 'There are two persons there (at Pechuia) who have fallen away from their Christian profession; but neither of them had from the beginning, as far as I learn, any marked evidence of a work of grace. The only really melancholy case that I know of, is one who was chapel-keeper, and afterwards a preacher, but who, there is reason to fear, has again fallen under the power of opium-smoking.' On the credit side he could add: 'I wonder more than ever I did at the reality and preciousness of the work of the divine Spirit at Pechuia and the neighbouring stations. May the time be near when new and like glorious manifestations of the Lord's saving power shall be witnessed in this and in all lands!'

After gentler means had been tried in vain, two of the offending members were cut off from the communion of the church, and two others were subjected to further discipline. The need for more regular organization was also seen, and a Session was constituted for the Pechuia church, the elders being elected by the congregation in open meeting; such a step having already been taken at Amoy and Chioh-bey. The Pechuia and Chioh-bey churches further joined in 'a season of solemn prayer and fasting, that they might seek the return of the Lord's favour to Pechuia.' There were large attendances, and 'it was evident that the Lord was in the midst of us'. The Amoy church made another advance in 1859, with the setting apart of two Chinese evangelists, whose support was guaranteed entirely by the local congregation. The gospel was thus taking root, and the church becoming indigenous.

In October of that year, Burns removed from Amoy to Fuh-chow, the provincial capital, where he continued for nearly a year. He quickly mastered the new dialect, then apportioned his time among the three established missions, helping specially in open air work. An American worker warmly commended him for 'his excellent influence upon our native assistants', and for 'success-fully introducing the use of colloquial hymns among us in our worship . . . The savour of his name is still fragrant at Fuh-chow'.

Returning to Amoy in September, 1860, Burns soon moved on to Swatow, where to his joy he found that the seed he had sown in faith and patience was already beginning to bear fruit. The evidence of this in his first service there affected him almost to tears. For the Swatow church also he compiled a hymnbook in the local dialect, which was to prove a real boon.

In 1861 he was in Fuh-chow again; his services next being re-quired in the Amoy district, where the Chinese Christians were suffering persecution and loss at the hands of their heathen neigh-bours, the believers in and around Pechuia being hardest hit. They were robbed of their property, including their cattle; the fields of rice and of sugar-cane which they cultivated were plundered and marred; their fruit trees were cut down; a believer who had refused to pay the festival tax for the support of idol worship was denied the use of the public well, and his son was beaten for attempting to obtain the needed water. Three female candidates for baptism were severely beaten by their relations. Though unconcerned about his own rights, Burns was deeply concerned to maintain the rights of others, and took prompt and vigorous action in the matter. A settlement entirely satisfactory to the Christians was secured from the Chinese authorities, through the interposition of the British Consul. But what had happened locally could easily happen generally; and it was deemed expedi-ent, therefore, that Burns should go to Peking, and place the matter before the British Ambassador, Sir Frederick Bruce, with a view to securing a general and permanent settlement. He reached the capital in October, 1863, and entered on a new phase of work in and for China.

Dr. S. Wells Williams, Secretary of the United States legation at Peking, later recalled that 'the purpose for which he came to Peking in 1864, to endeavour to obtain the same recognition of the civil rights of Protestants that the Roman Catholics had, was not attained in the manner he wished; but his mission was not fruitless. He made known the condition of the missions in Fokien province to the late Sir Frederick Bruce, and gave him a juster perception of the mode of carrying on missionary work than he had before, and the nature of the disabilities under which the converts then laboured. Sir Frederick declared that Mr. Burns was one of the most fascinating men in representing a case that he had ever met, and gave one a clear idea of whatever he undertook to describe'. He would no doubt have made a brilliant lawyer!

An L.M.S. missionary, the Rev. J. Edkins, gives a fuller picture of this 'Beulah land' period of the Scottish missionary's life: 'The Rev. W. C. Burns came to Peking in 1863, and at once opened to Sir Frederick Bruce the matter to attempt the settlement of which he had come. He went to stay with Rev. W. H. Collins (C.M.S.), who met him as he entered the city gate, and at once claimed him as a guest. It was not his object, however, to live with any of the mission families. He wished a house for himself. A small house with a little self-contained court was rented for him at 2/6d. a month. Here he lived for four years . . . This simplicity of living was happiness to our lost friend. He enjoyed quietness, and the luxury of having few things to take care of. He delighted to live on little, that he might have more to give to the cause of God. He was a generous friend to the poor, to hospitals, to various mission schemes.'

'We have a hot short summer, at an average of 90°, as we have a cold winter averaging 15°, when the ice never thaws till the opening of spring, but remains a foot thick through the season. Our friend had a small clay stove lit for the season. Here he sat summer and winter with his teacher, engaged for a good part of each year in hymn-making and translation. His first work in

Peking was a volume of *hymns*, about fifty in number. These were chiefly translations from home hymns, or hymns used in the south of China rehabilitated in the mandarin dialect. They have been extensively used since, and will continue to be so ... When he had printed this collection, he undertook a translation of the *Peep of Day* in fifty chapters ... This excellent little work of Biblical doctrine "has been widely circulated, and is found to form a very suitable introduction to the gospel history".

'*The Pilgrim's Progress* was his next work. Formerly at Amoy he had translated this book in a simple style. He now resolved to render it again into Chinese, adopting the dialect of Peking. The First and Second Parts are complete in two thick volumes ... In the Second Part, Burns attempted to increase the usefulness of the work to Chinese women by adding paragraphs showing the principles that should rule in Christian marriage. Immediately after the completion of this work, he commenced a translation of the *Psalms* from the Hebrew ... It is composed in four-word sentences throughout, so as to assume a regular appearance of symmetry; but this advantage has been gained at the expense of smoothness. To each psalm there is an introduction stating the argument. There are also many text-references to the New Testament and other parts of Scripture. These additions add much to the value of the book.

'While engaged constantly in these literary enterprises Mr. Burns never intermitted preaching when not physically incapacitated for it. He preached much at the chapel of the London Mission hospital, within two or three minutes' walk of his residence ... He preached also very frequently at a chapel of Dr. Martin's outside of the east gate, and at another more than a mile north of the London Mission hospital, belonging to the American Board. He also officiated occasionally at Mr. Collins' chapel, belonging to the Church Missionary Society, on the west side of the city. His services at all these places were very acceptable, and given with the greatest good will and the most catholic spirit.'

He also went on tour at least four times, in connection with the rural work of the L.M.S. He spent three weeks at Shen-cheu, one hundred and seventy miles south-west of Peking; ' and when he left, thought that at least two of the natives were suitable for baptism. The Bible distributor who was with him thought there were four. Mr. Burns was very cautious in giving an opinion with regard to the fitness of applicants for baptism. His habit was to be stern in requiring decided sacrifices on the part of the inquirer, such as would constitute indubitable proof of his sincerity.' The only extant photograph of him, in Chinese dress, was taken at this time, contrary to his own inclination but to gratify his mother's wish.

But the Peking field was fairly well occupied; and again this intrepid missionary felt the urge to pioneer. Edkins further writes: 'When Mr. Burns left Peking for Tientsin, in the autumn of 1867, it was still an open question whether he would go to Nieu-chwang or to Shan-tung. . . . But his sense of duty and his know-ledge of the need of a missionary at Nieu-chwang, led him there in preference. The captain of the native junk in which he went would take no money from him for the passage. This was on account of his character, and that of the catechist. Going not for trade but to do good, it appeared to this heathen sailor unreasonable to accept payment of passage money. Arrived at Nieu-chwang they began to seek a house, and found one at last in the outskirts. Here they became domiciled, and public and private services were daily held. Many persons attended, and the hearts of our departed brother and of the catechist were cheered. On Sundays Mr. Burns performed worship in English at the Consulate as long as his health allowed.'

A Christian seaman, the first mate of a trading vessel, met Burns at this time, and has left on record an interesting glimpse of him in his last 'parish'. 'In October, 1867, I left Che-foo, in the barque *Lady Alice*, for Nieu-chwang, where we arrived about the 6th. I had learned from the missionaries at Che-foo that a mis-sionary of the name of Burns was at Nieu-chwang.' The mate sent a message to Burns, who invited him to his residence. 'I landed at the appointed time, and was conducted accordingly to the mis-sionary I had never seen. I shall not soon forget it, for we seemed to meet as friends that had been acquainted for a long time. I felt perfectly at home with him. Mr. Burns walked up and down the yard of his house arm in arm with me, and talked to me as a friend, brother or father, in the most kind and familiar manner. As iron sharpeneth iron, so did the countenance of a man his friend that day. He told about how the Lord had guided him to that place. He had many friends, he said, where he had been staying for four years before, and was very comfortable; but he wanted to come to Nieu-chwang because there was no one labouring there. He said we must not study comfort: they that go to the front of the battle get the blessing; the skulkers get no blessing.'

Burns returned the mate's visit next day; 'and in the evening, when all the crew were with us, he gave an address about the Saviour and the woman of Samaria. There was one illustration I remember which shows his homely and forcible way of putting things. He compared the woman of Samaria to a fish with the hook in its mouth, twisting about, trying to get loose; but the more it tried to clear itself, the firmer hold the hook got of it. The whole of the address was very interesting and very earnest, and was well received . . . After our meeting was ended, not one offered to move; and our dear friend, sitting at the head of the table, told us about his travels in China . . . This was one of the happiest evenings of our voyage'. When the mate tried to thank him as he went ashore, he said: 'Don't mention it, don't mention it! Our meeting is providential.'

On November 21, Burns wrote to his friend and colleague Carstairs Douglas: 'Your letter of August 31st reached me this p.m. per steamer *Manchu*, and as she is the last vessel for this season, I hasten to send a few lines by her to Shanghai.' Like Douglas, he has grown a beard, because it 'both saves a great deal of time and trouble, and, in this cold latitude, the hair is a protection to the throat'. With his eye on over-all strategy, he adds: 'It seems to me that no place more suitable (or perhaps so suitable) could be recommended to the Irish Presbyterians than Nieu-chwang, and Manchuria beyond, a vast, open and unoccupied field, with a fine climate, and a population comparatively well off in a worldly point of view. In writing home, I have already made this suggestion, and I hope that on consideration you will see your way to second my proposal. If the Irish were here, would this not be a fine place to come to from the south for a change of air? . . . Romish priests are found here and there, but the only representative of the Protestant churches is my solitary self!'

He kept a record of the texts of his sermons at Nieu-chwang, from September 15 (John 3. 16), through December 1 (Luke 15 – 'a good day'), to December 29 (the last entry, when the portion expounded was, appropriately enough, Revelation 20. 11–15). Thus his last public testimony was to the same great truth to which he had witnessed so effectively on the streets of Newcastle twenty-seven years earlier, and the overwhelming conviction of which had so often imparted a peculiar grandeur and solemnity to his words.

To his mother he wrote on January 15, 1868: 'At the end of last year I got a severe chill which has not yet left the system, producing chilliness and fever every night, and for the last two nights this has been followed by perspiration, which rapidly diminishes the strength. Unless it should please God to rebuke the disease, it is evident what the end must soon be, and I write these lines beforehand to say that I am happy, and ready through the abounding grace of God either to live or to die. May the God of all consolation comfort you when the tidings of my decease shall reach you, and through the redeeming blood of Jesus may we meet with joy before the throne above!'

Towards the end, a friend noticed 'a decided change for the worse, and great distress in breathing'. For the sufferer's benefit, he 'repeated several portions of Scripture, among others Psalm 23. Hesitating at the words, "Yea, though I walk through the valley of the shadow of death", Mr. Burns took it up, and in a deep strong voice continued and finished the psalm . . . On closing the exercise with the Lord's Prayer, Mr. Burns suddenly became emphatic, and repeated the latter portion and doxology, "For Thine is the kingdom, and the power, and the glory", with extraordinary power and decision'; this being his last distinct utterance.

So this 'Greatheart of China' passed over, at Nieu-chwang, on April 4, 1868; and we may be sure that 'all the trumpets sounded for him on the other side'. At the simple service of interment, in the foreign cemetery, his physician, Dr. Watson fulfilled the late missionary's request by reading over his mortal remains the great passage, 1 Cor. 15. 42–57: 'So also is the resurrection of the dead ... Thanks be to God, who giveth us the victory, through our Lord Jesus Christ.' The inscription on the headstone concludes with the reference: '2 Corinthians, chap. 5'.

As we pass this eager life in quick review, certain features stand out, and call for comment. First, this man of God had a goodly heritage. He was a son of the manse, and the aims and aspirations of father and son were identical. There is powerful moral momentum in such a godly ancestry, as many have the happiness to know from experience.

Then, too, young Burns grew to manhood at a singularly favoured time in his nation's and his Church's history. If the latter half of the eighteenth century belonged to the Moderates, the first half of the nineteenth century witnessed an Evangelical resurgence, which reached its climax in the Kilsyth Revival and its aftermath, and poured out full spate in the Disruption, making the Church of Scotland *Free*, and a powerful force for world evangelization.

Burns came to the kingdom for such a time as this. But he was not only a product of the times. Under God, he helped to shape and mould them. His own conversion was literally a right-about-turn, being clearly the work of sovereign grace. Conversion, he soon saw, spelt complete consecration to the service of the Master. It was but his reasonable service, therefore, to be willing (and desirous also) to go abroad as a missionary.

He was only twenty-four years of age when the Lord of the harvest anointed him for, and used him as, the human instrument in the great revival that swept North Britain and kindled the heather during and after 1839. The same grace that thus honoured and exalted him, kept him humble; while he showed remarkable commonsense and balanced judgment in those hectic and exciting days.

Two notes in his Revival ministry stand out prominently, both reflecting his own spiritual pilgrimage, and particularly its critical moments. Thus he was deeply impressed, both with the natural condition of man as a sinner, and with his desperate need of a Saviour; and he pleaded with men immediately to close with God's gracious offer of salvation, and receive Christ as their Saviour. But he would have his converts receive a *whole* Christ – a Christ who would be not only Saviour but Lord. In fact the initial outpouring of the Spirit at Kilsyth directly followed his ringing challenge: '*No Cross, No Crown!*'

That Burns should have been able to step down from spearheading such times of refreshing and revival, to undertake, and more than fulfil, the pressing duties of a busy Edinburgh pastorate; and that he should have been equally at home in evangelistic ministry, unsustained by the fires of revival, in Ireland and Canada, are but further illustrations of the fact that he was no ordinary man, but one who was bound to make his mark in almost any calling or sphere.

The sphere in which he has made an indelible mark, however, is – even more than that of Revival ministry at home – the foreign mission field. His life was early yielded to God for this work. Yet there was a ten-year delay in the acceptance of the offering; and half-a-dozen doors of entrance into other lands (including India, Arabia and European Jewry) had to be closed, before it was made clear beyond even the shadow of doubt that the King and Head of the Church would have him serve in China, then slowly and reluctantly opening to the Gospel.

In China, too, we marvel that he could so quickly and fully adapt himself from the role of reaper to that of sower. For – though he was privileged to reap not a little of the crop from the seed he himself sowed – his principal work during his twenty years there was that of preparing a highway for our God, and sowing the good seed of the kingdom, by voice and pen. Continually the pillar cloud led on; and he died, as he lived, in a frontier situation, and on a bridge-head into the regions beyond.

It is impossible not to admire Burns' scholarly ability and application to the study of the language (including the mastery of new dialects as he moved about the country); his increasing identification of himself (in dress and other ways) with the Chinese people; his true catholicity, and delight to work in har-

[167]

mony with all who loved the Lord; his personal influence on the newly-arrived Hudson Taylor (destined to be the founder of the great China Inland Mission); his moral courage, that made him almost oblivious of any danger to life and limb; his outspokenness on public questions, such as the opium trade, slavery, and civil rights; his refusal to compromise his missionary position and standing, by accepting a military chaplaincy or other preferment; and his indifference to money matters and unconcern about normal furlough.

Probably few modern missionaries have more closely resembled the apostle Paul than Burns. Both remained single throughout their lives, for the kingdom of heaven's sake. Both were finished scholars and forceful preachers. Both recognized the power of the pen as mightier even than that of the sword. Both regarded evangelism, rather than baptism – the planting of new churches, rather than their nurture – as their primary order of reference. Both were in their element as pioneers, delighting most of all to blaze the trail over fresh horizons. Alongside Paul's yearning, 'I must also see Rome' (Acts 19. 21), we may set Burns' parting word, as he left home for his second and final term on the foreign field: 'Now for China!'

If we may thus compare Burns in these and other ways with the great Apostle to the Gentiles, we are bound to think of him also as the spiritual son of Paul, as well as of Augustine, of Calvin, and of Knox. In particular, he was 'of old Knox's principles', being a true child and product of the thorough-going evangelical Reformation, with which God favoured His Kirk in Scotland. In proclaiming the whole counsel of God, Burns' trumpet therefore gave no uncertain sound.

It scarcely needs to be added, that his life squared with his doctrine; and that he practised what he preached. A fellow-missionary to China, while on leave, was once asked if he knew William Burns? 'Know him, sir?', this man exclaimed, with pardonable hyperbole; 'All China knows him! He is the holiest man alive!'

A recent writer has dubbed him a 'fiery revivalist'. *Fervent evangelist* would be a much truer description. He was both a burning and a shining light. And, though we will soon celebrate the centenary of his passing, the after-glow remains: 'Being dead, he yet speaketh', calling an ease-loving, self-pleasing generation to 'have done with lesser things', and 'give heart and soul and mind and strength to *serve* the King of kings.'

'O William Burns! We will not call thee dead,
Though lies thy body in its narrow bed
In far-off China. Though Manchuria keeps
Thy dust, which in the Lord securely sleeps,
Thy spirit lives with Jesus: and where He,
Thy Master, dwells, 'tis meet that thou shouldst be.
There is no death in His divine embrace!
There is no life but where they see His face!'

– H. Grattan Guinness

BIOGRAPHY OF JOHN ELIOT

by

NEVILLE B. CRYER, M.A.

I. A Farmer's Son Learns Christ

On February 29, 1704, there occurred in New England an event which in our day would have earned a sensational place in our more popular newspapers. On that leap-year day, at Deerfield, Massachusetts, a party of Red Indians descended on the English settlement there and, with the help of their French allies, surprised and burnt it to the ground, killing forty-nine people, the men by scalping, and taking one hundred and eleven back to their encampments in the North as hostages. A painting of the scene which reconstructs dramatically the events of the day leaves us in no doubt about the tragic nature of this encounter between European settlers and their Red Indian neighbours, and to those who know no better it might well seem as if, in the manner of most 'Westerns', this had always been the case. It is to dispel this view and to show how, by the ministry of one man in the preceding century, many Red Indians came both to know Christ and to share in Christian fellowship with their new neighbours from the Continent of Europe that these pages are written.

It was in fact just one hundred years before, in another Leap Year, and on August 5, 1604, that a newborn child, John, was christened in the Parish Church of St. John the Baptist, Widford, Herts., by the Rev. John Payton. The child was the third of what was to be eventually a family of seven born to Bennett and Lettye Eliot who lived in the parish. Bennett Eliot was a yeoman farmer stemming from a family of Norman origin, and by the time his son John was born this typical product of the English countryside had already acquired land in the surrounding districts of Eastwick, Ware, and Hunsdon in Hertfordshire and of Nazeing in Essex. Such application in the building-up of the family holdings marks out Bennett Eliot as a man of energy and ambition and certainly as one whose influence on his son John is plainly to be seen in later years. A few glimpses at the kind of yeoman farmer that John Eliot's father was may indeed help us to appreciate the more not only the mettle of his son but also the kind of people amongst whom John Eliot served in Massachusetts Bay during most of his life.

Briefly stated, a yeoman was such an one as a certain John Morshead described a few years earlier, who 'always maintained a good house, a good plough, good geldings, good tillage, good rearing and was a good husband', the latter in both senses of the word. The house of the yeoman might vary as much as the tenures and rights of the land on which it was built, but most yeomen would have a one-and-a-half storey home with a milkhouse, a malthouse and other small buildings attached to the dwelling at the side or rear. Some houses, and John Eliot was throughout his life accustomed to such, would be half-timbered, of brick or stone and rectangular in shape. Such a house, simple in arrangement but solid in construction, and with furnishings as lasting, represented the character of the man who owned and used it, and it would be handed down with pride to the eldest son, who would normally inherit the house and estate on his father's death.

Such a man as Bennett Eliot would almost certainly have three or four workers in the fields, not to mention the sons who, unlike John, did not leave home, and there would also be an apprentice or two sent by the Overseers of the Poor to learn the skill of farm-labouring – a practice which was to be turned to good effect in New England when John Eliot sought to train his Indian converts in the ways of 'civilization'. The average yeoman had ample work to keep him busy all the year – ploughing and harrowing his acres, setting trees and hedging, sowing wheat and rye, and numerous other such occupations. Idleness, the disease of some in a higher class of society than Bennett Eliot, was not likely to be his failing, nor, by example and heritage, that of his son John. Very early in life John Eliot must have learned to scorn the ways of the sluggard. No less impressive was the yeoman streak of thriftiness, a natural quality in those who lived to a large degree on the food they raised and who clothed themselves with the fleeces of the sheep they reared. It is true that such an attitude of thrift could easily turn to hard-fistedness and George Herbert is recorded as saying that the besetting sin of the yeomen was covetousness, or to put it more plainly, stinginess. The liberal open-handedness of Eliot across the water was to earn for him some stern rebukes from those who measured more carefully the contributions to the mission field of New England.

Industry, homeliness and thrift, with a not-to-be-forgotten gift of being a good neighbour in a very practical way – these were the ideals and often the marks of that class from which John Eliot sprang. These too were the traits of the English folk who went to New England; most of those who went into business or politics were, because of such qualities, influential and prosperous. Their level-headed and practical approach to life we shall see in evidence in the subject of our story.

It was just such a concern for the practical welfare of the members of his family which led Bennett Eliot, like many others of his class, to bestow some acres of his hard-acquired land upon a younger son. In John Eliot's case his father bequeathed profits from his land to the sum of £8 per annum (in the values of the time) in order to maintain the boy at the University. An entry in the father's will of November 5, 1621, records this for posterity. So far as we know, John was the only son of the family to be favoured with this superior education, but the value of his father's judgment and provision was amply proved by later events, and doubtless the boy had already shown by his early schooling the promise which a period spent at Cambridge was to reveal.

But before we pass to this next stage of preparation in the life of this young Puritan 'apostle', who had doubtless already acquired the stocky build, long curly hair and smiling face which are so often attributed to him later, we must paint in the religious backcloth against which John and his family should be seen. That they were Anglicans we have already seen by the early attendance of the family at the parish font after the birth of the child. Such scant evidence of John's childhood as we have – and it is as meagre as that of the dear Lord he served – would suggest that he was taken faithfully to the Parish Church and there catechized and taught by the local minister in all that the Bible and Prayer Book had to tell of the marvellous acts of God in Christ. It is likely that his family were Puritan in outlook, which meant that they desired the ministry of the Word of God to be in the care of learned and godly men preaching the gospel of conversion and repentance; they believed that the Bible provided a God-given pattern of life and that Christians were, like Enoch, to walk daily with God. Were they not to live as 'pilgrims and strangers' who, after the fashion of those who sailed in the *Mayflower*, 'should lift up their eyes to the heavens, their dearest country, and quieten their spirits?'

Such were the patterns of the religious upbringing which John Eliot would know as he reached his teens – a religion of day-to-day godliness, the longing for a good man as one's local minister, one who, being skilled in Greek and, if possible, Hebrew, could search the Scriptures at their source and bring to light the life-giving Word of the Most High. It meant to walk each hour with a mind filled with the 'things of the Spirit of God', to read the Word of God and to seek His face in prayer, for, said John Preston, 'if we pray continually, though God is not changed, we ourselves will be!' It is not hard to believe that the normal pattern of family prayer was one which inspired John Eliot as he grew up.

The zealous Puritan watched the health of his soul as some of our contemporaries watch their blood pressure. Yet the normal Puritan of John Eliot's day – such an one as he himself became in these formative years – was not by any means a religious eccentric. He was a man of parts and a man of integrity. He believed particularly in the careful use of time. Certain hours must be set apart for specific spiritual exercises and the remainder must be devoted to his calling; the two aspects were not divorced but intimately linked. His calling was to be diligent in his worldly business and thus to support his family, but mere pastimes and worldly pleasures which served neither his soul's interest nor his calling earned his displeasure. Much casual evidence makes it clear that Puritans were the best of workers, and an examination of almost any of the new centres of industry in the land shows that where trade was humming the inhabitants were largely men of Puritan sympathies.

Such in outline was the domestic, social and religious life with which our 'apostle' became familiar as he grew up. For him it was a life without any certain prospects other than those which his

William Chalmers Burns

John Eliot

*(This portrait is reproduced by courtesy of the
Henry E. Huntington Library, San Marino, California).*

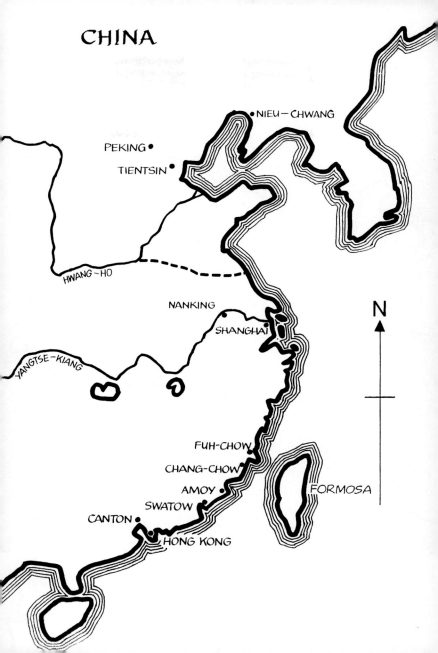

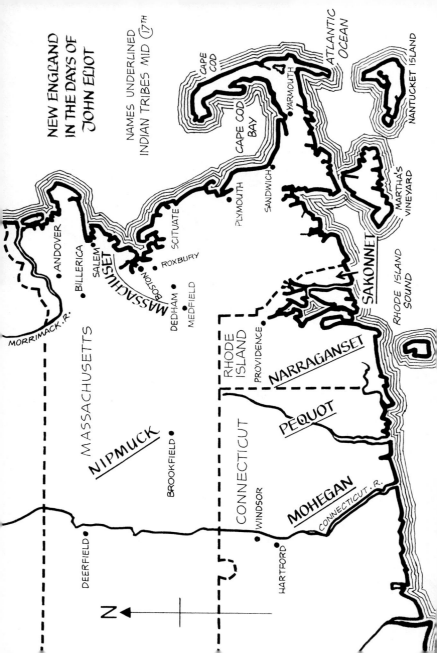

John G. Paton

Henry Martyn

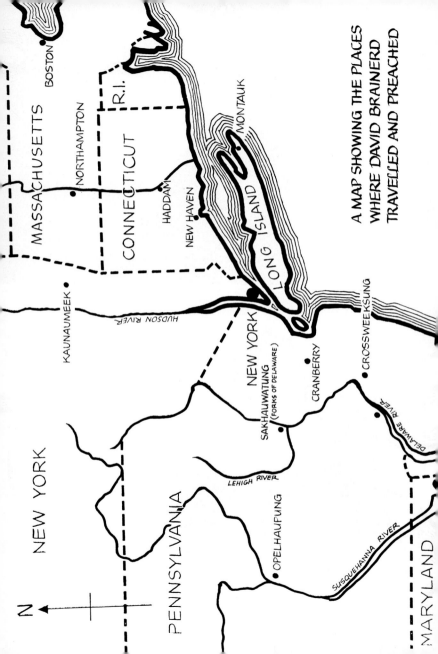

A MAP SHOWING THE PLACES WHERE DAVID BRAINERD TRAVELLED AND PREACHED

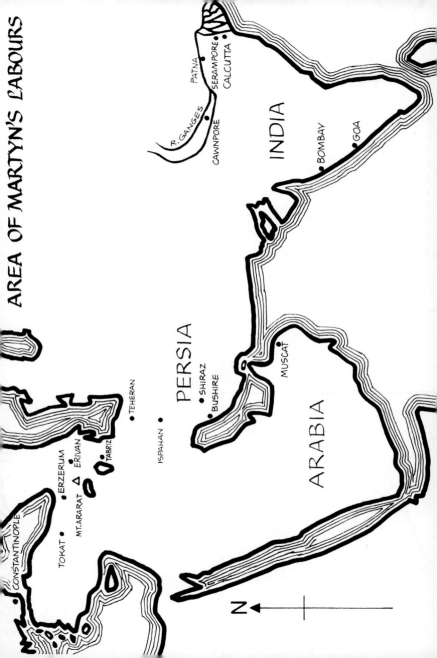

AREA OF MARTYN'S LABOURS

CONSTANTINOPLE

TOKAT

ERZERUM

MT.ARARAT

ERIVAN

TABRIZ

TEHERAN

ISPAHAN

PERSIA

SHIRAZ

BUSHIRE

MUSCAT

ARABIA

INDIA

R.GANGES

PATNA

SERAMPORE

CALCUTTA

CAWNPORE

BOMBAY

GOA

N

THE NEW HEBRIDES

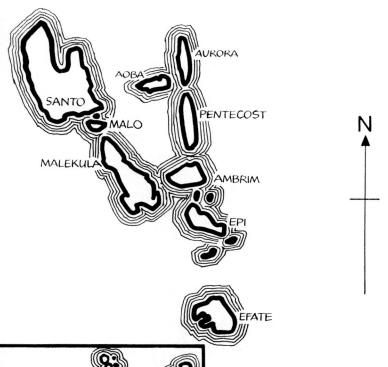

N

SANTO

AOBA

AURORA

MALO

PENTECOST

MALEKULA

AMBRIM

EPI

EFATE

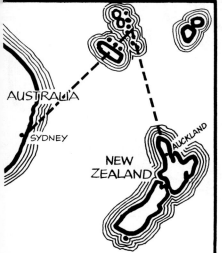

AUSTRALIA

SYDNEY

AUCKLAND

NEW
ZEALAND

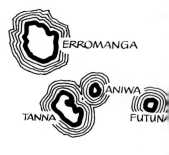

ERROMANGA

ANIWA

TANNA

FUTUN

ANAME

ANEITYUM

ANELGAUHAT

own applied talents could secure. Yet he had many sure guides – a happy home, a firm faith, a godly ancestry and, above all, an early and constant acquaintance with the Lord in prayer and the reading of His Word. It was with such a heritage that he left Widford in the early spring of 1619 when approaching fifteen years of age and travelled to the University of Cambridge, some thirty miles away.

John Eliot entered Jesus College as a Pensioner on March 20 and was enrolled for the four-year course leading to the degree of Bachelor of Arts. These simple facts tell us more than we might at first imagine about the man whose story we record. Cambridge in 1622, with sixteen colleges already and some 3,050 students, was in fact larger in proportion to the population of these islands than at any time afterwards until the University of London and other provincial universities began. Nevertheless, it was only at this date that the sons of yeomen were beginning to reach this distinguished educational centre, whose buildings, says one contemporary, 'were fitted to be the abodes of knights, lords and lawyers rather than of clerks', weavers' and butchers' sons.' It is true, of course, that there were grades of undergraduates and more of them than now, there being not only gentleman commoners, who might bring servants and horses with them, but also scholars, exhibitioners, sizars, pensioners and, lastly, battelers who were the poorest of them all and who worked their way through the University by doing some of the meanest tasks and being themselves fed, not in Hall, but in the kitchen. Eliot, we are told, was a pensioner, whose fees would therefore be paid by his father, but who would not have or expect much in the way of pocket-money for luxuries and 'diversions'. Most boys worked diligently as was essential if they hoped to fulfil the requirements for a degree. The backbone of the training was Rhetoric and Logic, two disciplines which God was to use powerfully with his new servant at College; for the rest, Cicero's orations were to be studied for style, as an invaluable aid to statesmen, the arguments of the Greek Aristotle and other classical authors being absorbed for the final 'public disputation' which replaced the written examination papers of today.

To this routine of scholastic endeavour John Eliot applied himself with all his native vigour. He slept, not in a private room of his own, but underneath or at the side of the truckle bed of the College 'fellow' who was in charge of him and the other five or six students in their 'company'. He would rise at 5 a.m. in the summer and at 6 a.m. in the winter as the College bell rang out, would partake of a frugal breakfast and then proceed with his studies until dinner at eleven. If he went out in the afternoon before supper at 5 p.m. he must only go out with a companion or in a larger group, and by 8 p.m. or 9 p.m. he must be in College or be severely punished for late arrival. That he worked long hours in his room after this hour would seem very likely if we look at the bills incurred for candles.

That John Eliot worked diligently during his time at Cambridge is everywhere attested and he is known to have been particularly interested in Hebrew and Greek as well as finding philological studies absorbing. In his fourth year, as anticipated, he graduated as a Bachelor of Arts . . . at the age of eighteen!

The period that follows is the only remaining period of his life for which we have no clear evidence of his activities or his whereabouts. In many ways this is not unlike the hidden years of the Lord Jesus Christ or the period of desert preparation experienced by the Apostle Paul. When he clearly reappears in 1629 as an usher at the small grammar school at Little Baddow, near Chelmsford, in the countryside of Essex it is clear that, during the intervening years three important crises have occurred.

The first and most important concerned his personal salvation. We have already remarked that John Eliot came from a God-fearing and sound Anglican home and owed much to the example set before him in the Hertfordshire homestead. Moreover there can be no question that the youths at the University talked much of religion in their leisure hours for it was a topic of immediate and practical concern in the England of those days. As pupils in a system which provoked enquiry and debate, comment and counter-comment, there would be little left of a man's faith by the time he bade farewell to the fields and courts of Cambridge if it were not firmly based on the evidence and arguments of

Scripture, and could be defended against the ruthless searchings of one's nearest companions. A graduate had something done to him that was more than intellectual. It was not only that when he attained the B.A. degree he was entitled to be called 'gentleman' whatever his previous station in life; much more than this, a boy grew up – or to use the motto long familiar to the scholars at New College, Oxford, 'Manners makyth the man'. When John Eliot emerges once more into the clear light of history we see him on the side of the Master whom he is to serve for the rest of his days – he knows assurance, the blessed assurance of one who has come to know the reality of Christ's victory on the Cross and who has been enabled to make his calling and election sure. It is only such an assurance which can account for his later ministry.

Such heartfelt belief, however, could not be contained. One eminent divine of that age, Dr. Edmund Staunton, used to greet his associates in the morning with the words, 'Come, friends, what shall we do for God this day? How shall we trade with our talents for the furtherance of His glory?' They were impatient folk, these Puritans; eager to get on with the Lord's work, and they could forbear no opportunity to promote the interests of the kingdom of God or to share the knowledge of divine grace with those who knew not of it. To an earnest Puritan the main burden of this task of delivering Englishmen from otherwise certain damnation fell upon the ordained ministry. It is not at all unlikely therefore that in these years the decision to be ordained was the natural outcome of John Eliot's deep personal faith. It is true, as William Kellaway has pointed out in his book on the New England Company that John Eliot's name does not occur in the Diocesan Registers of London and that his growing admiration for the more outspoken Puritan divines hardly suggests that he would be willing to subscribe to the Thirty-Nine Articles, as he would have had to do at his ordination in the Church of England. Persuasive as this reasoning may be, there are strong contrary evidences. What is certain is that Eliot's name was clearly included in the lists of the emigrant clergy given by Neal (in Anderson's 'History of the Colonial Church'); that the diary of John Winthrop clearly accepts Eliot from the outset as a fully-accredited 'minister of religion', which could for him only mean an Anglican clergyman; and finally, the admiration of John Eliot for the Rev. Thomas Hooker and his friends was the admiration of a younger man for one who had already subscribed to the Thirty-nine Articles of Religion and was not averse to being both the incumbent of Esher in the County of Surrey and subsequently Rector of Little Baddow, where we duly find Eliot in his school. A search in the Diocesan registers of Ely might prove to the world that John Eliot so soon as he was canonically eligible, in 1628, at the age of twenty-four years, had decided on his life's work – to preach with full authority an evangelical Christianity, and extend a religion of prayer and reading of the Scriptures, with meditation and self-examination.

What is most revealing when we meet him clearly again is the close relationship between John Eliot and the man with whom perhaps he was serving his title – The Rev. Thomas Hooker. Concerning the latter, surprisingly little is known, in spite of the important work that he did and the influence that he wielded during a masterful life. Like John Eliot he was sprung from yeoman stock and was a scholar and later Fellow of the same University, though at first a batteler of the lowest degree. It was as a 'lecturer', or popular preacher, that he made his name amongst English Puritans before being expelled by Archbishop Laud, only to become the most stimulating preacher in the colony of New England. He was so much an embodiment of the moral fervour of the Reformation that protested against 'dumb priests' that Cotton Mather once said of him, 'He is a person who, while doing the Master's work, would put a king in his pocket.' It is hardly surprising that such a man should draw to himself the admiration and discipleship of men like John Eliot who were full of zeal and new to the ministry. Indeed, a letter of May 20, 1629, written by a court supporter to Laud's tool, Chancellor Duck, says as much: 'All would be very quiet here if he (Hooker) would depart ... His genius will still haunt all the pulpits in the country, where any of his scholars may be admitted to preach. ... There be divers young ministers about us ... that spend their time in conference with him; and return home and preach what he hath brewed ...' – and there is a great deal more in the same vein. It was indeed to this man that New England Congregationalism and New England democratic institutions owed their greatest debt. The decision to consider the one, even if he could not fully embrace the other was for John Eliot due in no small measure to the short but certainly impressionable period during which he was the chosen subordinate, or usher, at Hooker's school in Little Baddow.

On May 31, 1638, Thomas Hooker preached a remarkable sermon on popular sovereignty from the text, Deuteronomy 1. 13, also used later by John Eliot for his notable book on Christian Government. Hooker elaborated the thesis that 'the foundation of authority is laid, firstly, in the free consent of the people' and therefore that 'the choice of public magistrates belongs unto the people by God's own allowance', and 'They who have the power to appoint officers and magistrates, it is in their power also to set bounds and limitations of the power and place unto which they call them.' Such preaching, let it be noted, was in Hartford, Connecticut, in the New World, and it was doctrine which sounded hard even to some of the emigrants from the land of Charles I and Archbishop Laud. Back in Essex John Eliot must have been early warned by Hooker that should Laud find it possible to apply his policy of 'thorough' there could be little freedom for Puritans in the years ahead. With such counsel and the news that Hooker could provide from ministers who had already left England's shores for the freer air of the American continent, the eyes of John Eliot must have slowly lifted from the hedgerows of Essex to the still largely unexplored horizons of the America of which he heard.

To this young man, committed to Christ and like Hooker unwilling to be muzzled, unafraid of hard work, and of yeomen stock, a graduate of repute and an ordained minister of God's Word, the way forward began to become clear. When Puritan emigrants, friends of Thomas Hooker, invited him to join them as they sailed to Boston, and when the woman to whom he was by now engaged agreed to follow, the way was open, and John Eliot, the man of God, at twenty-seven set out upon his life's career.

II. Following in the Mayflower's Wake

On August 16, 1631, the two hundred and fifty-ton *Lyon*, which had been laden at Gravesend and had there received John Eliot as one of her passengers, was riding off the quay at Deal in Kent, her flags flying, her newly-painted poop shining with red and blue, the lion rampant on her prow sparkling with new gilt. It was here that the principal passengers and emigrants were to board her – no less than the family of the Governor of Massachusetts Bay, John Winthrop. It can be imagined that in their hearts, no less than in the heart of the young curly-headed minister of twenty-seven, there must have been much questioning about the prospect that faced them across the sea. Though more than a century had passed since the momentous arrival of Columbus in the islands of the West Indies, the Age of Exploration was still in full spate. It was an age that encouraged wild stories and vivid fantasies, for truth itself was wonderful. The two images that were constantly being projected by reports from the new lands of America were on the one hand that of an earthly Paradise in which colonists would benefit 'from one of the most pleasant, most healthful and most fruitful parts of the world . . .' and on the other, that of a Howling Wilderness in which the first settlers could be envisaged as 'blazing their way into an unknown land, absorbing the rigours of a primitive countryside' and, in their encounters with the Indians – 'the savages', as they more usually called them – 'know how men lived whilst the world was under the Law of Nature'.

One seventeenth century traveller, John Josselyn, who approached the North American coast in 1638, tells us that he and his fellow-travellers were regaled with news from two passing vessels that there had been a general earthquake in New England and that a monster had been born in Boston. On landing in Massachusetts Bay he goes on to relate the stories told him by certain 'neighbouring gentlemen', such as the one describing a sea-serpent coiled up like a cable on the rocks at Cape Ann, which an Englishman in a passing boat would have shot, had not two Indians dissuaded him, saying that if the serpent was not killed outright they would all be in danger of their lives. John Eliot and his companions would be no less well informed than others in England of these strange shores that awaited them, and certainly John Winthrop, Governor, kept his family fully aware of what was happening in Massachusetts Bay.

There was, however, one aspect of this New World which differed from all others, for the colonists here had to face not only the hazards of nature but also the sorceries and strange practices of the 'red' natives who roamed the woods. These primitive people were called 'redskins' by the first travellers who encountered them because most of the Eastern tribes were fond of painting their faces and bodies with red ochre or red vegetable pigment in order to emphasize their sharp bony features, their part-Mongoloid eyes and above all their long, aquiline noses. If we are inclined to smile at these primitive habits we do well to recall that the inhabitants of Britain were once such people well within the bounds of recorded history, and one such northern group of British tribes was described by this very custom – the Picts or 'Painted ones'. These Red Indians of the Eastern American seaboard, however, should not be thought of as the magnificently attired, nomadic horsemen, hunters and warriors of romance. The Indians of John Eliot's acquaintance were more nearly like the aboriginal people of Northern Australia today, scantily clad, the men with only a dark ridge of hair down the middle of their otherwise shaven heads, living in dome-shaped or cylindrical huts of bark and grass, and depending for their food, clothes and general livelihood on the hunting which formed almost the wholetime occupation of the male members of each tribe. Here, at last, says William Wood in his *New England's Prospect* (1634), 'is a creature unspoiled by civilization ... in a state of nature.'

Some Europeans were quite prepared to equate these 'savages' with devils, or at least to regard them as people who were devil-possessed, and to give as much credence to the divining and conjuring-up of spirits practised by the Indian 'shamans' or witch-doctors as the Red Indians themselves. William Wood, in the book already mentioned, recounts what he hears of one shaman, Pissacannawa, who can 'make water burn, rocks move, trees dance and metamorphize himself into a flaming man'. Along with 'pow wow' magic and demon sorcery the colonists marvelled at the fanciful myths of the red man, and were left in no doubt that the entire background and philosophy of the Christian religion differed fundamentally from the native beliefs of the Indians. These aboriginal people had little thought of the hereafter and did not base their ethics upon their religion. Moral principles were not sharply defined. Dreams and visions, induced by fasting or drugs, wherein they regularly saw and spoke with individuals known to be dead, were proof enough to the Indians of the existence of a soul and an afterlife.

The religion of the Indian was entirely practical and was designed to help him to live, not in the future, but in the immediate present. Thus, when the Indian thought himself plagued by an evil spirit, it seemed to him that the obvious way to rid himself of his difficulty was to propitiate the spirit with offerings. Underlying all his other religious customs and practices there was the somewhat mystic conception of an impersonal supernatural force which spread throughout all Nature and animated all the things which control the destiny of man. In the countryside, and amongst the tribes of the Algonquin Indians which were to become so familiar to John Eliot, this force was called 'Manito' and it is this same concept which Eliot's forerunners had already named, 'The Great Spirit'. There was at least here for John Eliot in Massachusetts what Paul had encountered in the 'Unknown God' of the Athenians.

Interesting and in many ways essential as this preview of the Red Indians and their ways of life may be, space forbids that we should dwell on it at any greater length. What might well have exercised the imagination of the young minister of the Gospel as the *Lyon* ploughed the Atlantic was the prospect of living in the near proximity of such apparently primitive people. Stories of Indian cruelty and barbarism were seriously weighed by the

Pilgrim Fathers some ten years previously when they embarked at Leyden and it is therefore not surprising to discover that there stands today, close to Plymouth Rock, a more than life-size statue of the great Wampanoag chief, Massasoit, who was the first stranger to approach the Pilgrim Fathers as they landed, and who remained such a constant friend of the English settlers there for forty years that he has become known in history as the 'Protector and Preserver of the Pilgrims'. Edward Winslow, writing of the early experiences of the settlers in the immediate neighbourhood of Eliot's later home around Boston, says, 'We walk as peaceably and safely in the woods as in the hieways in England.'

Whatever then might be the differences and difficulties which Englishmen perceived between themselves and these ancient inhabitants of the New World, there was nothing, in the opinion of many contemporary writers, to deter their fellow countrymen from making the journey to America. It was Winslow again who pointed out that 'the spiritual condition of the savage is itself an argument for immigration. Every Christian has a duty . . . to spread true religion among the Infidels, and to win many thousands of wandering sheep unto Christ's fold . . .' Other early New England historians and diarists write in this vein: 'Those men might as well be dead who lived in England for themselves alone and sit still with their talent in their napkin when that could be of service both to God and to their country by becoming colonists and using every effort to convert the heathen.'

The Puritans, then, who emigrated to Massachusetts Bay in 1630 and 1631 regarded themselves as chief actors in a world drama which was being staged under the direct call and supervision of God in the American wilderness. There they planned to erect a Bible Commonwealth of sanctified citizens obeying His revealed Word as laid down in the Scriptures. Thus would a community of 'visible saints' come into being, the only one in the world. It was this grand motive which also urged John Eliot, the Winthrops and others less well-known to throw in their lot with those who had gone before them and to help build a real 'colony of heaven' behind Massachusetts Bay.

As Eliot sailed during these long weeks which were to separate

[185]

him for ever from the land which had given him birth, a sound education and a future wife, and in which he had come to a true faith in the Lord, there must have been a great deal to occupy his mind and conscience as a minister of the Gospel. He was, on board ship, and would be unquestionably on land, responsible for the first time in his life for precious souls whom Christ by His blessed Atonement had rescued from eternal death. There was much food for reflection there as he pondered how he could best minister to God's elect and feed their hungry spirits. He was, at the same time, reminded by the presence of the Governor's relations that the new Colony had a government in which he, as a minister, would have no little part to play. How could he best assist men to rule in righteousness and live in brotherly love? Some of his fellow-passengers, we are assured, did not know Jesus Christ as their Lord and Saviour and some were travelling to this New World impelled by nothing but the most mercenary of motives. They too would be his neighbours on that foreign shore and to them no less his ministry must extend. But above all there turned and tumbled in his mind the knowledge that he had gleaned already, through Thomas Hooker's friends, of those new and deluded people who had never heard of Christ and yet were now to be within a horse's ride of where he must reside – the Red Indians. Perhaps already there was forming in his mind the sentiment he was to express to a friend, Sir Simonds D'Ewes, a year or so later, when, speaking of the Indians, he wrote, 'I trust, in God's time, they shall larne Christ'.

As the *Lyon*, after ten weeks at sea, sailed along the coast of New England the Captain repeated the names of the places they passed, names such as Piscataqua and Agamenticus, uncouth Indian words which interested Eliot with his love of languages, even though the places seemed to his untrained eye to be unrelieved forest to the water's edge and there was no sign whatever of human habitation. At last, on Wednesday, November 2, 1631, the *Lyon*, being unable to enter Boston Harbour against a strong west wind, dropped anchor in the Nantasket Roads. They were still six miles from the English settlement but they had arrived safely in the New World and Eliot was rightly called on to offer praise and thanks to God for their deliverance from the hazards of their long sea journey.

It was that same day, as many of them hung over the side of the ship and stared away into the distance towards Boston, that a birch-bark canoe glided alongside, paddled by two feather-topped figures. Their dark faces were tattooed on the cheeks and painted with the usual ochre stripes. Their heads were shaved except for a long scalp lock stiffened with bear's grease and pierced with the feathers of a pheasant. Around the neck of one there were several necklaces of blue, shell, wampum beads and one of wolf-claws. the other was less splendid and wore nothing but a skin mantle and a simple breechclout.

The Captain introduced them with the words, 'Your first savages, ladies and gentlemen. The one with the necklaces is Sagamore Chickatabot, chief of these parts on the Bay. He lives by the Neponset River and is a very good Indian'.

'Is he a Christian?' asked John Eliot earnestly.

'Bless you, no, sir', replied Captain Pierce. 'They believe in a kind of Great Spirit called Manito, and a devil named Obbomock – that's all I know.'

It was then, doubtless, that John Eliot realized how far they were from Widford and the College courts of Cambridge, not to mention the pupils of Little Baddow. If he had never realized it before, he had reached his journey's end – the brave new world in which he would end his days amongst the people for whom he, more than anyone else in his generation, would lay down his life. In one sense the ship was as good as in port; in another sense John Eliot's ship had only just set out.

III. Working for God in Massachusetts

On Friday, November 11, 1631, little more than a week after the passengers of the *Lyon* had made land, John Eliot was praying and lecturing in the First Church of Boston on what had been proclaimed by Governor Winthrop as a day of General Thanksgiving. The Church was but a temporary affair, a small thatched building with clay-daubed walls and no steeple, and standing at the corner of what was but a wide muddy lane, though called King Street, and another similar thoroughfare called High Street, which led off to the district known as Roxbury. As John Eliot ministered in the Church on that warm and misty morning to 'the much edifying of Boston folk' (as the record runs) it could never have occurred to him that he stood at the point of a further change of direction in his life which would locate him in Roxbury for nearly sixty years! For the time being however, and at the personal invitation of the Governor, he was to work and preach in Boston, for the usual minister, Mr. Wilson, had recently returned to the home country.

John Eliot ministered in Boston for almost a year and was to prove, during that period, an acceptable member of the Massachusetts community. Social life in the early years of the colony was simple; a mid-week lecture in Church was considered the high-water mark of leisure activity and among minor indulgences could be counted a stroll on Boston Common 'where the Gallants a little before sunset walk with their Marmalet Madams ... till the Nine-a-clock Bell rings them home' – an event which would take John back in memory some ten years or more to the closing time of his College gates! Class distinctions were solemnly respected and when in 1631 Mr. Josias Plaistowe was convicted of stealing corn from the Indians, the court ordered his servants to be flogged, but upon him levied only a fine, though directing that henceforth 'he should be called by the name of Josias, and not Mr. as formerlie'. No kind of social gradation, however, was more jealously guarded than seating in Church according to 'dignity, age and estate'. There were most complicated rules of precedence such as that 'the fore seat in the front gallery shall be equall in dignity with the second seat in the body'. Even at Deerfield, where we began our story, rules were scrupulously worked out by a committee on Church etiquette, with this as a typical order: 'Brother Richard Jackson's wife to sit where Sister Kempster was wont to sit. Ester Sparhawke to sit in the place where Mrs.

Upham is removed from. Mr. Day to sit the second seat from the table, Ensign Samuel Greene to sit at the table. Goody Gates to sit at the end of the Deacon's seat. Goody Wines to sit in the gallery.' People who crowded into pews above their station were ejected and sometimes heavily fined.

Such an attitude of social distinction spilled over into many spheres in the City life of Boston. In the college founded in 1636 and named in honour of the Reverend John Harvard, the son of a butcher, students were listed for more than one hundred and thirty years according to their social rank. It should not be forgotten that though the 'Mayflower Pilgrims' were people of extremely humble origin, born and bred in poverty and living chiefly by manual labour in Nottinghamshire and the adjoining counties, the capable leaders who created the early institutions of Massachusetts Bay were Jacobean Englishmen of middle station, halfway between the aristocrat and the burgess and showing the main characteristics of both.

This was the society in which John Eliot first set to work in what was henceforth to be his homeland, and the fact that he was invited to be Mr. Wilson's colleague, on the latter's return from England in the summer of 1632, shows clearly that this young man of twenty-eight was, both as a person and a preacher, highly acceptable to this new but not uncritical congregation. The lifelong respect which this short year's service earned for him became, as we shall see, a very useful factor in his later work amongst the Red Indians.

It is clear, however, that Eliot did not feel free to become assistant to Mr. Wilson. He refused the invitation and instead became the first minister of the Congregational Church at Roxbury, a district which is today but one of the many suburbs of Boston but was then a separate township on the edge of virgin countryside. It was there in November, 1632, that he was 'ordained', or rather appointed and commissioned in Congregational fashion and became officially the 'Teacher' of Roxbury until the day he died. Having already welcomed his three brothers and three sisters to the colony in the months previously, and on September 4 caused the first marriage to be recorded in the Roxbury Church archives by being himself married to Hannah Mumford (or Mountford), John Eliot might well have interpreted these events as the clear direction of God in regard to his life's work. This was now 'home' for him, and here in the midst of his nearest and dearest ones he must work at encompassing by God's grace the salvation of those who were now his flock and his neighbours.

It may be valuable to consider here the probable reasons which led John Eliot to forsake the promising invitation made to him to stay in Boston, as they will enable us to understand still further the mettle of the man whose talent for missionary work was now about to find wide scope. Foremost in his mind must have been the desire for a greater independence. Had Eliot wished to remain in tutelage to an established society, to the local squire and the company of a fixed Anglican mould he need hardly have left his native shores, always assuming that he could have subdued his natural zeal and fervent spirit under the watchful eye of the Laudian informers and the Caroline gentry. To come so far across the sea to escape such limitations was for him an open sign of his desire to preach and teach and minister as God would lead him. And, as mentioned above, the society of Boston was, it would seem, already fast seeking to reproduce a colonial form of social etiquette which such a spirit as his could not easily stomach. Moreover he was naturally ambitious and would soon have a wife and family to support. A post as colleague in Boston must necessarily be limited in influence and reward, and the opportunity to find a fuller and freer scope in this New World was not one which a man with his gifts and the desire to use them for God was able lightly to set aside. Here at Roxbury were all the ingredients of an exciting and in many ways 'apostolic' task – a pioneer area, a first generation of settlers to be reared in the ways of the Lord by one who shared their earliest strivings, a church to be built, a school to be erected and a whole community waiting for leaders to create its standards and produce its laws. Here was a man's work, not easy, ready-made or definable, but rather a work which would be costly in time and effort, open to experiment and development, and with possibilities which were in themselves a compelling invitation to service. And not least, for we cannot but believe that in the back of this evangelist's mind the suggestion already lurked, albeit still unformed and tentative, there was here a step towards the wilderness country beyond, in which there lived the Red man and his squaw with their papooses. That this matter was not far from his mind is shown by a letter to Sir Simonds D'Ewes during Eliot's first year at Roxbury, in which he says, 'We are at peace with the natives and they do gladly intertaine us and give us possession, for we are as walls to them from their bloody enemies and they are sensible of it . . .'

It is hard to believe that John Eliot was unaware of what the assuming of a ministry so near to the edge of 'colonial civilization' would mean in terms of the natives of the land. It may be strange, as someone has remarked, that it took another fourteen years for his ministry to the Indians to begin in earnest. What is clear to anyone who will read between the lines of the evidence is that John Eliot did not avoid the call of God to Roxbury when it would very well involve him in missionary work in 'the regions beyond', whereas to have stayed in Boston's principal Church might have meant with certainty that he need never find himself a 'debtor' to bring the Gospel to the Redskins.

His immediate work, however, was that of a Pastor to the flock committed to his care – the flock which had so graciously called him as their 'Teacher' and was now to support him, frugally enough indeed, for the rest of his days. Out of his modest salary of £60 per annum, he provided from the start, as Richard Baxter, his friend and contemporary, suggests in the 'Reformed Pastor', for a 'competent assistant, rather than the flock that you are over should be neglected'. His choice fell upon Thomas Welde whom he employed as an assistant minister until 1641. Later we shall notice other worthy men who came to join him in the work of the pastorate though not continuously. No better analysis of the work into which John Eliot so fully launched himself, at least so far as his European congregation were concerned, can there be than is to be found in Richard Baxter's masterpiece of pastoral practice. In a section entitled, 'The Pastor's Labours' there are given in great detail the wisest counsels about the various aspects of the Puritan pastor's ministry. 'One part of our work,' he writes, 'and that the most excellent because it tendeth to work on many, is the public preaching of the Word; a work that requireth greater skill and especially greater life and zeal than any of us bring to it. It is no small matter to stand up in the face of a congregation and deliver a message of salvation or damnation as from the Living God, in the name of our Redeemer. It is no easy matter to speak so plain, that the ignorant may understand us; and so seriously that the deadest hearts may feel us; and so convincingly that the contradicting cavillers may be silenced . . .' In such wise vein he recommends the administering of 'the holy mysteries or seals of God's covenant, Baptism and the Lord's Supper; the guiding of our people in public prayer; being aware of our people by visiting their homes, by giving or lending books or by giving spiritual counsel and advice to those who come to us with cases of conscience, for a minister is not only for public preaching, but to be known as a counsellor for their souls . . . so that each man that is in doubts and straits should bring his case to him and desire resolution.' If there are any who wonder what all this may have to do with John Eliot, it would be well for them to know that from the pen of this acknowledged Puritan minister and saint, Richard Baxter, there came also these words written later about the minister of Roxbury, 'There was no man on earth whom I honoured above him'. Obviously to Baxter's mind John Eliot amply illustrated the very principles of the pastoral ministry which the Puritan divine has so powerfully outlined.

Yet the 'devotion to his religious obligations', so far as his immediate flock were concerned, did not blind John Eliot to the wider concern for the needs and affairs of men in the Massachusetts Bay Colony of which Roxbury was a part. The correspondence with Sir Simonds D'Ewes in England referred to above was in 1632 already concerned with the need for wider educational facilities in the colony than had existed hitherto. The emphasis upon reading the Bible and pious books had been a characteristic of English Puritans from the outset and this was naturally shared by most Protestants who had made the personal interpretation of the Scriptures a tenet of religion. The ability to read the Scriptures, therefore, was a way to salvation, and men and women had a religious obligation to teach their children this essential art. The Massachusetts Bay Puritans also had the initial advantage of a strong centralized government backed by church pastors who had firm opinions about training the young in a knowledge of the Bible and 'other parts of good learning'. However, there was a further problem, as stated in the tract called *New England's First Fruits* (1643). It was this: 'After God had carried us safe to New England and we had builded our houses, provided necessaries for our livelihood, reared convenient places for God's worship, and settled the civil government, one of the next things we longed for and looked after was to advance learning and perpetuate it to posterity, dreading to leave an illiterate ministry to the churches when our present ministers shall lie in the dust.' John Eliot was amongst the first of those, if he was not actually the very first, to promote the idea that has since blossomed into one of America's most honoured institutions, Harvard College, which was, from the first, like his own beloved Cambridge, distinguished for fine scholarship. His enthusiasm for this project was, as we shall see, to extend itself to the needs of his Indian converts.

In 1634 there is recorded the first of what were to be a number of plain-spoken criticisms of the Colonial Government's policy in one direction or another. In this instance Eliot's 'active and aggressive spirit' was aroused over a treaty which had been concluded, without public referendum, with the Pequots, a dangerous and warlike tribe who, with the Mohicans and less well-known Narangasetts, were to prove 'a very false people' in the years to come. It was not, however, on any issue of policy in regard to the Indians that John Eliot really stood opposed, though events were to show that the policy adopted was not of the wisest. What troubled his honest and individual spirit was the lack of consultation which the Boston oligarchy countenanced in reaching their conclusions. Here emerges the temper of a young man who had soaked up the teaching of Thomas Hooker, 'that the foundation of authority is laid, firstly, in the free consent of the people'. So outspoken an opposition to official policy by a minister of the quality and standing of the Teacher of Roxbury was not something that the Governor and his council could ignore. They called upon

Mr. Eliot for a public retraction of his views and he was not unwilling both to explain and acknowledge his concerns in the affair. The details of the settlement which was soon reached to the satisfaction of all concerned need not trouble us. The important thing was that John Eliot had discharged his conscience, revealed his watchful zeal for the proper governing of his flock, and been given a fair hearing in the public forum. Cotton Mather, one of his contemporaries, wrote, 'He that would speak of Eliot must speak of charity or say nothing,' for Mr. Eliot was never the man to harbour grievances.

This concern for public righteousness is no less amply illustrated by the many petitions in his own handwriting which are still extant. A time-worn manuscript volume, now in the keeping of the New England Historical and Genealogical Society of Boston, contains these and other records of his vast and varied Church work at this time. The energy of the man is beginning to emerge. Here was a man moreover to whom life was all of a piece and whose ministry set forth the concern of God for the whole life of his redeemed creatures.

John Eliot never was, and indeed never could be, simply a 'pious' man in the sense that his religious duties were divorced from the daily round. Social injustices, legal rights, public amenities and conditions of labour were as much his secondary concern as the preaching of the gospel of God's grace whether in the congregation or in the open air was his first. In an age like our own in which men try once more, and at times with an apparently desperate earnestness, to show the relationship of Work and Worship, Religion and Life, there is need to stop and consider such a man as this who, like many others in the seventeenth century, was 'engaged in adapting the forms of social and political institutions to that revolutionary principle' evoked by Luther – the priesthood of all believers. Preaching and practice were two sides of the same coin for John Eliot. He was concerned 'to discover a new system of social organization that should adjust equitably the rights of the individual to the needs of the political state and to society'. There is nothing in the least 'narrowly parochial' about him!

But there is one other development in the life of the colony which cannot be ignored. It was the front-page story of 1637 and the talk for months both before and after the event. This was the trial of Mrs. Anne Hutchinson, a mystic and 'enthusiast', against whom John Eliot was called in evidence.

In 1631 the General Court of Massachusetts Bay decided that 'No man shall be admitted to the freedom of this body politic, but such as are members of some of the churches within the limits of the same'. Church membership thus became a requisite for being made a freeman of the Commonwealth. Restriction of church membership to those who could give proof of their conversion, and the accompanying restriction of suffrage to 'believers' looked like a perfect plan to keep the Commonwealth in the hands of the righteous. Yet, try as they might, they could not prevent perverse and unorthodox ideas from invading the minds of men, even clergymen. Roger Williams is perhaps the most remarkable of these 'Antinomians' or Separatists, as many of them were called, but we cannot here enlarge upon his views so clearly expressed in his many sermons and writings. Mrs. Anne Hutchinson was another of the same mould, though perhaps in a more genteel fashion. She held meetings in her home, discussed and criticized freely the sermons of men like Wilson and Cotton and expounded 'the revelations privately vouchsafed to her by the Holy Spirit'. Her views were not unlike those held by the Quakers and other extreme pietists. By declaring that an 'inner light' was more important in salvation than moralism, law and external demonstrations of devotion, she came into conflict with the great majority of ministers and was sentenced to banishment. The significance of all this in regard to John Eliot is that as a witness for the prosecution it shows him, for all his own sense of individual rights and personal convictions as inalienable privileges of the human soul, to be a supporter of the established forms of government and not an innovator or revolutionary. His fervency and evangelical ardour by no means constituted him a firebrand or extremist. Perhaps his stand in this instance serves to reflect yet another comment of a later biographer, 'He united fervent piety and love of learning to burning enthusiasm for evangelization, these qualities being tempered with worldly wisdom and shrewd common sense. Eliot was truly of a saintly type, without fanaticism, spiritual pride or ambition.' He was certainly a man to whom the community would pay heed and thereby profit. His sons – by 1640 two had been born to him – would in due time stand up and call him blessed.

IV. The Redskins Receive the Gospel

In 1640 there appeared the first complete book to be printed on New England soil. The volume was *The Whole Book of Psalms*, published at the new Cambridge Press in Massachusetts, and popularly known nowadays as *The Bay Psalm Book*. The faithful in the colony wanted a literal version of the psalter which they could sing in their church services, a version better than the one in use. John Eliot, assisted by Thomas Welde and Richard Mather, who was linked with Eliot later in his Indian work, was one of the principals in this first venture of American printing and was particularly involved in the translation of the Hebrew original into singable English. The purpose of the work was stated plainly to be that of 'teaching God's Word in song, and not to titillate the ears with sweet rhythms'.

'Taking into account the nature of his life, his literary activity is remarkable,' says a biographer, and Eliot's devotion to his studies is indeed a fine testimony to the way in which, despite his many commitments as a pastor and a public figure, he never allowed his ordination vows to 'be diligent . . . in reading of the Holy Scriptures, and in such studies as help to the knowledge of the same', to fade or be neglected. He was accustomed at this time, some twenty years after he had left College, and at a time in life when many a man might think himself legitimately entitled to slacken his mental efforts and rely upon the accumulation of past knowledge for his normal ministry, to read the Old Testament and the New Testament daily in their original languages. At the same time he read steadily in older and more recent authors in Latin and English, and gathered together thoughts, ideas and projects which found practical expression in one form or another for the next FORTY years! Indeed Eliot maintained that the one universal language which the world needed, as a kind of contemporary Esperanto, was the tongue which God Himself had chosen – Hebrew, though even he was to balk at the prospect of putting his theory into practice when he was faced with the task of communicating the Word of God to those who knew little or no English.

In 1644 the studies of John Eliot took a new and exciting turn. He began, for the next two years, to give his wholehearted attention to a study of the Massachusetts dialect of the ALGONQUIN language. In the manner of his father in the days at Widford or Nazeing, John Eliot's home was always ready to receive within its shelter those needing help and charitable care. In return for the teaching of a young Indian the ways of civilization and the skills needed to follow a trade in the towns, John Eliot himself began to learn from his young friend the language spoken by the Red Indians of the Bay Colony. Like most primitive languages it was difficult to master, being unwritten and without systematic grammar. Between it and the languages commonly known to the white man there seemed not the slightest resemblance. When we add to this array of obstacles the fact that very few Englishmen had in any case attempted so far to familiarize themselves with more than the words of greeting such as 'How, netop!' (Good-day, friend) or the more familiar terms which have persisted, like pow-wow, wampum, squaw, papoose or tomahawk, and that Roger Williams was the only man who had hitherto produced any book which might assist possible students like Eliot (*Key into the Language of America*, 1643), we can see something of the magnitude of the task which John Eliot undertook, and appreciate the more the glory of the work to which, with his usual dedication, he applied himself. Yet the achievement of John Eliot does not lie in the learning of a new and difficult language, good and praiseworthy as that labour was. What does mark him out is his

[197]

determination to speak Algonquin for the sole purpose of preaching to Indians the Word of God, so that they might hear and receive the gracious promises of the Lord whose Gospel was to be 'preached to every creature which is under heaven'. It is this which makes this new period of study and application so decisive in the story, and marks out John Eliot as a pioneer missionary of the first order. If men and women use Algonquin then in that language he will set forth the Gospel! It is typical of the man that, having determined on his course, under God's guidance, he never ceased to use the gift he acquired – a Pentecostal gift indeed – throughout the whole of the years left to him on earth.

As we think of the minister of Roxbury, aged forty, studying in his spare time with the help of his Indian companion and slowly learning to translate the Ten Commandments and the Lord's Prayer, it will be as well to consider more fully the people with whom he is to spend so much of his later days. The first people to inhabit America probably arrived several thousands of years ago, drifting after wild game across the bridge of islands that exists between Siberia and Alaska. In course of time other migrating peoples followed them, mainly from central and northern and south-eastern Asia or the islands of that Continent. These bands and tribes pushed into one another, fought, merged, quarrelled and split apart, until the last waves of conquerors, prior to the arrival of the white folk, probably reached North America only a few centuries before Columbus. It took the white men generations to realize that the Indians were not all one people. For long they persisted in thinking that the natives had a common heritage, suggesting among other romantic notions that they were the descendants of the 'lost tribes' of Israel, or possibly survivors from the sunken continent of Atlantis.

The first Indians to come into contact with the strange civilization of Europe were the people of the North-eastern woodlands. They are described by the Norsemen, who visited the New England coast during the first two decades of the eleventh century, as 'Skraellings' or 'savages', and from their customs, dress and habitations we can recognize them as the same race of Algonquins to whom John Eliot was to minister six hundred years afterwards.

The Algonquin were certainly the most widely extended and fortunately the least warlike of the American Indians, as a comparison with the French and Jesuit encounters with the Iroquois in the southern provinces of Canada makes very plain. The Massachusetts tribe of the Algonquins not only gave their name to the colony of the first Puritans but also suffered from a plague of smallpox brought by the English settlers and many of them were at once wiped out by this scourge. This disaster and the coming of further epidemics of measles and chickenpox were the first reasons for whole tracts of the coastal territory being swept clear of their Indian occupants and the comparative ease with which the first settlers were able to establish their unfortified communities. To these aboriginal people, indeed, their decimation by a scourge against which they had no racial resistance whatever led also to the ready welcome they gave to those who with strange weapons could enable them to defend their lands against the more warlike tribes to the West and North. But the introduction of alcohol by the white man did much to break down the pride and resistance of the Indian, who seemed unable to control his thirst. Since, in return, the Indians either bartered their land or taught the white men their native skills – how to make canoes, use seaweed as fertilizer, cook food in the ground overnight or cure tobacco – we ought not to be surprised to note how rapidly the distinctive qualities of these native people disappeared.

It was, however, the social, economic and psychological factors which led to the ultimate confrontation of the two races, white and red, and brought to the Indians, alas, swift destruction. It is to the eternal credit of John Eliot that he saw these things and was ready, alongside the preaching of the Gospel, to set his mind to the domestic, public and personal welfare of the people to whom he ministered. Clearly, he held that Faith must be wedded to Good Works.

The new culture from over the sea undoubtedly tended to obliterate the basic occupations of tribal life. The prestige enjoyed by a man in his tribe was determined principally by his skill as a hunter and fisher, and by his standing as a warrior. These skills were not leisure pastimes for an overfed 'brave' – they were the only way by which he could ensure that his family would be fed at all. In a region where game is still relatively abundant it was much more so before the coming of the white man with his firearms, but the Indian with his primitive weapons and tools was often hard pressed to find enough to eat and he was therefore a man 'full of occupation'. The more rapid devastation caused by the white hunters left little place for the skilful 'deerstalker' or the 'intrepid' Redman. It is not to be wondered at that even by the time Eliot began his ministry amongst these people there were plenty of his English contemporaries who could only criticize the many Indians who were unemployed, who loafed about the streets or lay at the doors of houses, swigging their cheap alcohol and becoming morose and rebellious as they thought of their past skills and interests fading away. When we realize also the large part that their women had always played in labouring in the fields, cooking the food, weaving the clothes and blankets, making the domestic pots and bringing up the children, we can even better appreciate the social problems which beset the Indians of Massachusetts in Eliot's day.

And the English had not come merely to trade and to hunt. They had come to occupy and work land as they had once worked land in the home country. Moreover they came determined to create a better version of England than the one which they had left for conscience or adventure's sake, and as they grew rapidly in numbers they needed ever more land. Naturally the Indians foresaw the loss of their territories and of their independence. Since time immemorial the Algonquins had been a nomadic people, ranging at will over the territories of their tribes, erecting for a period in one area their simple stockade, their barrel-shaped bark and skin wigwams and cultivating their primitive fields, but moving on to another area when the game ran short, the soil seemed thin or the local fish were more difficult to catch. Telling the simple Indians quite plainly and honestly that the land on which they lived was theirs, but then paying them in goods and currency, or guns and spirits for the exclusive ownership of the same by Europeans, and then hauling the Indians into a colonists' court and sentencing them before hostile strangers to a humiliating set of punishments, from flogging to the stocks – all in a language that they barely understood – was a process that could scarcely fail to promote deep and lasting resentment amongst the younger Indians.

It was against this background of growing suspicion of the white man's motives, a subtle sense of inferiority as they saw the settlers' growing wealth and achievement, a developing opposition to the further encroachment of the white man on their tribal possessions and ancient landmarks, and not least the taunts of the 'sachems' or leading men of the tribes whose influence would be broken if a European way of life were introduced, that John Eliot's work of preaching and ministry to the Indians of Massachusetts must be seen. It would require courage, singleness of purpose, tactfulness, utter sincerity and endless patience to win these primitive people to the knowledge of Christ and the consequent acceptance of much that they already associated with the life of the intruders. The story that now unfolds is all the more dramatic because these qualities are revealed at every stage of the account. The events of the next years may with all reverence be called the 'Acts of the Indian Apostle'.

In the September of 1646 John Eliot, accompanied by Richard Mather and John Allen, fellow ministers, mounted his horse and set off across the countryside to the north-west of Roxbury on his first visit to the Indians under the sachem, Kitshomakin. His young Indian companion also accompanied the ministers and was used as an interpreter when Eliot preached on this occasion. It may have been this experience which prompted the historic event of a month later, when on October 28, 1646, in Eliot's own words, 'Four of us went to the wigwam of Waaubon (the Wind) and there met a company of Indian men and women and children gathered from all the quarters round about.' The site of this turning point in the whole approach of some of the Puritans of the Bay Colony to their Indian neighbours was actually the area called Nonantum, a place only four or five miles across open country from Roxbury, but on the south side of the Charles River and near to the settlements of Newtown and Watertown. The site is fittingly marked by a commemorative monument.

The visit lasted three hours and opened, after a cautious welcome by the 'sachems', with John Eliot praying for fifteen minutes in English, since, as he also remarks later, he was 'not so farre acquainted with the Indian language as to express our hearts herein before God or them.' This was followed by the first sermon ever preached in an Indian tongue by an Englishman. It lasted, in true Evangelical style, for seventy-five minutes, and, in the words of one of the other ministers present, 'it was a glorious, affecting spectacle to see a company of perishing, forlorn outcasts, diligently attending to the blessed word of salvation then delivered.'

The Sermon, which began with the text from Ezekiel 37. 3, 'Can these (dry) bones live?', contained 'all the principal matter of religion, beginning first with a repetition of the Ten Commandments and a brief explication of them, God's wrath at those who broke his commandments, Jesus Christ the redeemer of our sins, the last Judgement, the blessed estate of all those that by faith believe in Christ, the Creation, the Fall of Man, Heaven and Hell: these things and more were expounded – not meddling with any matters more difficult, and which to such weak ones might at first seem ridiculous, until they had tasted and believed more plain and familiar truths'. In the light of such a contemporary summary it is clear that John Eliot was not a man to lose an opportunity to set forth the Gospel, nor lacking in courage to be able to persist for so long a period in expounding the Gospel in so difficult a medium. The sheer effort reveals that, as Governor Winthrop has recorded in his diary earlier, 'Eliot took great pains to get their language' – and what he got he gave.

This instructive evangelistic address was immediately followed by a set of fascinating questions which filled another hour and a quarter. These Eliot attempted to answer in their own tongue, while the other ministers gave assistance by using the interpreter. These questions were described by Eliot as 'curious, wonderful and interesting', and details of them in the tracts of the period confirm his impressions. Some asked how they might come to know Jesus Christ, to which Eliot answered that they could do this principally through the Bible, which the Indians must consequently learn to read, but also through what they were taught by ministers like himself, linked with prayer and repentance. Other questions were: whether Englishmen were ever at any time so ignorant of God and Jesus Christ as themselves were? How could there be an image of God when the making of images is forbidden in the Second Commandment? and, How came the world to be so full of people, if all were once drowned in the Great Flood? Interesting questions indeed and such as show that once the Indians had overcome their initial astonishment at hearing an Englishman humbly labouring in their awkward idioms, they must have given him their whole-hearted attention and keen interest. Wonder it would certainly be if a congregation of English folk would listen for so long to the Gospel being preached even by the most eloquent minister and then make such pointed queries about the logic and the implications of what had been said. The effort was honourable indeed before the Lord. Eliot had opened 'the door of faith' to these children of the wilderness and the grace of God was finding entrance into their hearts. The occasion contained rich blessing for John Eliot himself for, following the questions, God opened his heart to pray in this Indian tongue before they departed, in proof that if they thus prayed God could understand them. Many affirmed that they had 'understood' the message and would wish to put more questions to their visitors, to which Eliot replied that 'we resolved to leave them with an appetite'.

Before the Englishmen left the encampment an appointment was made for another meeting, and apples were given to the children, whilst small portions of tobacco were handed to the men. It is instructive to note that whilst Eliot was personally a non-smoker and a strict teetotaller he was not averse to these pipe-smoking menfolk having a moderate portion of their favourite 'weed', though he would never encourage them in the taking of drink. His judgment here was that whilst smoking was a natural habit of the Indian, to drink spirits was an innovation started by his own countrymen which was by no means to be encouraged. It is unfair to suggest that such gifts as these were an early kind of 'rice-Christian' technique – they were but simple tokens of the friendship felt for these simple people. As such they were accepted with pleasure, and future visits always saw papooses digging into the deep pockets of John Eliot in search of sweetmeats or titbits of fruit.

Three more meetings were held in the two succeeding months. After the last of these, several Indians came forward, declared themselves converted, and showed themselves very willing to receive the Gospel. One thing which they asked was that their children might live with white friends in order that they might be trained 'in the right way' and some of their adults sought employment within the English colony so that they might receive further instructions in Christianity more easily and frequently. The results were indeed encouraging and the series of Tracts which now began to be published, based largely or wholly on Eliot's own experience in the work, reveal to the reader a moving and dramatic tale.

The 'Indian Tracts', for so they were called, bear long and descriptive titles, such as *The Day-breaking, if not Sun-rising, of the Gospel with the Indians in New England* (1647), or *The clear Sun-shine of the Gospel breaking forth upon the Indians in New England* (1648). *Strength out of weakness, or a Glorious Manifestation of the further progress of the Gospel* appeared in 1652 and (the last before Eliot died) *An Historical account of the doings and Sufferings of the Christian Indians in New England*, in 1675–77. It is through a close study of these first-hand accounts that the missionary methods and spiritual objectives of John Eliot and his colleagues become apparent.

By the close of 1646 the impact of the ministry of John Eliot and his friends was beginning to tell, and the Tract for 1647 informs us in detail of the orders and requirements drawn up for the Indians around Concord at that time. These points of private and public conduct numbered over thirty and included the following: –

2. No more powawing . . .
8. Monogamy to be the rule . . .
13. The Lord's Day to be strictly observed . . .
15. They were to wear their hair comely as the English do . . .

16. There was to be no more greasing of their bodies, or howling . . .
17. No more killing their lice between their teeth . . .
19. There was to be no more lying with a beast . . .
26. No Indian or Englishman to enter the other's house or wigwam without first knocking . . .

In 1648 Thomas Shepard, the author of *The Cleare Sun-shine of the Gospel* . . ., and the minister at Cambridge, Massachusetts, gives us much information about the further progress made during another year. Charmingly, however, he tells us that he has not much first-hand experience of the Indian work because, he says, 'of the neare relation between me and the fireside all the winter time . . .' (!) How can we disbelieve a man so honest as that?

On March 3, 1647, nevertheless, he describes his attendance at a conference with Indians at Nonantum conducted by three ministers, Mr. Wilson, Mr. Allen and Mr. Dunster. The women, he explains, were forbidden by custom to address any remarks to any other man than their relatives and so their pointed queries were made through a tribal interpreter. Wampooa's wife asked whether she had to pray aloud when her husband prayed, if she liked what he said and could add no more? Totherswampa's wife, with tact, since she could hardly risk another rebuke, asked, 'Should a husband still be angry with his wife when he was a praying man, even if he was less so?'

It was at the opening of the Synod at Cambridge, Massachusetts, on June 9, 1647, that John Eliot was able to demonstrate to a great concourse of his fellow English ministers, settlers and their wives the progress which these new 'children of his in the Gospel' were making. Whereas there had previously been only an English sermon on the morning that the Synod began, there was on this occasion an afternoon address in Algonquin for the benefit of the many Indian converts who were present. 'It was not unreasonable', says Shepard, 'that the reports of God's work begun among them, might be seen and believed of the chief representatives. . . who could hardly believe the reports they had received concerning these new stirs among the Indians, and also partly to raise up hereby a greater Spirit of prayer for the carrying on of the work begun . . .' The questions following the Sermon on this occasion included the following: –

'How they might lay hold on Christ, and where He was, being now absent from them?

Whether the devil or man were made first?

Whether a squaw could pray in a private place in the woods when her husband was away, because she feared to pray before company?

Why did God not kill the devil that made all men to be bad, God having all power?

How they should know when their faith and their prayers were good?'

'Indeed', says the writer of the tract, 'The Lord hath at last an enquiring people among these poor naked men,' and he goes on to tell how John Eliot on April 25, 1647, having gone to speak with Waabon Sachem at sunrise, on his return heard a father in a wigwam at prayer, at which he was so much affected that he could not but stand under a tree within earshot, hearing but part of the words and yet considering that God was fulfilling His promises in the Psalms, viz. 'the ends of the earth shall remember themselves and turn unto Him . . .' And Eliot himself has recorded how in the following September he saw a father calling in his children from the fields to say grace over their humble fare of corn stalks, which prompts him to comment, 'I wish the like heart and ways were seen in many English who profess themselves Christians, and that herein and many the like excellencies they were become Indians, excepting the name.'

Another tract includes a letter from John Eliot to the author which, says the latter, 'I think is worthy of all Christian thankfull eares to heare, and wherein they may see a little of the Spirit of this man of God, whom in other respects, but especially for his unwearinesse in this work of God, going up and down among them and doing them good, I think we can never love and honour enough.'

[206]

The letter reads as follows: –

'That which I first aymed at was to declare and deliver unto them the law of God, to civilise them . . . (Galatians 3.19), to convince, bridle, restrain and civilise them and also to humble them . . . Some Indians have thought it would take forty yeares but my heart moved within me, abhorring that we should sit still and let that work alone . . . and I therefore told them that they and we are one, save in two things, which make the only difference . . .

'First, we knowe, serve and pray unto God and they doe not; secondly we labour and work in building, planting, clothing ourselves, and they do not. They said they did not know God . . . and I told them if they would learn to know God, I would teach them; unto which they being very willing I taught them . . . and was invited to their wigwams.'

It all seems so disarmingly simple and obvious – and therein lies the genius of this man of God. In an age of Church expansion, when there were many ready to state that the Puritans were doing nothing for the Indians, John Eliot's devotion to the task of their conversion provided the most conclusive answer; 'It was', says William Kellaway, 'his continued devotion and enthusiasm which lent distinction to the New England mission in the seventeenth century'.

V. 'Cities of Refuge' for 'Praying Indians'

There was one tailpiece to the historic meeting of John Eliot with the tribe of Waabon Sachem which we have so far overlooked, since it raises the most difficult problem and the most burning issue of the whole Indian question. Before Eliot and the other ministers left Nonantum they were asked point-blank by the Indians of their audience for ground on which to build a town.

Eliot and his colleagues were very much encouraged by this request, for it suggested that these Indians had grasped what Eliot believed very firmly – that the Indians could never hope to progress in faith or Christian character until they ceased their nomadic existence and settled down to a more stable way of life. Eliot indeed went so far as to promise that he would petition the colonial government for this very purpose, and the journal of Governor Winthrop records that Eliot thought it 'absolutely necessary to carry on civility with religion, and induced the Massachusetts courts to set land aside for Indian residents, being voted £10 to prosecute the work'. Land tenure and the whole issue of land grants was from now on to be as much a concern of this minister of the Word as more theological matters. To quote from Kellaway again: 'The English asserted that the only land to which the Indian had any inherent right was that which he cultivated; uncultivated land was public domain in the Crown's gift ... But to the nomadic Indian the allotment must have seemed as incomprehensible as the English claim to the soil of America by right of discovery. Eliot never expressed himself fully on the theoretical aspects of Indian title to land; to the practical issue of how to secure land for the Indians he devoted himself *tirelessly*' – as by now we should expect!

The court that made the above grant of land at Eliot's request also directed that two ministers should be elected annually by the other ministers to be 'preachers to the Indians' though, whether elected or not, in actual fact Eliot was to visit some Indian tribe or other every fortnight during the next forty years, to teach or preach, until in 1687 he declares himself too tired to go more than once every two months – at the age of eighty-three!

The next two years were spent in establishing new settlements for the Indians, 'properly fenced off to prevent English cattle from eating their crops'; in providing industrial occupations and instruction in 'Letters, Trades and Labours such as Flax and Hemp-dressing, planting Orchards, building, etc. ....', and in seeing to it that they had a supply of decent clothes and materials for more permanent houses. Help for this work came also from the Home country, for in 1647 the Long Parliament ordered efforts to be made to promote piety among the inhabitants of the American, New England colony, and published an Act for 'The encouragement and advancement of learning and piety in that quarter'. Since, as was suggested earlier, there were not a few who surmised that the Red Indians were descendants of the lost tribes of Israel, there was 'an additional incentive for efforts to convert them'. On July 27, 1649, the final draft of the Act was published and became law. In the preamble it speaks of what is being achieved in New England where 'some Godly English of this Nation' are preaching to the Indians in their own language. The English in New England having exhausted their resources, it was stated, it was 'incumbent upon England to further the work'. A Corporation of sixteen persons was therefore set up, to be called by the name of 'The President and Society for the Propagation of the Gospel in New-England'. The Commissioners appointed were empowered to receive and disburse the money sent across the Atlantic by the Society. Finally it enacted that a collection should be taken up in all parishes of England and Wales to further the work.

The safe passage of such an Act as this, comments William Kellaway, 'at a moment when Long Parliament had little time and less inclination to discuss the conversion of New England's savages, must stand as a monument not only to Winslow's persistence and powers of persuasion but also to those who, if only for a moment, abandoned their sectarian quarrels in order to promote a common Christian cause.' It is not the last time that united effort amongst Christians has been achieved by an adequate missionary objective.

The beginning of 1650, the turn of the century, was the start of a new and constructive period in the life of John Eliot. He had been joined now by the Revd. Samuel Danforth who was to give him faithful support for the next twenty-five years.

A previous event, moreover, may be of some interest to record.

John Eliot was proud to call himself a Protestant and a Reformed Christian into the bargain. Yet John Eliot was also and above all else a man of love. To quote Everett, 'Since the death of the Apostle Paul a nobler, truer and warmer spirit than John never lived.' That winter proved this eulogy not to be misplaced. For just prior to Christmas a Jesuit Father, Gabriel Druillettes, of the French mission to the Iroquois in Canada, had occasion to stay briefly with John Eliot of whom he had heard so much. The two missionaries talked long into the night and rejoiced in their fellowship, so much so that next day John Eliot begged the Roman Catholic to spend the winter season at his house. Regretting, perhaps tactfully, that he had to be at a certain mission station for the Christmas ceremonies the Jesuit took his leave but not before he had expressed to Mrs. Eliot that it had moved him greatly to spend a day in 'the house of an Apostle'. This so far as one can tell was the first occasion that anyone had so described Eliot, and the source is of interest.

In this same year the book *Iewes in America*, by Thomas Thorowgood, who was, incidentally, the first Protestant to give John Eliot the apostolic title, set out to prove to his own satisfaction that the Red Indians were indeed the distant but definite descendants of the lost tribes of Israel. Whether this had its effect or not on the pious imagination of English churchgoers we cannot record, but what satisfied Eliot was that at the first appeal of the Society for the Propagation and Advancement of the Gospel in New England a sum of £1,100 was forthcoming. It encouraged him to go forward with an even more ambitious plan in his settlement of the 'praying' or Christian Indians, and this he did in the following year.

Eighteen miles south-west of Boston, and not very far from Roxbury, though Eliot thought it to be 'remote from the English', there was granted the land for the first Indian township of Natick – today, an experimental centre for Atomic Research. The town stood on the Charles River and one of the first signs of the community at work was the building of a bridge across that river and the construction of a Town Hall close by. These were followed by the completion of the Fort in August, 1651, with residences, a meeting house and a school also being completed. For the first time also Eliot was able to encourage them to set up a simple form of civil institutions 'under the government of the Lord, having a Church and the Ordinances of Christ among them', as he wrote in the tract, 'the light appearing . . .' It was here that Eliot was usually to be found on his regular fortnightly visits to the Indian centres, though he also travelled as far as the River Merrimac to the North, to Cape Cod in the East, to the Narrangasett country in the South, and to Brookfield, sixty miles west of Roxbury, and beyond Natick.

The work did not proceed smoothly, however, for the success of the growing township caused its English neighbours at Dedham to contest the Indians' right to the tenure of their land. Hence, in October, 1651, Eliot was again petitioning the Massachusetts General Court on the Indians' behalf so that they would be able to develop in security and without the fear of being crowded out by their more powerful English neighbours. This petition was effective. Two thousand acres were guaranteed to the Indians, provided that if any Indians possessed land in Dedham itself they should surrender this, and the Indians were not to set traps on land which was not enclosed. It is at this stage of greater stabilization amongst those more northerly of the Massachusetts Algonquin tribes that we also begin to see greater resistance by the sachems in the areas less effectively touched by the Gospel than the Bay colony, and it is at this time also that the Indian King Philip, the warlike son of Massasoit, refuses to entertain English missionaries as his father had sometimes done. He, with his quite remarkable gifts of courage, oratory and statesmanship, was to give the colonists many moments of anxiety ere long, for being racially as proud as an Indian ever was, he saw clearly what the colonists were doing to his people, and from the start regarded them as enemies who would have to be thwarted.

Philip's uprising, however, was not yet, and in good confidence John Eliot made constant efforts from 1652 onwards to obtain further land grants for the establishing of some twelve townships on the Natick model. These grants were always made on the condition that the Indians should not subsequently dispose of the land without the consent of the General Court, a proviso intended to ensure that the interests of the Indians would be protected, as well as to avoid speculation in land and endless requests by the Indians for more. But the good intentions of the lawmakers were not always apparent to the Indians and as late as 1673 we find John Eliot saying that the Indians showed great reverence for the English 'but the business about land giveth them no small matter for stumbling'. The new towns emerged nevertheless, such as Ponkapog, in 1654, specifically placed under Eliot's direction by the Court, though in this case he much valued the help of Major Daniel Gookin who was to assist in the Indian work until Eliot died.

It is at this stage in our story, with the 'Indian Apostle' proclaiming the Gospel to the Red man with an enthusiasm that brought thousands under its influence, that we shall do well to consider, if only briefly, the varied methods which Eliot employed to further the work of the Lord. Civilizing the Indian, setting up walls around his communities so that he could live a more stable and thriving existence, was from the very outset a strong conviction with Eliot, in accordance with the generally-accepted Puritan view, and there were many occasions on which he declared that otherwise it would be impossible to bring them over to Christianity.

A later but typically Puritan expression of this same view is provided in 1662 by John Winthrop, Jun., for the New England Company, in some *Proposals concerning the Employing the Indians in New England*. The advantages to the Indians from such a scheme are plainly set forth: 'They would be furnished with such necessaries as may make their lives more comfortable, as civil people have'; they would provide a market for English goods and would be able to supply such commodities as hemp, flax, tar, wheat and prairie grass for the English market. Winthrop's confidence in these proposals seems inexplicable in view of the prevailing notion in the colony at that time that the Indians were constitutionally unfitted for any kind of serious labour. Indeed the proposals have two serious flaws – they do not indicate exactly *how* the Indians were to produce their goods for the English and hence they do not explain how the Indians are to become people able to buy goods *from* the English. These are serious problems in any new community, and not least such communities as we are considering, since, as we have already hinted, the so-called idleness of the Indian menfolk was probably due not so much to a natural indolence as to the complete disturbance of the earlier tribal pattern by the incursion of the white man with his enclosures which prevented hunting, his firearms which increased food, and even his supply of ready-made clothing which limited the scope of the women who were the really stable workers in Indian society before the English came.

It is to Eliot's credit that his essentially spiritual outlook on life was wedded to an ability to grapple with mundane problems. He saw to it that the Indians at Natick and the other Indian townships were encouraged to follow rural pursuits of various kinds, including basket-making, spinning and weaving. Gookin was also one of the few persons who actually took practical steps to employ the Indians and, with Eliot's backing and influence, he persuaded the Commissioners of the New England Company to supply materials for 'spinning and other manufactury'. To John Eliot idle hands were 'unchristian hands' and Eliot used every endeavour to see that, as far as possible, tools and implements were provided for the hands of his converts.

Yet the Indians must not only be employed; they must also be educated. Indians' minds must be trained so that their powers of reasoning could master the intricacies of Protestant theology and logic. For according to Eliot's view – and he was a man of his time in this above all – regeneracy, though an act altogether divine, normally came only after the rigorous preparation of the mind. Hence schools were among the first buildings to be erected in every township which he supervised. Yet schools and buildings are themselves of small value if there are not the teachers to staff them. It is here that Eliot initiated and promoted a vigorous scheme of 'self-help'. He was constantly searching for new colleagues from the English side, though he writes in 1671 in the *Indian Dialogues*, 'I find few English students willing to engage in so dim a work as this is.' But he was determined that lack of response from his own countrymen should not be permitted to hold up the work. It had ever been his custom on his visits to the Indian wigwams to link the distinct preaching of the Gospel with plain teaching from the Catechism, and when the Indians desired an extension of the teaching Eliot counselled them to pass on the instruction he gave them. 'I told them', he is reported as saying, 'to meet nonetheless, and the best men to pray, and one to teach what he knows, and all to ask and answer questions, or to ask of me when I should be next come.' His instructions took effect, as the changed lives of many Indians bore witness, and it was probably true of this part of the work as of his most sacred duty, that 'he studied to instruct with all plainnesse and brevity, unto which many are very attentive.'

This, however, was not the full extent of the educational concern of Eliot for his Indian converts. The charter of Harvard College, when drafted in 1650, contained allowance for 'all other necessary provisions that may conduce to the education of the English and Indian youth of this country in knowledge and Godliness'. This mention of 'Indian youth' may have been premature, but the Society for the Propagation of the Gospel in New England was anxious to see some Indian youths educated, and in addition to suggesting that mixed schools of Indians and English were well worth considering, it shortly proposed that six Indians might be put into Harvard to learn English and teach the Indian language to the English! One suspects that Eliot, whose son Joseph was later to graduate at this College, was not unconnected with such a proposal, though it is recorded with all due formality in the College archives. In 1653 the Commissioners replied that the College was full and therefore it would be necessary 'to raise some building' for Indian students. They reckoned the cost would be £100 and desired that 'the building may bee stronge and durable, though plaine'. In fact the Indian College was of brick and was completed in 1654 or 1655. The only difficulty was that there were no Indian students to fill it, hence the President of Harvard asked permission to grant the use of it for English residents, and this, we are told, was granted temporarily on the advice of the Massachusetts Commissioners *and* Mr. Eliot, who now plainly appears on the scene. It is indeed necessary to add that though some Indian students at the Grammar School at Cambridge, Massachusetts, were able to translate Isaiah into Latin and then construe it – a formidable feat even for English teenagers – and some, like Caleb Cheschanmuk, did eventually reach the graduate stage, none of them actually inhabited the 'Indian College' and its only connection with that race will be seen as a printing house in another connection.

One of the questions early put to Eliot by his Indian questioners as he visited the wigwams was this: 'If we leave off Powowing, and pray to God, what shall we then do when any are sick?.' This prompted the practical minister of Roxbury to recognize the need to teach them 'Physick' and he 'stirred up the wiser sort to get this skill' by himself instructing them in anatomy and the general principles of medicine – thus revealing again his remarkable all-round capacity. Yet, he reflects, they need teaching less by precept and rules of art than by sight, sense and experience, and he adds significantly, 'I have had many thoughts in my heart of some or other of God's people in England to give some maintenance towards some school or collegiate exercise this way . . .' and later, 'by this meanes we should traine up these poore Indians in that skill which would confound and root out their powaws, and then they would be farre more easily inclined to leave those ways and pray unto God, whose gift Physick is and whose blessing must make it effectuall.' With what amazing and studied simplicity Eliot shows, as one of the implications of his own preaching, the connection between physical and spiritual health! It is in connection with this instruction concerning the blessing of forsaking the 'shamans' (or witch doctors) that we have the delightful example of Eliot's graphic teaching methods with these simple folk. In order to show the contrast between those who do, and do not, know the gracious power of the Lord in salvation, he lifted up his hand before them and showed them first his small finger and then his thumb, as symbolic of the state of a person before and after conversion to Christ.

It should be stressed that Eliot took no credit to himself for the work of conversion. He was careful to declare that 'God hath bowed their hearts who were as averse and farre from God as any heathen in the world, and their hearts bow more and more'. To show that this was so, and also to promote his further projects of Native Indian churches, Eliot began in 1652 to encourage the Indians to 'make confession before the Lord of their former sins, and of their present knowledge of Christ, and experience of His grace'. The substance of these first confessions makes up that amazing tract to which we can only make passing reference, *Tears of Repentance*. Yet the hearing of these confessions, or rather the reading of them, by selected ministers from Boston did not convince them that the Indians were ready for forming into a Church, and it was not until 1659 that it was at last decided that 'a few Indians should be seasoned in Church-membership in communion with our English Churches, before they should be Churches among themselves'. They were therefore admitted to Church membership at Roxbury strictly on trial, and significantly, in opposition to the wishes of a substantial part of the Roxbury congregation. It is interesting to note that many years later Eliot still championed the idea of mixed congregations, though he also added characteristically, 'I am quiet in the plea of the diversity of language.'

The establishment of a separate Church community by the Indians at Natick in 1660 was certainly a triumph for Eliot and the fruit of long and patient waiting upon the Lord with his Indian 'disciples'. No other Indian community afterwards had a comparable struggle to attain Church status, partly because Natick created a precedent and partly because the next generation of Puritans were far less conservative in outlook than their fathers. Certainly there were grave doubts about the effectiveness of Eliot's methods and the quality of his results. The sane Daniel Gookin had to admit that 'there may be some of them hypocrites that profess religion, and yet are not sound-hearted'; but it would have done good to the Commissioners of Charles II, who came to report on the state of New England and who were critical of the conversion methods which hired Indians to 'come and heare sermons . . . and by appointing rulers amongst them, over tens, twenties, fifties, etc.', to listen, as Eliot and his fellow ministers did, to a query asked by one, Wabbakeoaett, who said, 'Why did the English not teach Indians sooner in their twenty-seven years in New England?' John Eliot had little with which to reproach himself, despite official sarcasm.

The Church and ecclesiastical organization of Natick was to

last until 1716 when the last Indian pastor, Daniel Takawombpait, died. By the time of the Stuart Restoration in 1660 there were seven 'old' and seven 'new' praying towns, embracing approximately 1,100 souls, 'yielding obedience to the Gospel'. Twenty-four Indians had been trained as Evangelists to their own people and their influence on the domestic and social life of the Indians – in saying grace at meals, in Sabbath observance which was most sternly applied, in morning and evening prayers as a family, and in much stricter and more seemly behaviour towards the women folk – is attested, not only by the Tracts but also by other observers who were not inclined to show undue bias on the one side or the other.

In 1676 a certain Edward Randolph was sent from England to report on the Massachusetts Colony. In his first report to the Committee for Trade and Plantations he accused the magistrates of Boston of 'imprudent zeal . . . in Christianizing these heathen before they were civilized and injoyning them the strict observation of their lawes which to a people so licentious and rude, hath proved even intollerable'. 'To Eliot,' says William Kellaway, 'the criticisms of Randolph . . . must have been hard to bear.' To us, who at this distance can see them in their context, they appear little less than cant. One wonders whether the Royal master of Mr. Randolph ever asked the question put to Mr. Eliot by one seeking Indian, 'Whether any of us shall go to heaven seeing we find our hearts so full of sinne and especially of the sinne of *lust* (manwunwudsquas=mad-after-women)?' It was easy for the visitor from the 'ivory tower' of England to throw stones at the humble folk living in the stockades of the new Praying Towns.

VI. The Bible for 'The Sons of the Morning'

'Mamusse Wunneetupanatamwe Up-Biblum God naneeswe Nukkone Testament kah wonk Wusku Testament. Ne quoshkinnumuk nashpe wuttinneumoh Christ noh assowesit John Eliot.' The meaning of these strange words is as follows: –

'The whole Holy his-Bible God, both Old Testament and also New Testament. This turned (translated) by the-servant-of Christ, who is-called John Eliot.'

The writer of the article on John Eliot in the *Dictionary of National Biography* says aptly, 'This marvellous monument of laborious piety is of considerable linguistic value, although no-one using the language has been living for many years.'

There are indeed few things in the life of John Eliot of which it can truly be said that they set a seal on his work as much as did the publication of the entire Scriptures in the language of this despised and hitherto neglected tribe of Red Indians. Of all Eliot's doings it was the most renowned. 'But scarcely less remarkable was his achievement in getting that translation printed. Although he had little or no encouragement and often direct opposition, he persuaded the New England Company that to finance publications in the Indian language was one of its most important functions.' The amazing truth is that as we consider today the list of volumes, tracts and booklets in the Algonquin tongue (Cotton Mather called it 'the Indian Library') we have to pay the chief honour for its inception, and largely its execution, to one man, our 'Indian Apostle'.

Though Eliot was by no means the first settler to think of printing books for the Indians, just as he was not in a technical sense the 'first' missionary to the Red Indians, yet it is with him that the project moves from the realm of wishful thinking into the realm of reality. This indeed was always the mark of John Eliot. He was not just a dreamer, but a doer; not just a prophet, but a practical man of affairs. In 1649, after Eliot had been for three years a visitor and missionary to the Algonquin tribes, Winslow received a letter from him which in part runs thus: 'I do very much desire to translate some parts of the Scriptures into their language, and to print some Primer in their language, wherein to initiate and teach them to read . . . and printing such a thing will be troublesome and chargeable.' He went on to say something else, 'that translating the Scriptures is a sacred work to be regarded with much fear, care and reverence'. As in so many other fields, we here see that John Eliot had grasped the great challenge that faces Bible Societies today as new translations are needed in the smaller tribal languages which have not hitherto been transliterated. It is not simply a case of producing a local translation; the task before the Church which ministers the Word is to teach natives to read even their own tongue. There were some later who were to question very warmly whether it would not be easier and wiser to teach the Indians to read and speak English. The interesting thing is that this issue was never even considered at the outset and Eliot decided that it was asking too much of the Indians to require them to learn not only a new religion but a new language as well.

It was 1654 that the first Indian book ever printed appeared in New England. It was the 'Catechism' in Massachusetts Algonquin, translated by Eliot and printed by Samuel Green, the printer to Harvard College. By 1655 Genesis had been printed as a trial issue, as also had St. Matthew's Gospel. Eliot submitted copies of these two works for the perusal of others in the colony who were familiar with spoken Algonquin. Their favourable reports spurred Eliot on to proceed even more vigorously with his work, so that by December, 1658, at the same time that he was both a faithful minister to his English congregation *and* responsible for the establishment of an increasing number of Indian towns, their schools and future Church leaders, the WHOLE Bible in the Massachusetts dialect was ready for the press. Negotiations were put in hand with London, a sample sheet of the New Testament was despatched for approval, and by September 5, 1661, the printing of the New Testament was complete. As it was a common practice of the time to include a complete set of metrical psalms with the whole Bible, John Eliot was now charged by the Company to provide these before the Old Testament was added, and hence it was 1663 before the complete translation of God's Word could be printed and despatched to England.

On April 21, 1664, Robert Boyle took a presentation copy to the King, and in a letter very soon afterwards explained that, though the King looked 'a pretty while upon it . . . yet the unexpected coming in of an Extraordinary Envoyé from the Emperour hindered me from receiving that fuller expression of his grace towards the translators . . . that might have been expected'. But Charles II was not qualified to pass comment upon this book, whether he had time or no. Not only was it the first Bible in Algonquin but it was also the first Bible printed in any language on the North American Continent; in the matter of being first or best John Eliot was most certainly becoming a typical Yankee prototype! J. H. Trumbull, a nineteenth century expert on translation work, has said, 'On the whole, his version was probably as good as any *first* version that has been made, from his time to ours, in a previously unwritten and so called "barbarous" language'. Praise indeed, and yet we may by now find it hardly surprising, for thoroughness was all but a synonym of John Eliot's name.

His energy and imagination were also apparently boundless. On July 6, 1663, he was writing to Richard Baxter in England, 'My work about the Bible being . . . finished (he means the Indian Bible), I am meditating what to do next for these sons of the Morning – they having no books for their private use, of ministerial composing. For their help, though the Word of God be the best of books, yet Humane Infirmity is, you know, not a little helped, by reading the holy Labours of the Ministers of Jesus Christ.' He then asked permission to translate Baxter's *Call to the Unconverted*, which seems highly appropriate; and when Baxter agreed, submitting the use of the translation wholly to Eliot's wisdom, we are treated to the (no less) surprising news that it was ready for the press by December 31 of the same year and appeared in 1664 under the ferocious title of *Wehkomaonganooa asquam Psantogig kah asquam Quinnupegig*.

Space forbids that we should do more than mention briefly the other major works in 'the Indian Library'; the translation of Lewis Bayly's *Practice of Piety* in 1665; the Indian Grammar, for the use of English readers, which required great 'sweat of brow' but in which he was helped by his two sons, John and Joseph, the latter of whom was now ordained as minister of Guidford, Connecticut; the Indian Primer, for native proselytes; whilst the last work of this kind, a translation of *The Sincere Convert*, by Thomas Shepard, was published a year before he died. In addition there were two books in English, the *Indian Dialogues* and the

Logick Primer. These in themselves constitute a labour worthy of any man but when set in the context of all his other occupations, interests and the 'care of all the Churches' his achievement becomes almost incredible. To say also that in 1680, when he was seventy-six years of age, he undertook a complete revision of the entire Indian Bible with the assistance of John Cotton only gilds the lily and stifles the voice of praise.

The truth is, of course, that this impetus given to a spate of books designed to promote missionary work amongst the Red Indians and thence to increase their faith is but one facet of a multi-sided servant of God. In 1678, he produced a Harmony of the Gospels with a variety of instructive stories from his rich and dedicated life; in 1679 he produced a telling retort to a small controversial handbook by J. Norcot on Infant Baptism, whilst sometime earlier he had written a useful booklet entitled, *A Christian Covenanting Confession*. But it is the two books, *The Christian Commonwealth* of 1659, and the similar *Communion of Churches* of 1665, about which we must say something more before we leave John Eliot, as always, busy in his study. Did ever a man more faithfully fulfil his ordination vow to teach and study the things pertaining to the Kingdom of God?

The Christian Commonwealth was, in its way, the determined and sincere, if also idealistic attempt of John Eliot to set his religious seal on the political practices of his age. It appeared however, at the very time that the New England magistrates were under the especially censorious eyes of the newly-restored Stuart monarchy, and thus inclined to be particularly critical of any deviation from the plain acceptance of the re-established order. On May 22, 1661, the General Court, held at Boston, ordered, 'that the booke written by Mr. John Eliot, being justly offensive and in speciall relating to the kingly government in England . . . be totally suppressed and the Author's acknowledgement recorded . . .' The book had in fact been written in 1650, at the time when the Indians were first being successfully converted and formed into organized communities by Eliot and his co-ministers, and this may largely explain what prompted the 'Indian Apostle' to commit himself to yet another field of human study and debate. It was neither love of argument nor any Renaissance desire to be a man of many parts which drove Eliot into print or practice. All that he did was related to ONE sole purpose, the better setting-forth of what God had done for men, and could again do for those who were, in His providence, 'called to be saints'. So far as Eliot was concerned, 'the idols had been broken by the hammer of Cromwell; the malevolent powers of this world were brought low; it remained now only for the people of God to enter into a solemn covenant to establish a commonwealth after the true divine model'. Eliot therefore sets out a Christian Utopia, sanctioned by Mosaic and other example, with chapter and verse, as a suitable guide for the godly, and the newly-saved 'Sons of the Morning', his Indian converts.

The theory is indeed wholesome and plain – Christ is King of kings before whom all earthly authority must bow, and Scripture *alone* reveals the Law of God. Eliot therefore lays down the following thesis: 'There is undoubtedly a forme of civil government instituted by God Himself in the Scriptures, whereby any nation may enjoy all the ends and effects of Government in the best manner, were they but persuaded to make trial of it . . . Much is spoken of the rightful Heir of the Crown of England and of the injustice of casting out the right Heir; but Christ is the only heir of the Crown of England (Psalm 2. 8) and of all other nations also (Rev. 11. 15).' It is not difficult to see that what would have been acceptable in 1650 was ten years later accounted sedition indeed.

From his scriptural premises Eliot then proceeded to formulate a system of government remarkable for its naïve simplicity. Since the source of law is finally given in the Bible there is no need for a legislature, and since Christ is King there is no need for an earthly throne. All that is needed is a magisterial system to hear causes and judge between differences, and in order that this may be properly done, he advises the division of society into groups of ten, fifty, a hundred and a thousand people each, with their own elected leaders, they in turn electing representatives to rule the whole nation.

A somewhat critical assessment of this work and its logical provisions, by a modern American scholar, Vernon Parrington, is worth mentioning if only to show how easy it is to judge a man's whole life by one part of it which may not be its most pleasing or edifying facet. He says, 'Curious as this little work is – testifying rather to the sincerity of Eliot's Hebraism than to his political intelligence or his knowledge of men – it is characteristic of the idealist who consecrated his life to the Indian mission. How little disturbed he was by the perversities and limitations of everyday fact is revealed in the policy which he laid down for his Indian converts: 'that . . . being a people without any forme of government and now to chuse; I would endeavour with all my might, to bring them to embrace such government, both civill and Ecclesiasticall, as the Lord had demanded in the holy Scriptures . . . that so they may be the Lord's people, ruled by Him alone in all things!" One is only tempted to comment that had John Eliot been unduly "blown about by every wind of public opinion and worldly doctrine", and not kept to his command from God to preach the *Gospel* to every creature, it is questionable whether we should even have heard his name, let alone poured scorn on what was at least an attempt to relate Politics to Piety and Government to God!'

But we have now reached the period when all John Eliot's work amongst the Indians of New England was to be put to the test as never before. Throughout the years in which he was ministering to the new Praying Towns, translating the Scriptures into Algonquin, and settling land disputes and money matters with the New England Company, a serious change of policy was developing to the South in the area of Narrangasett Bay. The Chief there, Massasoit, whom we mentioned as welcoming the Pilgrim Fathers and becoming their Protector and Friend, remained in that happy relationship as long as he lived. During that time he profited in wealth and prestige and the Wampanoags ('Eastern People'), whom he ruled, were in their turn protected by the white settlers from the neighbouring Narrangasetts. Massasoit acquired many European assets, guns, horses and manufactured goods. Yet it was all at a price, and by the time he died in 1661 and was succeeded by his son Metacom, known to history as Philip, the Indian villages in southern Massachusetts were tightly hemmed-in by the towns and holdings of the white settlers who had bartered goods for land with the old Chief and were now aggressively seeking still more of the Indians' territory.

When to this situation is added the friction which naturally arose between two cultures in the new and unusual settings of the towns, where Indians could drink and gamble, fall into debt or become hired servants or even quasi-slaves, and where some of the worst and most materially-minded of the settlers would exploit these simple people to the full, the outcome proved to be an explosive combination which could and did cause untold horror. For thirteen years Philip kept the settlers on edge, and yet, when challenged openly, denied all rumours of betrayal and revolt, and seemed outwardly to be following the general line of his trusted father. Yet in truth he seems to have been preparing for the war of 1675 over a long period, and would in fact have prepared for even a longer time had not circumstances precipitated the conflict. It is significant that it was a Christianized Indian who started, and another who ended the war, though the former was dead and the latter one who wished to stay alive.

The detailed story of King Philip's war is not our concern though it has much to recommend it as a tale of Indian courage and adventure. The really vital matter is that, had the war gone in favour of the chief of the Wampanoags, as quite often seemed likely, the whole English race might well have been driven off New England soil. The merciless warfare of those days left memories that were to haunt the colonists for decades. The Indian warrior with his flaming arrow, bloodstained tomahawk, and barbaric war-whoop, erased the benign image of Massasoit and the more hospitable natives. The silent forest became the dread abode of skulking savages, thought of as no better than wild beasts, and the fierce sieges of frontier settlements provided enduring nightmares of dawn attacks and fiendish atrocities. There was a time when out of ninety white settlements in the land, fifty-two had been attacked and twelve completely obliterated. King Philip's design of removing the hated and superior white man from the ancient land of the Indian seemed well within reach of fulfilment.

It was in the context of this desperate situation that the work of John Eliot with the Praying Indians began to make its mark. Immature in his political theories he may have been, but the Apostle to the Red Indians had created the only military force which could and did save the whole English community in Massachusetts from extinction. In the early days of 1675 many of the Praying Indians near Boston had already pledged their support to the English to bring this trouble-making King Philip to justice. The mere fact that they were Indians was regarded as treachery to their common race. It says much for the Praying Indians that a year later they were in large measure still willing to be used by what was then a completely desperate Colonial Government, and it was only their skill as trackers and hunters which really halted the appalling onrush of the forces from the south joined by the warlike Mohicans from the North. William Stoughton and Peter Bulkeley, Government agents for Massachusetts, are on record as saying of the Praying Indians at this time; 'though some very few of them have not so closely adhered to the British, yet the rest of them have been upon all occasions very faithful'. The seal of a common loyalty to a common Lord does seem to have been set on the hearts of these still young Christians, and John Eliot, though the uprising must have dismayed him, had much for which to give praise to God.

In regard to the Indians it left him with heavy and new tasks to undertake. The blow dealt to the Praying Indians by the war was enormous. The general feeling of the English towards them was one of mounting hatred and when one group of those despised folk did actually desert to Philip's forces the rest of the Massachusetts converts were first of all ordered to stay in their villages, then moved, in October, 1675, to Deer Island in the harbour area of Boston, and their fields ravaged. Eliot wrote to Robert Boyle on December 17 describing the 'bleake bare Island' on which the Indians had been interned, and the sufferings and hardships which they had to endure without adequate food and fuel. The Indians had gone, we are told, 'patiently, humbly and piously without complaining against the English' and their fortitude does Eliot great credit. It was not until May, 1676, that they were allowed back to their towns on the mainland and by then only four out of the previous fourteen settlements had survived. For his part in the protest against the treatment meted out indiscriminately to the Praying Indians, Eliot was treated to vitriolic abuse, and Daniel Gookin, who supported the protests, was, though an assistant Governor of the colony, so threatened that he was at times 'afraid to go about the streets'.

It was the plight of those Indians who were seized by trickery and shipped off to Tangier that specially occupied the attention of Eliot, apart from his own local problems of re-establishing the Praying Town communities. To release these unfortunate prisoners from their exile to that narrow strip of British territory, with its heat and disease and constant threat from Barbary pirates and the natives of the hinterland, Eliot wrote constantly to Boyle and others urging them to use their influence at the English court to advance the return of these folk to their own land as soon as 'may suit your persons'. Against such traffic in slaves, whether in America or Tangier, Eliot wrote, 'The design of Christ in these last days is not to extirpate nations but to gospelize them; to sell souls for money seemeth to me a dangerous enterprise.'

By May, 1678, the numbers of Praying Indians, which had been some 3,600 before King Philip's War began, had been much reduced, though a large proportion of the Indian people in the Bay colony were considered to be civilized. A seal had, however, been set on the previous rate of progress and there was to be no major revival of the work that John Eliot and others had seen in the years before. Indeed, after Eliot's death the extinction of the Massachusetts Indians was very rapid. Up to 1733 all the town officers in Natick were Indians but by 1760 the Indians were reduced to one family, and in 1846, the two hundredth anniversary of Eliot's first service at Nonantum, there was in the town only ONE GIRL as the surviving Indian representative!

This was not the end, however. Dankers and Sluyter, agents for the Labadist sect, who stayed at the Eliot home in 1680, recorded that, 'though he is a very old man he is the best of the ministers of whom we have yet heard in the town and vicinity of Boston'. By that time the title of 'Indian Apostle', first used some thirty years before, had secured universal and perpetual acceptance. In 1685, John Dunton, the bookseller, speaks of Eliot's still wonderful success with the Gospel amongst the Indians, and says that he is 'the glory of Roxbury, as of all New England'.

There is a tailpiece which we must by no means omit. It was in 1685, the year that John Eliot's first and most famous grandson was born, that this indefatigable servant of the God who is ever compassionate arranged for the first negro servants and boys to be sent to his home for care and instruction. Hence the story of one such foundling, rendered blind by falling into a fire, who was taught the Bible so well by Eliot that within a year the lad could repeat whole chapters by heart. In an age in which there was no such blessing as Braille script, there was all the more need, as Eliot knew, to fill the child mind with good and sound doctrine from the Word of the Lord. By 1689 Eliot sealed this new step by making, somewhat in the same manner as his own father had done at the beginning of the century in order that John could go to Cambridge, a grant by deed of seventy-five acres 'for the maintenance, support and encouragement of a school and schoolmaster at that part of Roxbury commonly called "Jamaica, or Pond Plain", for the teaching and instructing of that end of the town (together with such Indians and Negroes as shall come to that school) . . .' Naturally the outcome of this venture could not be appreciated by the Teacher of Roxbury but it once more shows how to the end he was sensitive to the needs of the under-privileged, eager to promote sound learning, and aware of the social problems that the rapidly-moving American society was creating at every stage. In the school of this little 'Jamaica' district, de-segregation was the only ground a Christian could allow for the imparting of knowledge to Christ's little ones of any race in the seventeenth century.

VII. A Glorious Sunset

It was in the latter part of 1687 that Mrs. Eliot died. At her graveside the husband spoke of her as his 'dear, faithful, pious, prudent, prayerful wife' and all these things she must indeed have been. She had travelled far across the sea to follow the man she loved and to set up a home in a land that neither of them knew, and yet were prepared to give their lives and their children to serve. She had seen her husband censured in public, criticized in the press and scorned by passers-by. From her presence he had gone out to meet the 'savages' without any certainty that he would return alive. And at the last she had to die knowing, as John Eliot himself knew, that much of his labour had been destroyed and that only one of their children was likely to survive them. She had uncomplainingly shared all the hardships of the ministerial life, for ministers, though respected for their calling and their learning, were amongst the poorest members of society and their pay was largely in kind. In 1673, runs the record, the Roxbury pastor, John Eliot 'Apostle to the Indians' was given thirty-four pounds weight of copper coins, the same being by estimation £1 13s. 4d. 'lawfull money'. This would hardly be the equivalent of more than National Assistance standard in our modern England, and yet on this Mrs Eliot raised a family. Her husband's words, as her body was laid to rest, represented not sentiment only, though we can well believe that he felt them deeply; they were an accurate and fitting tribute to a courageous and no less Christian spirit.

By this time also the spark of his previous energy was beginning to fail John Eliot. He found it increasingly difficult to devote himself to the Indians with the fervour of former years, for even when his missionary labours were at their most onerous, he never neglected his ministry to the people of Roxbury, a burden which was much harder to bear when Samuel Danforth died in 1674. It is believed that at one time he would have liked to have devoted himself entirely to the Indian work, but a letter to Richard Baxter in 1670 suggests that when he seriously raised this possibility his Roxbury congregation or part of it were opposed to releasing him. Indeed, the view of ordination held in New England at that time – that the bond between pastor and flock was indissoluble – would alone have deterred him from pressing his wish further. Even so, the desire of the congregation in whole or in part to retain his services does suggest rather pointedly that they knew a true minister when they saw one. His assiduity in pastoral labours would doubtless put to shame many who, with only a small fraction of his responsibilities upon them, account themselves overworked.

Like most fathers, John Eliot would have liked his sons to follow in his footsteps, but not one of them lived long enough to make any considerable mark in the missionary field. His youngest son, Benjamin, assisted him for some years, but when the father suggested him to the Commissioners as a possible student for training in the Indian work, he was almost wholly disregarded. John, his eldest son, became the pastor of a small English congregation at Cambridge, Massachusetts (again another strange link-up with the father's earlier days) and helped his father by preaching in the Indian language at Natick and elsewhere every fortnight, but he also died young, in 1668. His departure cast another dark shadow on the 'Apostle's work' for he had described this son to Baxter 'as a good workman in the vineyard of Christ, my assistant in the Indian work, a staff to my age'.

In 1682 the Commissioners saw fit to provide John Eliot with 'a Servant to attend him when he goes on his journeys amongst the Indians' and they also provided a horse. Even so, his strength decreased steadily, and from 1685 onwards it would appear that his visits to the Praying towns became more infrequent, until, by 1687, he is only found there once every two months. It was that same year that the Indians, who out of deference for their 'Evangelist', had never hitherto elected a minister for themselves chose one of their own number to maintain the work. About the same time Eliot produced his last complete tract, *The Dying Speeches of Several Indians*, printed at Cambridge, Massachusetts. In the following year Nehemiah Walter was ordained as Eliot's colleague at Roxbury, which relieved the old man of most of his labours there.

The glorious sun of Eliot's warm-hearted and attractive ministry was indeed now near its setting. In the spring of 1688 the Dutch scholar Leusden dedicated his Hebrew-English Psalter to John Eliot in the most fulsome terms. He spoke of the man's piety and learning, his love of the Bible and his zeal in languages, and we are led to note that a man who could be ignored as a preacher in the backwoods of a virgin colony, a Congregationalist Independent who meddled in an obscure tongue and dabbled with political theory, was thus singled out by one who was admired in Europe as a scholar to be the focus of his latest piece of useful, pastoral study. It was in a sense a farewell homage to a man whose own emotions are recorded in a letter he sent to Robert Boyle on July 7 of the same year, in the words, 'I am drawing home'.

On May 21, 1690, Eliot died at the age of eighty-five, and was buried in the parish tomb already occupied by his wife and children in the old burying ground at Roxbury. Of his six children—five sons and one daughter—only Joseph survived him. From Joseph sprang several who bore the name of Eliot with distinction in American society in the following two centuries; Fitzgreene Halleck, the poet; Charles Wyllys Elliott, the author; and Ethelinda Eliot Beers, the author of an American classic, *All quiet along the Potomac*, but especially Jared Eliot, the Apostle's first grandson, who was a most renowned member of the stock, being several times Moderator of the Congregational Churches of New England, a theologian, physician, agriculturist and author.

Thus, then, for forty years John Eliot, minister of Roxbury, had played his indispensable part in the great adventure of the first Indian missions. 'His energy and will-power had overridden Company and Commissioners alike, so that in the end it was he who decided at almost every point what steps should be taken to convert the Indians. Perhaps more than any other missionary, he persisted to the end in believing that their conversion was possible.' William Hubbard, a Harvard Graduate of 1642, comments that, 'some judicious persons have conceived no great harvest is to be expected of reall converts ... there being little progress made that way for the present, notwithstanding that many endeavours have been made in that kinde'. (Massachusetts Historical Society's Collections.) These endeavours were supremely Eliot's, and yet his deathbed words show his own assessment of them, 'There is a cloud ... a dark cloud upon the Work of the Gospel among the poor *Indians*. The Lord revive and prosper that work, and grant that it may live when I am dead. It is a Work, which I have been doing much and long about. But what was the Word I spoke last? I recall that Word. *My Doings!* Alas, they have been poor and small, and lean Doings, and I'll be the man that shall throw the first stone at them all.'

The sun sets but it does not expire. John Eliot's life on earth closed nearly three hundred years ago but his influence lives on. Beyond the grave he rejoices in the company of the spirits of just men made perfect. His writings survive. In their early editions they are almost priceless. Even more invaluable is his example, that of a simple-hearted labourer for the Lord who, 'after he had served his own generation by the will of God, fell on sleep'. 'They that be wise shall shine as the brightness of the firmament – and they that turn many to righteousness as the stars for ever and ever.' Such, surely is the only verdict we can pronounce on John Eliot, 'Apostle of the Indians'.

HENRY MARTYN

by

RICHARD T. FRANCE., M.A., B.D.

I. The Making of a Missionary

The secular historian seldom feels obliged to take any notice of the work of God. But in at least one period of British history it can neither be ignored nor denied: that is, the eighteenth century. The names of John Wesley and George Whitefield are known to almost every schoolboy, and the change which came over the life of the nation at that time is common knowledge. Nowhere was this more felt than in Cornwall, whose miners, farmers, and fishermen, previously notorious for vice and depravity, were so affected by the power of God that John Wesley could write in 1781, 'I hardly know any part of the three kingdoms where there has been a more general change.'

But what the schoolboy and his teacher do not always realize is that God's work did not stop at that. The history books seem to imply that the fire burned for a while, spluttered, and died out; the revival was over, and England was herself again. If it had been simply the impact of a group of enthusiastic preachers, this might have been so, but the true work of God does not die out. The story that follows is only a small part of the ever-widening continuation of that work, unknown to most of secular history, but an essential part of that great whole which is the eternal purpose of God, and which will be completed when 'a great multitude which no man can number, from every nation, from all tribes and peoples and tongues' shall shout together their praise, 'Salvation belongs to our God who sits upon the throne, and to the Lamb'.

The story begins in Cornwall.

* * *

Truro had had its share in the great change in the life of Cornwall. Since the conversion in 1747 of its curate, Samuel Walker, and his faithful labour in that city, it had gained the reputation that 'you might fire a cannon down every street in

Truro in church time, without a chance of killing a single human being'. Among the many keen members of his church was the cashier of a Truro merchant, by name John Martyn, a remarkable man who, by his honest hard work, had risen to be a respected and reasonably wealthy citizen of Truro, dividing his leisure time between the prayer-meeting and an avid study of mathematical problems.

Henry, born on February 18, 1781, was the son of John Martyn's second wife, who died when her son was only two years old. It was from her that Henry derived his almost constant poor health. The tuberculosis which killed her and Henry's two sisters was evident in him for at least the last five years of his life, and was in part the cause of his death too. At the age of twenty-eight he was the last survivor of the family.

John Martyn had great hopes for his son, recognizing in him something like his own quick mind and love of learning. This opinion was shared by Dr. Cardew, headmaster of the Truro Grammar School, to which Henry was sent at the age of seven, who recalled that 'his proficiency in the classics exceeded that of most of his school-fellows'. Henry himself seems to have recognized his own talent, and not being as yet very much addicted to hard work, he used to trust in his ability, and 'was frequently known to go up to his lesson with little or no preparation, as if he had learned it merely by intuition'. His school-fellows thought of him as the idlest among them.

'Little Harry Martyn' was not a popular boy. His academic ability, and a certain reserve and shyness, together with his small physique, made him an obvious target for the school bullies, and though not a coward he inevitably had the worst of such encounters, when, to the delight no doubt of his attackers, he would break out into the violent rages of a highly-strung small boy; Martyn never did anything by halves. Fortunately, he was placed under the protection of one of the older boys, John Kempthorne, who 'had often the happiness of rescuing him from the grasp of oppressors, and had never seen more feeling gratitude than was shown by him on those occasions'.

Truro Grammar School had a well-deserved reputation for

turning out some of the best classical scholars at the universities. Dr. Cardew recognized in Martyn an unusually able scholar, and at the age of fifteen he was sent up to Oxford to compete for a scholarship at Corpus Christi College, which, despite his youth and lack of the expected connections in the university, he very nearly gained. Looking back some years later he saw this failure as a divine deliverance, for it was in Cambridge that he was brought face to face with God.

Two further years at school were spent in acquiring additional classical knowledge, as well as in 'his favourite employment of shooting, and ... reading for the most part travels and Lord Chesterfield's *Letters*'. His protector, John Kempthorne, had gone on to St. John's College, Cambridge, and in the summer of 1797 had just reached the highest mathematical honour, in becoming Senior Wrangler. There Martyn was to follow him, and there he too was to change his classical studies for mathematics. But he could not bring himself to prepare in advance for this, 'attributing to a want of taste for mathematics what ought to have been ascribed to idleness, and having his mind in a roving, dissatisfied, restless condition, seeking his chief pleasure in reading, and human praise'.

So when he arrived in Cambridge his tutor found him 'utterly unable as it seemed to make anything of even the First Proposition of Euclid'. A second-year man was detailed to help him to see the light, but all his efforts proved useless, and Martyn, in desperation, was all prepared to book a seat on the next coach back to Truro and abandon his academic career. His instructor persuaded him to make another effort, and records how next day 'light seemed suddenly to flash upon his mind, with clear comprehension of the hitherto dark problem, and he threw up his cap in joy. The Second Proposition was soon taken, and with perfect success; but in truth his progress was such and so rapid, that he distanced everyone in his year'.

This was October. In December his name appeared in the first class in his college examinations, and in the following summer he was the second name within that first class. 'Rapid progress' indeed, and so much did he take it in his stride that by the summer of 1799 he expressed himself 'nettled to the quick' to be again only in second place. December, 1799, saw him at last in first place, which 'pleased my father prodigiously'. All this was the result of hard work; his former idleness was now abandoned for ever. He had set himself to follow Kempthorne in his academic distinction, and his father's eager interest made him the more industrious; it was not long before he was known in college as 'the man who never lost an hour', and this was a characteristic which, in different spheres of service, never left him. It was indeed easy in the Cambridge of those days, as it is today, to waste time pleasantly in good company. 'During the first term', he records, 'I was kept a good deal in idleness by some of my new acquaintances, but the kind attention of Kempthorne was a principal means of my preservation from excess.'

In all this, however, his motive was one of ambition, and desire for fame. In this he differed from Kempthorne, who, besides being a proverbially hard worker, was an earnest Christian, and 'attempted to persuade me that I ought to attend to reading, not for the praise of men, but for the glory of God. This seemed strange to me, but reasonable. I resolved, therefore, to maintain this opinion henceforth; but never designed, that I remember, that it should affect my conduct'. This was in 1799, before he had found that personal knowledge of God that so deeply affected every part of his life.

To his tutor he seemed 'a quiet youth'. To his acquaintance he was generally good company, with a lively wit, and sometimes a quick temper. It was seldom that they saw anything of the conflicts which raged below the surface, the surging passions, hopes and fears of this strong character on which the Spirit of God was already at work. Looking back in later years, he saw it as a time of misery, mastered by 'carnal lusts', directed by strong ambition. Occasionally the outward self-control was broken, as when in a rage he flung a knife at a friend; fortunately his aim was no more steady than his mind, and the knife quivered in the wall.

*   *   *

'Prodigiously pleased' though his father was at his son's academic success, he still had cause for concern at his spiritual state. Still more concerned was his younger sister, Sally. 'I went home this summer', he wrote of 1799, 'and was frequently addressed by my dear sister on the subject of religion.' The reaction of the elder brother could have been predicted: 'The sound of the gospel, conveyed in the admonition of a sister, was grating to my ears.' Of this same visit he records that his selfishness and bad temper were at their worst, issuing in harsh language to both sister and father. His father's patience was long remembered, though not yet understood. As for Sally, she extracted a promise that he would read his Bible, 'but on being settled in college, Newton engaged all my thoughts'.

It needed more than his sister's persuasion to bring the proud Henry Martyn to his knees. But she was also praying, and he afterwards acknowledged her prayers as playing a large part in his conversion. In January, 1800, his father died, and the young man who had been left unmoved by his father's words and life could not be indifferent to his death. He began to think of 'that invisible world to which he was gone, and to which I must one day go'. Unable to concentrate on mathematics, he took up his Bible, 'thinking that the consideration of religion was rather suitable to this solemn time'.

Once again John Kempthorne came to his side, and urged him to continue. He started with the Book of Acts, as he expected to find it 'the most amusing'. It held his interest, and soon, besides enjoying the narrative, he was examining the teaching of the apostles, and finding it the same as that which he had heard in his young days from his father and his evangelical friends. The same night, probably for the first time, he started to pray 'from a precomposed form, in which I thanked God, in general, for having sent Christ into the world. But though I prayed for pardon, I had little sense of my own sinfulness; nevertheless, I began to consider myself a religious man'.

This he continued for a little time, with Kempthorne's help. 'Yet still I read the Bible unenlightened, and said a prayer or two, rather through terror of a superior power, than from any other cause. Soon, however, I began to attend more diligently to the words of our Saviour in the New Testament, and to devour them with delight.' He found 'offers of mercy and forgiveness made so freely', and took the Saviour at His word. Henry Martyn became a son of God. The God who before had been a mere idea to him became real, and Martyn found he could call Him Father. He began to pray, and to enjoy praying, to submit himself gladly to the will of God. From this time God gradually took control of Henry Martyn; his character, his abilities, his whole life, all were brought into the new relationship. It was not that he ceased to be Henry Martyn: the strong emotions, the brilliant mind, the nervous tension, the industrious life, all are still recognizable, but now in a new light, and directed to a new end. It is Henry Martyn indeed, but Henry Martyn reborn.

Some years later he looked back to this as the time when God 'turned me from a life of woe to the enjoyment of peace and hope. The work is real. I can no more doubt it than I can my own existence. The whole current of my desires is altered, I am walking quite another way'.

*   *   *

Perhaps the most loved and the most hated man in Cambridge in the first half of the nineteenth century was Charles Simeon, vicar of Trinity Church from 1782 to 1836. He was an uncompromising evangelical, a ready source of amusement to the witty young undergraduates, who would come to his church to make fun of him. But others came because they valued his fearless and balanced preaching of the apostolic gospel, and throughout his long career there was always a considerable band of 'Simeonites', Christian students who looked to this wise champion of the faith for direction and help. Among these there now appeared the brilliant mathematician from St. John's. The famous conversation-parties, when Simeon poured out a sound mixture of devotional fervour and common sense, became for Martyn a regular source of spiritual refreshment. Here he met and learned to love other keen young Christians, some of whom were later, due to the influence of Simeon, his colleagues in India.

But his new faith was not allowed to detract from his study; Simeon always counselled hard work and Martyn's own academic bent was unchanged. Indeed he found it sometimes too strong, and felt in 1800 that the 'intenseness with which I pursued my studies, in which I was so absorbed, that the time I gave to them seemed not to be a portion of my existence' was responsible for his remaining spiritually 'stationary'. He envied the ploughman and the weaver, who may be wholly absorbed in religious thoughts even while hard at work. However, the facts seem to bear out his friend Sargent's suspicion that this was the excessive self-condemnation of a truly humble man.

January, 1801, brought the final examination, and Martyn was not exempt from the agitation which that crisis has brought to many. But as he entered the Senate House he remembered the text of a recent sermon: 'Seekest thou great things for thyself? Seek them not.' This calmed his nerves, and he worked triumphantly through the three gruelling days, coming out as Senior Wrangler in what was acknowledged to be an exceptionally brilliant year. His father's ambition and his own were fulfilled; until recently this had been the ceiling of his hopes. But now his values had changed: 'I obtained my highest wishes', he confessed, 'but was surprised to find that I had grasped a shadow.' Not that he despised learning, but he had now a higher love and ideal, nothing less than full Christian maturity, and from this he felt himself to be still very distant.

Mathematics had never been Martyn's chief interest, and now they were largely abandoned. His old love of the classics began to reassert itself, and it was as a classical scholar that Cambridge knew him for the rest of his academic career.

But the year 1801 brought other developments. Much of his now plentiful leisure was devoted to solitary prayer and meditation, to the enrichment of his fellowship with God which he felt he had neglected before his final examination. All through his life he loved to get away from men and alone with God. 'God was pleased', he recalled, 'to bless the solitude and retirement I enjoyed this summer to my improvement; and not till then had I ever experienced any real pleasure in religion.' The Fellows'

Garden at St. John's was later the scene of frequent close communion with his Father, and a walking tour on his own in the Welsh mountains in 1802 provided the opportunity for much reflection like the following on the road between Aber and Bangor: 'It was a remarkably clear day. The sun shone on every object around me, and the sea breeze tempered the air. I felt happy at the sight, and could not help being struck with the beauty of the creation, and the goodness of the God of nature.' Everything, from the storm on the Mersey, and the 'horror of the ascent' of Snowdon, to the tranquil beauty of the Dovey estuary, filled his mind with thoughts of God; and throughout his life he found the same delight in the beauty of the world, both for himself, and for its testimony to its Creator.

But also at this period he was beginning to discover and delight in the deeper revelation of God in the Bible. Staying with his brother-in-law at Woodbury in Cornwall, 'I passed some of the sweetest moments of my life. The deep solitude of the place favoured meditation, and the romantic scenery around supplied great external sources of pleasure. For want of other books, I was obliged to read my Bible almost exclusively, and from this I derived great spirituality of mind compared with what I had known before.' The book of Isaiah now, as later, was his special favourite.

Together with an increasing love for God and 'pleasure in religion', Martyn was at this time feeling his way towards his choice of profession. He had intended to study law, and enter that lucrative and respected profession, but now, through his growing friendship with Simeon, other ideas were suggested to him. Simeon never ceased to lay before his young followers the importance of the ordained ministry: his own life exemplified it. Their reactions varied. John Sargent, who had come to Trinity Church to mock 'the old hypocrite', but had been unable to resist the convicting work of the Holy Spirit, was one of the foremost, a close friend of Martyn, and later his first biographer; he longed to be able to answer Simeon's call, and it was only obedience to his parents' prohibition that forced him sadly to renounce it. Martyn, on the other hand, 'could not consent to be poor for Christ's sake', and preferred the legal profession, which Sargent decried. But it was while he was reading Isaiah in the solitude of Woodbury that his mind was made up and his ambition conquered. From now on the service of his Lord was his one desire.

Simeon had soon recognized the spiritual potentialities of the young scholar, and now invited him to serve as curate of Trinity Church. Much as the prospect delighted Martyn, he knew it would mean the loss of much of his popularity and respect, and after the decision was taken, he records his being ashamed to confess that he was to be Simeon's curate, through 'a despicable fear of man'. For by now Martyn was a man of importance, elected a Fellow of St. John's in April, 1802, establishing himself by further prizes as a leading classical scholar, and not long after his mathematical triumph appointed classical examiner for his college. No one could fail to recognize his brilliance, but this did not protect him from mockery, and the Fellows sometimes amused themselves in the Common Room by baiting their resident 'Methodist'. The great work of God which had so transformed the life of the working people had as yet had little effect on the universities, where 'enthusiasm' was frowned on, and a little morality together with the statutory chapel services was seen as the sum of religion. To such men, Martyn and his like were incomprehensible, and therefore to be ridiculed. For his part, he understood them no better. 'It sometimes appeared astonishing that men of like passions with myself, of the same bodies, of the same minds, alike in every other respect, knew and saw nothing of that blessed and adorable Being in whom my soul findeth all its happiness, but were living a sort of life which to me would be worse than annihilation.' Martyn was indeed good company, and had many friends; his diary is full of references to callers who stayed sometimes longer than he liked, but essentially he was different, and as such was alone in the crowd.

* * *

Simeon, besides recommending men to enter the ministry, had a consuming interest in missionary work, especially in India and the East. Charles Grant, of the East India Company, had made Simeon responsible for finding chaplains for India, and through his constant presentation of this need a good number of young Simeonites eventually sailed for the East. Martyn could not be deaf to such appeals from his beloved leader. This was the exciting period when the church, or at least its evangelical section, was stirring, and waking up to its missionary responsibility. The sailing of William Carey for India in 1793 is generally regarded as the beginning of the modern missionary movement. The first missionary societies were beginning to be formed, though the Church Missionary Society, founded in 1799, had to wait until 1813 before it had an English missionary on its roll.

Into this concern for the long-neglected heathen Martyn now entered with all his heart. He began to read avidly the lives and views of missionaries and the reports of missionary societies, and Simeon fostered his interest. From 1802 his diary and letters are full of thoughts of the East, and it was especially China that claimed his attention. 'Read Sir G. Staunton's *Embassy to China*, and was convinced of the propriety of being sent thither.' 'I prayed to be sent out to China, and rejoiced in the prospect of the glorious day when Christ shall be glorified on earth.'

But perhaps the greatest force impelling Martyn to think of missionary service was the discovery in the autumn of 1802 of his hero, in the diary of David Brainerd. No one who has read the diaries of Brainerd and Martyn can be surprised at the appeal Brainerd had for him. Both are full of the same longing and striving for a closer communion with God, the same battles against a corrupt and selfish nature, the same absorption in prayer. Brainerd, like Martyn, was of weak health, and had a natural tendency to melancholy; like Martyn, he found in his college days a personal knowledge of God that transformed his whole life. It gave him a love for the souls of men that nothing could quench; he prayed, fasted, loved, and worked, and God sent his delicate servant into the 'hideous and howling wilderness' to preach to the Red Indians. Here, in constant discomfort and suffering, he prayed and preached, and was privileged to see a mighty work of God turning many Indians to their Creator. But it was too much for his weak constitution, and at the age of twenty-nine he, like Martyn, died of tuberculosis.

The name of Brainerd now constantly recurs in Martyn's diary. 'I feel my heart knit to this dear man, and really rejoice to think of meeting him in heaven.' 'I long to be like him; let me forget the world, and be swallowed up in a desire to glorify God.' The wish was fulfilled, for both in character and in experience Martyn came nearer than anyone to being a replica of Brainerd. How often the life of one servant of God has inspired another! And Martyn's in its turn has been much used by God: among those drawn out to the East by his example was John Wilson of Bombay; John Wilson's in turn drew out Ion Keith-Falconer to Arabia. So it goes on, and the chain is not even yet complete.

The idea of missionary work was not popular among Martyn's friends. Of course to the Cambridge Fellows it was sheer madness: one of them 'thought it a most improper step for me to leave the University to preach to the ignorant heathen, which any person could do'. Even among his Christian friends some were not keen on the idea of missionary work: one appears to have been in the tradition of the hyper-Calvinists who accused Carey of enthusiasm for thinking that God needed his help in converting the heathen; as this friend 'entered into the highest points of the Calvinistic scheme', Martyn found that his heart was 'much frozen'.

More serious was the objection of his sister, Sally. She did not object to missionary work as such, but felt that her brother was 'unqualified through want of religious experience', and faithfully told him so. He felt the force of the objection, and added to it the confession that 'the thought that I might be unceasingly employed in the same kind of work, amongst poor ignorant people, is what my proud spirit revolts at. To be obliged to submit to a thousand uncomfortable things that must happen to me whether as a minister or a missionary is what the flesh cannot endure'. On the other side he was aware of the danger of being carried away by the 'romance' of missionary work: 'I find greater pleasure at the prospect of it; I am conscious, however, of viewing things too much on the bright side, and think more readily of the happiness of seeing the desert rejoice and blossom as the rose, than of pain, and fatigue, and crosses, and disappointments.' It was well that he saw this danger, for he was never permitted to 'see the desert rejoice and blossom as the rose', and had a plentiful supply of pain and disappointment.

But his calling was on firmer ground, and so could stand the strain. Above and beyond all these arguments, he gradually became convinced during 1802 of the call of God to foreign missionary work, and despite his painful sense of unfitness, he never again seems to have thought of any other course. His life-long conviction of the sovereign wisdom and power of God lay at the back of this resolve: if it was God who called, he could not refuse, and the issue must be in God's hands. There he was content to leave the matter.

Henry Martyn was to be a missionary.

II. Missionary Designate

The candidate for ordination in 1803 had no great hurdles to leap. Many years were to elapse before selection boards, theological colleges, and written examinations were heard of. The squire's son would find a comfortable living in the well-endowed parish of which his father was patron, the ideal setting for a pleasant leisurely life, with a comfortable sense that he was doing good to his people. The jolly company gathered at the Bishop's Palace at Ely in October, 1803, were no doubt perfectly happy about the step they were about to take, and any suggestion that their vows might be open to the charge of perjury would have horrified them.

But one of the company was not in a jolly mood, and their frivolity only increased his gloom. Martyn's sensitive nature always made it hard for him to rebuke another, or to introduce religious questions with those who, he knew, would resent it, but 'at length I began to feel the shameful and cruel neglect and unconcern for the honour of God, and the souls of my brethren, in having trifled with men whom I feared were about to "lie to the Holy Ghost",' and so he took what opportunities he could to beg some of the candidates to take their ordination seriously, but with little success. So he 'went to bed with a painful sense of my hardness of heart and unsuitable preparation for the ministry'. He fully expected to fail the perfunctory oral examination in Greek, Latin, and Christian apologetics: 'I felt great shame at having come so confidently to offer myself for the ministry of the Lord Jesus Christ, with so much ignorance and unholiness, and I thought it would be but just if I were sent off with ignominy.'

The day of the ordination service he struggled in vain with feelings of pride and self-importance, and at the same time dreaded the 'weight and difficulty of the work which lay before me, which never appeared so great at a distance'. Walking back to Cambridge that night he 'could scarcely believe that so sacred an office should be held by one who had such a heart within'. With such feelings Martyn began his ministry at Trinity Church. The same feelings constantly recur in his diary, though they are generally happily combined with an acknowledgement of the faithfulness and mercy of the God who had placed this responsibility upon him.

Charles Simeon gave him, in addition to his work at Trinity Church, charge of the parish of Lolworth, near Cambridge. Between the two, Martyn's eighteen months under Simeon were fully occupied. Simeon was a man of action, and expected the same of his curates, and, difficult as he found it, Martyn worked hard, perhaps too hard for his weak health.

Martyn's character was essentially academic, and pastoral work did not come easily. 'It is my will rather to sit down, to please myself with reading, and let the world perish.' 'The work of visiting the people of Cambridge and reading to and praying with them appeared hateful to me.' Yet he did it, and his diary contains many examples of faithful visiting and pastoral care often in most uncongenial situations.

If there is one characteristic of Martyn which marks him out among God's most faithful servants, it is the shrinking which often preceded his service: some men delight to plunge into the thick of the battle for God; Martyn recoiled. He was a sensitive scholar. Yet at the same time he had a vivid sense of responsibility to deliver his message as Christ's ambassador, and, hard though it was, he did deliver it. To the end of his days it cost him an inward struggle to speak to an unwilling hearer about God, and occasionally he shirked it, but not often. Whether he was visiting in the workhouse, riding on the coach to Cornwall, or with the servant who cleaned his room, he missed few opportunities to present the gospel of the grace of God, and though he often met with scornful rejection, there were not a few who were 'much affected'.

But it was not success that drove him on: in 1804 he wrote, 'It has never yet, to my knowledge, pleased God to awaken one soul by my means, either in public or private; shame be to myself.' There were individuals later, but in general he never saw much fruit from his work. But that did not alter the commission to preach, and it was this which would not let him rest. His diary refers quite often to the figure of the watchman in Ezekiel 3, upon whom God lays the responsibility of the death of those whom he failed to warn. He had no doubt of the hopeless and lost condition of those who die without Christ, and he was commissioned by God to preach to them before it was too late. 'May the Lord be pleased to fix this in my mind,' he wrote, 'that I am in the midst of dying souls, who are thronging to hell. How cruel, how impious to let a brother perish for want of warning.' This was enough, and not even the attraction of his books could keep him from his duty.

Preaching, too, he found difficult. It was not lack of material; his constant study of the Bible and his longing to declare the good news of salvation ensured that. But his friends told him he was going far above the heads of his hearers, and he recognized that it was true: the Cambridge Fellow, much as he loved his country people, thought on a different wavelength. 'C. told me I was far above the comprehension of people in general. Nothing pains and grieves me more than this, for I had rather be a preacher of the gospel among the poor, so as to be understood by them, than be anything else upon earth.' Another accused him of an 'insipid, inanimate manner', and urged him to put more eloquence and power into his preaching. But it was especially the long, hard hours spent in preparing his sermons which distressed him. Towards the end of his Cambridge days he took to preaching extempore, which eliminated much of the academic polish, and made his presentation more forceful, but he still continued to write out at least one sermon a week.

It must not for one moment be imagined, however, that Martyn's ministry was one of unrelieved misery. Often, the initial struggle over, he 'preached the gospel of peace with great delight'. After a time he recorded with joy, 'Blessed be God, I feel myself to be His minister. This thought, which I can hardly describe, came in the morning after reading Brainerd. I wish for no service but the service of God, in labouring for souls on earth, and to do His will in heaven.' And again, 'I do not wish for any heaven upon earth besides that of preaching the precious gospel of Jesus Christ to immortal souls,' Now, as always, it was in private communion with God that he found his chief pleasure, as he humbled himself, and rejoiced in the grace and glory of his Saviour.

But while he was giving himself unsparingly to his ministry of the pulpit, the workhouse, and the village school-room, and concluding half unwillingly that 'it must be more acceptable to God to labour for souls, though the mind remains uninformed', Martyn was still the refined scholar, still living in his quiet suite of rooms in St. John's College, still enjoying the beauties of nature and of art, the superb music of the services in King's College Chapel, and his own occasional warblings on the flute. Perhaps he had little time now for these pleasures, but he certainly had no less inclination. 'Since I have known God in a saving manner, painting, poetry, and music have had charms unknown to me before. I have received what I suppose is a taste for them.' Yet he was constantly on his guard lest these earthly loves should diminish his love for God. Especially was this so when he was appointed classical examiner for the third time: reflecting on his examining in Xenophon, he wrote, 'I was obliged to reason with myself, and to force open my eyes, that I might see the excellency of divine things. Did I delight in reading the retreat of the ten thousand Greeks; and shall not my soul glory in the knowledge of

God, who created the Greeks, and the vast countries over which they passed?' So every part of his fertile mind and wide interests was feeling the influence of his ever-growing knowledge of God.

The influence of Simeon, and his own conviction of God's call to the East, were responsible for the growth at this time of a new interest, one which was later to become the centre of his work, the love of languages. 'Love' is not too strong a word, for it was with reluctance that he tore himself away from a Bengali grammar to write a sermon, and he had to reproach himself for wasting valuable time absorbed in an Arabic grammar. It was said of him that 'he read grammars as other men read novels'. Already proficient in Hebrew, Greek, and Latin, he was now eagerly devouring Hindustani, Bengali, Persian, and Arabic, and later the list became longer. It is worthwhile to quote from a letter which he later wrote from Cawnpore in 1809: 'There is a book printed at the Hirkara Press, called *Celtic Derivatives:* this I want; also grammars and dictionaries of all the languages of the earth. I have one or both in Latin, Greek, French, Italian, Portuguese, Dutch, Hebrew, Rabbinical Hebrew, Chaldee, Syriac, Ethiopic, Samaritan, Arabic, Persian, Sanscrit, Bengali, Hindustani.' Right up to his last journeys in Persia, comparative philology and the problems of translation, which an ordinary mortal would dread and avoid, were his favourite means of relaxation, and so absorbed his mind that he had to plead with God not to let them distract him from prayer.

Somehow too he seems to have found time for other reading. His diary and letters refer to the apologists Butler and Paley, the *Confessions* of Augustine, William Law and Bishop Hopkins, and particularly to that 'Puritan born out of due time', Jonathan Edwards. Together with these he eagerly read all the literature on missions that he could lay his hands on, especially delighting in Dr. Vanderkemp, whom he later met at Cape Town, and above all, now as always, David Brainerd.

*   *   *

Before the end of 1802, Martyn had made his first approach to The Society for Missions to Africa and the East, which later became the Church Missionary Society, with a view to being sent out to India by them. Early in 1804 this plan received a fatal blow, when Martyn found that he had lost the legacy left by his father. This left him with his younger sister entirely dependent on him, and a missionary salary would not be adequate for this. But already Simeon and his friends had been considering the possibility of his serving as an East India Company chaplain; the post carried a large salary, and while its duties were primarily among the Company's European employees, it might be expected to leave considerable scope for work among the Indians. This proposal was now put to Martyn, and he found it distasteful, at least as far as the salary was concerned. 'The prospect of this world's happiness gave me pain rather than pleasure.' 'I could have been infinitely better pleased to have gone out as a missionary, poor as the Lord and His apostles.' And this was the man who two years earlier 'could not consent to be poor for Christ's sake'!

This proposal, and the legal business connected with the legacy, necessitated several visits to London, where Charles Grant, a director of the East India Company, and a leading member of the 'Clapham Sect', a group of earnest evangelicals who made a strong mark on the nation in the early years of the nineteenth century, took charge of his application for the chaplaincy, which he had agreed to make, as being the only apparent way to get to India. And it was as well that he did adopt this course, because the East India Company, while willing to have its own chaplains, was becoming increasingly hostile to missionary work in its territory, and the group of British missionaries already at work in North India were confined to the minute Danish possession of Serampore. If Martyn had been sent out by the Society for Missions to Africa and the East, it is unlikely that he would have had the freedom that he in fact enjoyed. So even in the loss of the legacy we can see the hand of God directing His servant to the most fruitful course.

This confidence in God's direction of the decisions of men appears in his reaction to the news of his appointment: 'Found from Mr. Grant that I was that day appointed a chaplain to the East India Company, but that my particular destination would depend on the government in India. Rather may I say that it depends on the will of my God, who in His own time thus brings things to pass. Oh, now let my heart be spiritualized, that the glorious and arduous work before me may fill all my soul, and stir me up to prayer.'

India and its need more and more filled his thoughts: 'Ten thousand times more than ever do I feel devoted to that precious work. O gladly shall this base blood be shed, every drop of it, if India can be benefited in one of her children, if but one of these creatures of God Almighty might be brought home to his duty.' Once he found himself regretting his decision: 'I could not help saying, "Go, Hindus, go on in your misery, let Satan still rule over you; for he that was appointed to labour among you is consulting his ease" – "No", thought I, "hell and earth shall never keep me back from my work. I am cast down, but not destroyed".' He was appointed by God to work in India; that was his settled conviction, and from this nothing could turn him back.

A visit to John Newton, the former slave-trader, now for many years a warrior of the gospel, confirmed his conviction. The old man's epigrams were prophetic: 'On my saying that perhaps I should never live to see much fruit, he answered, "I should have a bird's-eye view of it, which would be better". When I spoke of the opposition that I should be likely to meet with, he said, he supposed Satan would not love me for what I was about to do. The old man prayed afterwards with sweet simplicity.'

Once appointed a chaplain, Martyn had to be ready to sail with the fleet due to leave in the summer of 1805. He returned to Cambridge in April of that year for the last time, to say goodbye to his friends and parishioners. He left his Lolworth people still, he feared, in 'general hardness of heart', and added with characteristic humility, 'yet so it hath pleased God, I hope, to reserve them for a more faithful minister.' That night he preached for the last time in Trinity Church, and afterwards 'Mr. Simeon commended me to God in prayer, in which he pleaded, amongst other things, for a richer blessing on my soul. He perceives that I want it, and so do I'. Humbly conscious, as always, only of his unworthiness and failure, he was unaware as he walked down the aisle that the kneeling congregation rose and turned to catch a last sight of the young scholar whom his Lord was taking away from Cambridge to a far less comfortable sphere of service.

Three months in London soon passed, and Martyn was summoned to Portsmouth, where the fleet was preparing to sail. He met his London friends for the last time, fully convinced that he was leaving England for ever. Even at this date his diary contains hints of the probability of an early death, and a fainting fit on his way to Portsmouth made the probability more real; 'Death appeared near at hand, and seemed more terrible than I could have conceived before, not in its conclusion, but in itself. I felt assured of my safety in Christ.' But however many years he lived, he had no intention of returning to England. His friend Sargent said that 'He went forth to preach the gospel to the heathen, and it was his fixed resolution to live and die amongst them. When he left England, he left it wholly for Christ's sake, and he left it for ever.'

To some this resolution might seem comfortably heroic; to Martyn it was agony. 'Shed tears at night, at the thought of my departure, and the roaring sea that would soon be rolling between me and all that is dear to me upon earth.' Martyn's affectionate nature recoiled from such a separation, and though he made many friends in India, he never forgot or became reconciled to the loss of his English friends. Sargent, who knew him perhaps better than anyone, paints a vivid picture of his dejection and misery in saying his last farewells, his last eager gazing on the English coast, and his agony when it had disappeared. And the diary amply bears this out: 'England has disappeared, and with it all my peace.' 'Oh my dear friends in England, when we spoke with exultation of the mission to the heathen, whilst in the midst of health and joy and hope, what an imperfect idea did we form of the sufferings by which it must be accomplished.' The romance of the mission field was well and truly shattered.

Simeon and other friends came down to Portsmouth to see him off, and there for a week they waited, saying repeated farewells until the fleet at last set sail. An odd bunch this group of devoted Christians, praying, preaching, and singing hymns on the way to the ship, must have looked among the blasphemous high spirits of the soldiers, sailors and clerks all bound for India. And so at last Martyn found himself alone, seasick, miserable, watching the coast of Dorset and Devon slip away.

But that was not to be the end. Further orders were awaited from Lord Nelson, and the fleet could not proceed without them. They reached Plymouth, and eventually anchored in Falmouth harbour. To Martyn the delay was both welcome and painful, for here he was in the middle of his native county, and every mile of the wooded shore held memories. He had said his farewells in Cornwall a year ago; now he was to have both the pleasure and the sorrow again.

But there was one person in particular whom he longed to see, and yet half dreaded it, for only twenty miles away, at Marazion, lived Lydia Grenfell, with whom for over a year Martyn had been deeply in love. Indeed this was the deepest element in his sorrow at leaving England, that the ship was not only separating him from friends and country, but from the woman whom he loved with a devotion that amounted in his mind to idolatry. Yet now here he was again a short horse-ride from Marazion. He had steeled himself to renouncing Lydia for ever; did God intend otherwise?

*   *   *

Lydia Grenfell was his cousin's sister-in-law, the daughter of a respected leading citizen of that old, dull town. At the time when Martyn's fleet anchored in Falmouth harbour she was already thirty-one, six years his senior. Five years earlier she had fallen in love and become engaged to a local solicitor. In that same year she had also found Christ, and later discovering that her fiancé was not all that she had thought him to be, she broke off the engagement. In 1804 this solicitor became engaged to another woman, but until he actually got married, which he in fact put off until 1810, Lydia felt herself bound to remain free from other ties; it was this unreasonable scruple which was responsible for so much of the sorrow in Martyn's life and her own.

Since her conversion, Lydia had become a devout and active

Christian, worshipping in the local Methodist chapel, and visiting the poor and sick of the neighbourhood to bring practical help, and to read and pray with them. Her diary has much in common with Martyn's, being full of critical self-examination, and revealing a longing for more holiness of life and fellowship with God. But it far exceeds his in what can fairly be described as morbid brooding. However, there is not much exaggeration in Sargent's estimate of her as 'one of whom less ought not, and more can not be said, than that she was worthy of him'.

When Martyn first became aware of his love for Lydia is uncertain; it suddenly erupts into his diary in July, 1804, on his farewell visit to Cornwall, and from then on it is a constant theme. During that month he spent some time with her, walking, visiting the sick, and 'conversing on spiritual subjects'. Even as he talked with her his mind was wrestling against the attachment which he felt to be both idolatrous, and the cause of his losing the sense of God's presence; but yet 'I felt too plainly that I loved her passionately. The direct opposition of this to my devotedness to God in the missionary way excited no small tumult in my mind'. He struggled by every means to forget her, but it was a losing battle – 'In dreams her image returned, and I awoke in the night with my mind full of her.'

Yet he said nothing, and left Cornwall determined that this must be the end of his love. 'Parted with Lydia, perhaps for ever in this life, with a sort of uncertain pain, which I knew would increase to greater violence.' He did confide, however, in Lydia's sister, Emma, his cousin's wife, and found that Lydia too had confided in her; 'I learned from Emma that my attachment to her sister was not altogether unreturned, and the discovery gave me both pleasure and pain, but at night alone I resigned myself entirely to the will of God.' Lydia's diary shows that 'not altogether unreturned' was an understatement.

But still Martyn tried to forget her. He was convinced that his missionary calling demanded that he should remain unmarried. It is startling to find frequently in his diary, side by side with expressions of his ardent love, a persistent conviction that it is better not to be married, as it allows a free and undistracted service of God. It was this conviction that caused him to brand his love as 'idolatry' and 'back-sliding', and it persisted even when he was waiting in India in the vain hope that the next mail would bring Lydia's consent to come out to join him. Even then he could write, 'My heart still entangled with this idolatrous affection, and consequently unhappy. Sometimes I gained deliverance from it for a short time, and was happy in the love of God.'

His friends were divided. One said he would be acting like a madman to go out to India unmarried; others urged the need of companionship in his future lonely life, and the chaplain David Brown wrote from Calcutta, 'Let him marry and come out at once.' Some, on the other hand, argued strongly for celibacy, foremost among them the unmarried Simeon. Both sides were represented in Martyn's own mind, and the struggle was long and hard. When he eventually sailed from Portsmouth he thought his 'idolatry' was finally conquered, but now in Falmouth the whole question was reopened.

The fleet remained there a full three weeks, and after initial hesitation Martyn rode over to Marazion, where he lost no time in declaring his love, hoping for a response there and then which would justify him later in sending for Lydia to India. He was disappointed; her old scruples and the suddenness of the proposal were too much for her, and she would not say what she felt. He returned to the ship in deep gloom, writing to Emma that 'another consequence of my journey is, that I love Lydia more than ever'. A further visit was later possible, and then a third. His hopes rose again: 'I was almost induced to believe her more interested about me than I had conceived.'

This final visit ended with tantalizing abruptness. He was sitting with Lydia and her mother, reading the Bible; 'She was then just putting into my hand the tenth of Genesis to read, when a servant came in, and said a horse was come for me from St. Hilary, where a carriage was waiting to convey me to Falmouth. Lydia was evidently painfully affected by it; she came out, that we might be alone at taking leave, and I then told her, that if it should appear to be God's will that I should be married, she must not be offended at receiving a letter from me. In the great hurry, she discovered more of her mind than she intended; she made no objection whatever to coming out. Thinking, perhaps, I wished to make an engagement with her, she said we had better go quite free; with this I left her.' Wavering and indecisive – that was always the character of Lydia's love. He never saw her again.

He galloped back to the ship, which 'was entangled in the chain, and was by that means the only one not under way when I arrived'. The next day, as Martyn preached on deck from the text 'Now they desire a better country, that is, an heavenly', St. Michael's Mount, on to which he knew Lydia's window looked, was gradually fading from sight, and with it England. He wondered whether Lydia had noticed the fleet passing: no doubt she did.

But though Henry and Lydia never saw each other again, that is not the end of the story. It would take a considerable volume to hold all the letters that passed between them, and the thoughts about each other with which their diaries abound. Both were truly in love, and both continued to be. Neither was fully reconciled to the separation until Henry's death, and that death was on a journey which had as its object England, and Lydia; the hope of returning to claim her as his bride was still alive in his mind at the end. When he arrived in Calcutta, and had seen the great advantages of being married, he wrote, as he had suggested at that last interview, asking Lydia to come out to India to marry him. But she never came; her mother's opposition, and her own unreasonable scruple about her first fiancé, still held her back, and kept them both in what has since seemed to many a quite unnecessary state of unhappiness.

Undoubtedly there was much in Lydia's hesitation that cannot be commended, and undoubtedly the company of a devoted wife would have added much to Martyn's happiness, and probably to his usefulness in India. But it must not be forgotten that the crowning achievements of his ministry came after he had left India, in conditions where a married man could hardly have gone. His lifelong conviction of the value of an unmarried state for missionary work was vindicated there, if not in India. And above all it must not be forgotten that both Henry and Lydia did what they did in the conviction that it was the will of God. Their diaries are full of prayers and appeals to God to show them the right way, and to confirm them in following it. Can we not accept their conviction that, hard as His ways seemed to them, He knew what He was doing? The easy way is not always God's way; this is one of the supreme lessons of the life of Henry Martyn.

So, on August 10, 1805, as the troop-ship *Union* followed the rest of the fleet out of Falmouth harbour, Henry Martyn left England, and Lydia, for ever.

III. The Missionary Imperative

Sea voyages in 1805 were, at the best, a tedious and uncomfortable business; at the worst they were dangerous, and even fatal. Storms and sickness were commonplace, but Trafalgar Year brought other dangers, and Martyn cannot have been surprised to find that this trading fleet was under the escort of four warships, and contained fifty transport ships carrying some five thousand troops. Somewhere between Britain and India a military campaign was planned, but no one knew where. From Falmouth they sailed to Cork, from Cork to Madeira, and from Madeira to San Salvador, in Brazil; a strange route for India, but one which provided welcome breaks from the monotonous squalor of life on ship, as they wandered in the orange groves, and enjoyed the hospitality of a friendly Portuguese landowner. But eventually the destination of the soldiers was revealed, and they set sail for the Cape of Good Hope, then in Dutch hands, to reclaim it for Britain.

Martyn has left us vivid descriptions of the battle of Blaauwberg, and the surrender of Cape Town in January, 1806; it was his only taste of war, and it revolted him. The only consolation was that it gave him the opportunity to meet one of his heroes of Cambridge days, Dr. Vanderkemp, whose work among the African people delighted him. He asked the doctor if he had ever regretted his decision; ' "No", said the old man, smiling, "and I would

[258]

not exchange my work for a kingdom".' The example of such men was a constant source of encouragement to Martyn.

They spent a month at the Cape, and then the voyage continued. It was not until May, 1806, that the *Union* at last sailed up the Hooghly to Calcutta.

The events of the voyage are all of great interest, but our aim is to follow one member of that huge fleet, perhaps the most incongruous figure of all, the refined, sensitive Cambridge scholar, going to preach the gospel of Jesus Christ to the people of India. It is not in the relaxation of Brazil, or the excitement of the Cape, that we see him best, but in the stench and the blasphemy of the lower decks, or facing the cold contempt of the ship's officers. This 'raw academic' had been appointed chaplain to the fleet – no wonder, as he was the only minister among them. But in practical terms his ministry was limited to his own ship, and there for nine months he struggled to do his job.

He could hardly have been less suited to his 'parish', nor the 'parish' less receptive to a Christian ministry. However hard he laboured to simplify his sermons, he was still told that he was going right above the heads of his hearers. He hardly spoke the same language. And the officers, who could understand his message, resented it. They told him 'they would not attend if so much hell was preached'. They wanted the sort of gentle moral homilies they were used to. But Martyn was not the man to cry 'Peace, peace' where there is no peace, and the day after the protest he took as his text, 'The wicked shall be turned into hell, and all the nations that forget God.' The officers showed their disgust, one by saying that he resented being shut up in hell, another by employing the time of the sermon in feeding the geese. That sermon is preserved, and there is no shrinking from the open declaration of man's natural corruption, the seriousness of revolt against God, and the imperative need for repentance, all the time balanced by a full declaration of the love and mercy of God and an urgent appeal to flee from the wrath to come. Martyn may have been 'more tried by the fear of man, than I ever have been since God has called me to the ministry', but the fear was gloriously conquered.

The captain only allowed one service on Sundays, but that was not the limit of Martyn's work. He was always to be seen among the men, rough, hardened old sailors and soldiers, raw young recruits, and even a shipload of female convicts for Botany Bay. They liked his teaching no more than the officers, and were more profane in their scorn. Their oaths wounded the sensitive young minister deeply, but, with a sinking heart, he rebuked them, and often the response amazed him. But usually it was short-lived, and though the *Union* became known in the fleet as 'a very praying ship', the epithet indicates rather the complete godlessness of the rest of the fleet than any marked improvement in Martyn's charges.

Whenever Martyn worked among Europeans he found the same response, a scornful rejection of his message by the vast majority, but a handful of men who, often in secret, came to hear more. There was the corporal who slipped into his hand a letter begging for spiritual help, a request he dared not make in the open; there was the chief mate who, though unable to understand much of Martyn's theology, stopped swearing, and became the chaplain's loyal supporter; there were the faithful five who joined him in his cabin for daily worship; there was above all Mackenzie, an officer of the cadets, who throughout the voyage was a constant visitor to the chaplain's cabin, and incurred ridicule by attending the hymn-singing which Martyn introduced among the lower ranks. A few did indeed find a true faith in Christ on that voyage; but the majority grew steadily more obstinate in their opposition.

Much as they disliked his message, however, they could not deny the sincere love of the man for his 'parish'. It was love for the blaspheming sailors that kept him busy trying to awaken their consciences. Such love is not easily recognized by men of the world, but they could not disregard his unselfish care for the sick and dying, who were always to be found in plenty on the troopships of those days. From the captain, who died on the way to the Cape, to the merest ship's boy, all claimed his unceasing care, and only when dysentery attacked Martyn himself was he forced to stop. Imagine it: the sweat and the dirt, the foul smell and the unbearable heat of the lower decks, and the Cambridge don in his meticulously neat black clothes moving from hammock to hammock, from sick boy to dying man, with food and medicine, and always with the Word of God. The men had never seen anything like it; nor had the officers, and they wrote him off as a mad enthusiast.

For Martyn it was, like much of his ministry, a hard service from which he often shrank. He felt inadequate, out of his element; he was afraid; and worst of all he was alone. He had never known such loneliness before, not even in the Senior Common Room at St. John's. But such problems never caused Martyn to despair of anything but himself, and only increased his trustful dependence on his God. The diary is still full of times of delight in the love of God, and of longing for more of His presence. He is confident that he is where God wants him to be, and, with all its hardship, he would choose nowhere else. 'I am so far from regretting', he wrote at the end of 1805, 'that I ever came on this delightful work, that were I to choose for myself, I could scarcely find a situation more agreeable to my taste. On, therefore, let me go, and persevere steadily in this blessed undertaking, through the grace of God dying daily to the opinions of men, and aiming, with a more single eye, at the glory of the everlasting God.'

The consciousness of his helplessness to influence the men around him turned his mind more to the almighty power of God. Returning to the ship from San Salvador, fresh from an encounter with Roman Catholic friars, listening to the praises of Muhammad sung by the Muslim Lascars who rowed his boat, and trying unsuccessfully to convince a fellow-passenger that it was not enough for men to be sober and honest, 'I turned away, and with a deep sigh cried to God to interfere in behalf of His gospel; for in the course of one hour I had seen three shocking examples of the reign and power of the devil, in the form of Popish and Mahomedan delusion, and that of the natural man. I never felt so strongly what a nothing I am. All my clear arguments are good for nothing; unless the Lord stretch out His hand, I speak to stones. I felt, however, no way discouraged, but only saw the necessity of dependence on God.' So God was teaching His servant in practice the truth of his theological beliefs, and the sovereign power of God to bring men to Himself became as ever more precious reality to him.

* * *

India, however, was the goal, and Martyn never forgot it. He prayed constantly for God to 'exert His power in the conversion of the Eastern nations', and felt that his prayers were being heard. He constantly prepared himself by his work on the Hindustani grammar, and supplemented this by talking to the Muslim Lascars, Indians employed on the ship, trying to turn his academic grasp of the language to colloquial use. This was the last straw for some of the officers: an educated Englishman talking with these 'blacks' – he must be crazy! But Martyn was not deterred, nor did he even notice, probably; he was far too concerned to reach the language, and through it the souls, of the Lascars.

And so, at last, Ceylon appeared, and before long they had anchored at Madras. Martyn soon escaped from European company into an Indian village, but he did not enjoy the experience: 'Everything presented the appearance of wretchedness. I thought of my future labours among them with some despondency, yet I am willing, I trust, through grace, to pass my days among them, if by any means these poor people may be brought to God. The sight of men, women, and children, all idolaters, makes me shudder, as if in the dominions of the Prince of darkness. I fancy the frown of God to be visible.'

Sailing on up the coast, they passed the great Pagoda of Jagannath (Juggernaut), 'employed for the worship of the spirits of darkness. Poor India erected a monument of her shame by this huge building on the coast. Here is heathenism staring the stranger in the face on his arrival off the land. The scene presented another specimen of that tremendous gloom, with which the devil has overspread the land'. With such thoughts Martyn approached Calcutta, but with an ever-increasing confidence in the power of God: 'How easy for God to do it; and it shall be done in due time. And even if I never should see a native converted, God may design, by my patience and continuance in the work, to encourage

[262]

future missionaries.' He did not know then how exactly he was summarizing the purpose of God for his brief work in India.

* * *

On May 16, 1806, he sailed up The Hooghly, the most westerly branch of the Ganges delta, to Calcutta, the city whose name was a byword for the indolent and oppressive lives of the wealthy Nabobs. The only type of European known to the Bengali people was the hard-headed clerk of the East India Company, who made his pile as quickly as he could, rose to the top in the Company, and, if he did not return to England to squander his fortune, settled down, surrounded by a vast retinue of servile natives, to a life of magnificently luxurious boredom, a man who had no religion, and little morality, but an imperious will and a lot of money, a man to whom the native was a mere chattel, to be used, but otherwise ignored.

In 1786, however, another type of Englishman had arrived, David Brown, a Yorkshire clergyman, sent out to take charge of an orphanage, but soon to become chaplain to the European community. Under the influence of this man, later joined by a fellow-chaplain, Claudius Buchanan, and aided by the Governor-General, Lord Wellesley, a change had begun, and church-going began to become fashionable. There, in the new Church of St. John, David Brown carried on a faithful ministry of the gospel to the British.

At the same time an Englishman had been sent by God to bring the gospel to the native people of Bengal. William Carey, the one-time cobbler and Baptist pastor, reached Calcutta in 1793, and was soon joined by others, notably Marshman and Ward. But the purpose of God to bring the gospel to the Indians was not the purpose of the East India Company: chaplains they could allow, but not missionaries. Carey was forced to become an indigo planter to remain in the country, and when later he gave himself fully to missionary work, he could only live in the minute Danish colony of Serampore, sixteen miles up the Hooghly from Calcutta. There, out of the jurisdiction of the British Governor-General, a great centre of missionary work and Bible translation grew up, the Serampore Community, which survived the attempts of Sir George Barlow, Governor-General 1805–07, and his successor Lord Minto, to crush out Christianity from all but the European community in North India. If Martyn had come as anything other than a chaplain, it is hard to see how he could have stayed in India, and, though he used it to provide plenty of scope for missionary work, he retained the post of chaplain as long as he stayed there. He had not liked the idea, but God knew best.

The chaplains were all congregated in and around Calcutta. There were many Europeans, both military and civil, at stations further up the Ganges, but they were spiritually neglected; to the Indians, of course, no thought had been given. For five months, much against his will, Martyn was kept in Calcutta. His one idea was to get among the Indians, and while there was scope for such work even in Calcutta, there were others there who could do it. But his fellow-chaplains disagreed: 'My dear brethren, Brown and Buchanan', he wrote on the day after his arrival, 'wish to keep me here, as I expected, and the Governor accedes to their wishes. I have a great many reasons for not liking this; I almost think that to be prevented going among the heathen as a missionary would break my heart.' Before long they sensed it too, and came to know the young chaplain well enough to know that it would be useless to try to keep him in Calcutta; negotiations were begun to appoint him to a station up country.

Meanwhile, as an East India Company chaplain, he was expected to preach to the Europeans in Calcutta, and he was never unwilling to preach God's Word. His first sermon in St. John's Church, before all the great men of Calcutta, 'excited no small ferment'. He was conscious, as usual, of the danger of preaching merely to please, but prayed that the sermon might be used to convert his hearers, and fearlessly preached on 'Christ crucified, a stumbling-block to Jews, and folly to Gentiles'. Calcutta society might have begun to go to church, but it had not abandoned its self-righteousness, and the opposition to the 'severe' and 'extravagant' views of the new chaplain was as strong as aboard ship. It was not long before another chaplain was openly denouncing him from the pulpit in his presence. The atmosphere of Calcutta society was stifling; he wanted to be away.

Between sermons and official visits, Martyn had his home at Aldeen, near Serampore, where David Brown and his family lived. During those five months, Martyn became a close friend of the family, and especially of the children. He was always fond of children, and it is quite a revelation to see the Cambridge don, often thought of as a morbid pessimist, delighting to play with them, and they in their turn, quick to recognize genuine love, 'jumping and shouting, and convoying me in troops to the house'.

He did not live in the Browns' house, but in what has ever since been known as 'Henry Martyn's Pagoda', an oddly-carved pile of crumbling masonry beside the wide-flowing Hooghly. It had not long since been the temple of a Hindu god, Radhabullub, but the sacred river had steadily encroached until the temple was within the prohibited range of one hundred yards from the bank; the 'little, ugly, black image' had had to find another home further from the river, and the temple was taken over by David Brown. Here Martyn lived and prayed. 'Thither I retired at night, and really felt something like superstitious dread, at being in a place once inhabited as it were by devils, but yet felt disposed to be triumphantly joyful, that the temple where they were worshipped was become Christ's oratory. I prayed out aloud to my God, and the echoes returned from the vaulted roof. Oh may I so pray, that the dome of heaven may resound. I like my dwelling much, it is so retired and free from noise.'

It was not always free from noise; the very next day the cymbals and drums from Radhabullub's new home invited Martyn to go and see the evening worship. There he found fifty people playing the instruments. 'At intervals they prostrated themselves, with their foreheads to the earth. I shivered at being in the neighbourhood of hell; my heart was ready to burst at the dreadful state to which the devil had brought my poor fellowcreatures. I would have given the world to have known the language, to have preached to them.'

Another day he ran out of the pagoda to a near-by funeral fire, only to find that he was too late to save the widow of the dead man, who had already thrown herself in the flames.

His indignation was roused by the vast Jagannath procession: 'Before the stumps of images, for they were no better, some of the people prostrated themselves, striking the ground twice with their foreheads; this excited more horror in me than I can well express, and I was about to stammer out in Hindustani "Why do ye these things?" and to preach the Gospel. The words were on my lips; though if I had spoken thousands would have crowded round me, and I should not have been understood. However, I felt my spirit more inflamed with zeal than I ever conceived it would be; and I thought that if I had words I would preach to the multitudes all the day, if I lost my life for it.'

There was no holding a man so possessed with a desire to reach the heathen, and soon his appointment was made to Dinapore, the European military settlement adjoining Patna, the second greatest city of Bengal, some three hundred and fifty miles from Calcutta up the Ganges.

Meanwhile he was enjoying long and frequent discussions on questions of missionary policy with the men of Serampore, and especially with Joshua Marshman, with whom he struck up a deep friendship. Chaplain as he was, he felt his affinity to be not so much with his official colleagues, but with these men, whose aim, like his, was to reach the Indians, and who had already had some success. Serampore already had its group of Indian Christians, and Martyn heard them preach: 'To see a native Indian an earnest advocate of Jesus, how precious! An Indian sermon about Jesus Christ was like music on my ear, and I felt inflamed to begin my work.' It was a sound he was not to be privileged to hear again.

*   *   *

At the same time, his mind was engrossed in another subject. The more he saw of the loneliness and yet comparative comfort of the life to which he had come, the more he felt disposed to agree to his friends' advice that he would be better married. On her side Lydia, despite her reticence at the time of his sailing, had not been able to contain herself, and had (as a cousin and a Christian friend, she no doubt told herself) started writing to him. These letters now began to reach him, and the conclusion was inevitable. Much as he still wrote about his complete happiness as he was, and the danger of 'idolatrous affection', he had soon made up his mind, and at the end of July wrote a long letter to her asking her to come out and marry him; at the same time he wrote to Simeon, and asked him to use his influence to the same end. And he does not seem seriously to have doubted that she would agree. He had underestimated her mother's opposition, and Lydia's submission to it. But there was no air mail in those days, and Martyn was able to live in false hopes for over a year. Lydia received his letter the next March, and her refusal reached him in October, 1807; further letters confirmed the decision, and by January, 1808, he was, for the time, resigned to it.

But for the moment he could still hope, and so in October, 1806, he set out for Dinapore, fully expecting to have a wife there within a year. A group of missionaries gathered in the pagoda to pray for God's blessing on his new sphere of work, and for the whole future of India. 'My soul never yet had such divine enjoyment. I felt a desire to break from the body, and join the high praises of the saints above. May I go "in the strength of this many days"!' In prayer the next day, 'I found my heaven begun upon earth. No work so sweet as that of praying, and living wholly to the service of God.'

* * *

The journey to Patna was a new experience. It was by river, in a 'budgerow', a type of houseboat towed up the river among the innumerable villages of Bengal. For six weeks Martyn found himself, as he had always wanted to be, among Indians, and Indians only. Much of the time was spent travelling, when he would study Hindustani, Persian, and Bengali, discuss Bible translations with his Hindu and Muslim language helpers, and hold long disputes with them. When they came to the shore, he would explore the neighbourhood with great delight, reporting strange birds and animals in his diary, but especially eager to contact the people, who often fled in panic at the sight of a European face. He distributed hundreds of tracts on all possible occasions, and in Hindustani and stammering Bengali he tried to tell the good news of Jesus Christ. To a fanatical Brahmin priest of the god Cali, he declared the falsehood of idolatry, and felt satisfaction 'that I could make known the truth of God, though but a stammerer; and that I had declared it in the presence of the devil'. Always, everywhere, he was the servant of Christ, and when he was not engaged actively in preaching the gospel, he was as busily occupied in preparing himself for the task, by prayer and by study; even on what could have been a delightful six weeks' holiday, we can recognize 'the man who never lost an hour'.

So he came to Dinapore, prepared for hardship, but confident in his God, ready to fulfil the wish with which he had landed in Calcutta: 'I have hitherto lived to little purpose, more like a clod than a servant of God; now let me burn out for God.'

IV. The Heat of the Day

At Patna all was pagan: the Indians were pagan, the Europeans were pagan. Once again Henry Martyn, God's messenger to the half million inhabitants of the fifth city of India, was alone, desperately alone, and it daunted him. 'Reached Patna this afternoon. Walked about this scene of my future ministry with a spirit almost overwhelmed at the sight of the immense multitudes.' The arrival at Dinapore was no more encouraging: its two regiments and numerous camp-followers seemed to be against him to a man. 'I have now made my calls and delivered my letters, and the result of my observations upon whom and what I have seen is that I stand alone.' Near by, at Bankipore, the European civilian community soon made it plain that it had little use for his ministry; he found that the judge there had married a Muslim woman, built himself a mosque, and openly renounced Christianity; nor was this an isolated case.

It was to the Europeans that Martyn's responsibility was officially restricted, and it was to them that he gave much of his time, despite his longing to be among the Indians, preaching to them in their own language. He soon acquired a bungalow near the barracks, and one room of this became the church of Dinapore. Here he held his official Sunday services, to which the troops paraded, an experience as unfamiliar to them as it was to him. They were a rough body, containing, as he soon discovered, a large number of Roman Catholics, but very few with even a nominal profession of Protestant Christianity.

As on the ship, he found the majority of both officers and troops scornful of his message, but, as on the ship, there were a few exceptions. He had the joy of watching Major Young and his wife blossom out into a genuine and joyful Christian experience, despite much sneering opposition. And among the lower ranks he had a few secret disciples: twice a week a small group of 'serious' soldiers would make their way to his house, taking elaborate precautions to conceal their destination, and there they would sing and pray, and learn from the chaplain, who always found time for this handful of sincere though ignorant seekers for the truth. At first six was a good number, but the presence of a man like Martyn inevitably has its effect, and by the time he left Dinapore, two and a half years later, there were thirty of them. Among them were some whose conversion could neither be denied nor concealed, and who excited considerable interest among the troops.

To the rest of the troops Martyn was an enigmatic figure, at first resented, but gradually more appreciated, especially in the hospital, where he found his main field for work among Europeans. More and more he spent his time there, and in that climate it was always well filled: 'Found fifty sick at the hospital, who heard *The Pilgrim's Progress* with great delight.' Such entries reveal a ministry which was not so unfruitful as his more pessimistic reflections might suggest.

Attached to any East India Company barracks was a large following of women, mostly Indian, whose marriage with the troops was forbidden, but whose attachments were often deep and permanent. Martyn soon decided that it was his duty to minister to these as well, and started a weekly service for them. He had translated into Hindustani much of the Church of England Prayer Book, and this he used. The women listened with reasonable attention, and continued to come, though in decreasing numbers, but he never found any real spiritual response among them, and though one applied to be baptized, he felt bound to refuse, as he saw in her no evidence of true conversion. But, discouraging as it was, he kept at this work; many would say it was not a strategic priority, and that these women, even if converted, would be of little significance in the cause of Christ. And Martyn would have agreed: 'The conversion of any of such despised people is never likely perhaps to be of any extensive use in regard to the natives at large; but they are a people committed to me by God, and as dear to Him as others.' And so he persevered.

*　　*　　*

But it was to the Indian population at large that Martyn longed to bring Christ. He saw them thronging the streets and markets of Patna, he saw them prostrate before wood and stones, and he could not rest. 'How awful the thought, that while perishing millions demand my every thought and care, my mind should be distracted about such an extreme trifle as that of my own comfort' – even when the trifle in view was Lydia!

But everything stood in his way. The Europeans opposed any such idea. Some thought it simply crazy; others saw it as pernicious: a converted Indian would be harder to keep under. 'They seem to hate to see me associating at all with the natives, and one gave me a hint a few days ago about taking my exercise on foot. But if our Lord had always travelled about in His palanquin, the poor woman who was healed by touching the hem of His garment might have perished.' They were sceptical of his ever making much progress, and in this they were right. But success was not Martyn's criterion: 'If we labour to the end of our days without seeing one convert, it shall not be worse for us in time, and our reward is the same in eternity.'

More serious was the hostility of the Indians themselves. Whatever his profession, and however great his love, Martyn was an Englishman, and no one could expect the Indian to love his oppressors or their religion. 'Here every native I meet is an enemy to me because I am an Englishman. England appears almost a heaven upon earth, because there one is not viewed as an unjust intruder.' It was this, as well as his still imperfect command of Hindustani as a spoken language, which caused him to refrain from open preaching. 'The thought of interrupting a crowd of busy people like those at Patna, whose every day is a market day, with a message about eternity, without command of language sufficient to explain and defend myself, and so of becoming the scorn of the rabble without doing them good, was offensive to my pride. The manifest disaffection of the people, and the contempt with which they eyed me, confirmed my dread.' Here speaks the man who always shrank from introducing the subject of religion with those who were not willing to listen; but surely also the voice of reason. It might have been dramatic to gather a hostile crowd, but not profitable. The great Patna massacre of 1763 was too recent to be forgotten.

Instead Martyn began schools for Indian children, staffed by Indians, but supplied by him with Hindustani translations of the Parables and the Sermon on the Mount, as well as the more traditional studies. These institutions survived much suspicion and trouble, but that, it seems, was as far as Martyn's direct work among Indians extended during his time at Dinapore. We can not know whether he would ever have begun the street-preaching which he both longed and dreaded to do, if he had been able to stay there longer.

But in his own household Martyn had two Indians with whom his discussions of religious matters were endless, one a Hindu, the other a Muslim, both brought from Calcutta as language teachers. His diary constantly returned to these two men. Often the work of translation would be laid aside, and the missionary would find himself defending and pressing home the truth of what was being translated. The Hindu was alternately scornful and apathetic, the Muslim uniformly scornful of what he considered to be a credulity no better than that of the Hindus.

Martyn's patience was often nearly exhausted by their intolerant rejection of his arguments, often based on the most patently absurd reasoning. It was valuable training, and he learned now lessons which proved their value when he was later engaged in constant discussions with Muslims. 'Above all things, seriousness in argument with them seems most desirable, for without it they laugh away the clearest proofs. Zeal for making proselytes they are used to, and generally attribute to a false motive; but a tender concern manifested for their souls is certainly new to them, and seemingly produces corresponding seriousness in their minds.' But even this was not enough: 'I wish a spirit of enquiry may be excited, but I lay not much stress upon clear arguments; the work of God is seldom wrought in this way. To preach the gospel, with the Holy Ghost sent down from heaven, is a better way to win souls.' Good principles, these, for any evangelist, and ones which later won an unprecedented respect for their author among the learned Muslims of Persia. These and other talks, especially with Muslims, helped to develop in Martyn that knowledge of Islam and sensitiveness to the Muslim mind which alone could enable him to fulfil his future work.

So in a climate where often his utmost efforts would not bring the thermometer much below 100°, with his hereditary tuberculosis beginning to tell more and more, and once at least bringing him within a hair's breadth of death, surrounded by suspicion, hostility, or apathy, with remarkably little visible success to encourage him, Martyn struggled on, and in the thick of it confided to his diary an unconquerable delight and trust in his God, and a genuine satisfaction with whatever God saw fit to appoint. Of himself he seems to grow constantly more critical, but at the same time he grows more confident in the One whose service is his supreme joy.

*   *   *

In April, 1809, God saw fit to move His servant. The move would never have come on his own initiative; he was too devoted to his ministry in Dinapore and Patna. But the military authorities, for reasons best known to themselves, decided to transfer the chaplain to Cawnpore, the modern Kanpur, another three hundred miles up the Ganges, with, if possible, a hotter, drier, and dustier climate than Dinapore. And the move came in the hottest season of the Indian year, when shade from the sun is little help against the burning winds that sweep across the plain. Martyn was never strong, and that journey nearly cost him his life. 'I transported myself with such rapidity to this place', he wrote to David Brown, 'that I had nearly transported myself out of the world . . . I was obliged to travel two days and nights without intermission, the hot winds blowing like fire from a furnace. Two days after my arrival, the fever which had been kindling in my blood broke out, and last night I fainted repeatedly'.

Happily for him, he found now, and throughout his eighteen months in Cawnpore, a Christian home constantly open to him. After his long exile from Christian fellowship, Mr. and Mrs. Sherwood of the King's 53rd Regiment of Foot were welcome friends, and they and Martyn lived almost as one family. It was they who nursed him back to at least a measure of health after that terrible journey, and who provided the sheet-anchor for his Cawnpore ministry; and it was Mrs. Sherwood's vivid auto-biography which gave to the world the most lifelike portrait of 'that simple-hearted and holy young man'.

She never forgot their first meeting at Dinapore. This is her description of the chaplain: 'His features were not regular, but the expression was so luminous, so intellectual, so affectionate, so beaming with divine charity, that no one could have looked at his features and thought of their shape and form; the outbeaming of his soul would absorb the attention of every observer . . . The conversion of the natives, and the building up of the Kingdom of Christ, were the great objects for which alone that child of God seemed to exist . . . Henry Martyn was one of the very few persons whom I ever met who appeared never to be drawn away from one leading and prevailing object of interest, and that object was the promotion of religion. He is one of the most pleasing, mild, and heavenly-minded men, walking in this turbulent world with peace in his mind and charity in his heart.'

After a short convalescence with the Sherwoods, Martyn acquired his own bungalow, and there carried on a ministry similar to that at Dinapore, preaching to the soldiers in an atmosphere where several men fainted, meeting a small group of 'serious' soldiers in his house, trying to make contact with the Indians. Here, as at Dinapore, he found no church building, and here again he agitated for one, with more success: the temporary structure was completed just as he had to leave Cawnpore; its dedication service was his farewell, a typical experience of the man who seemed to be called by God always to labour so that others could enter into his labours, but seldom to see any of the harvest himself.

A new form of service opened up here. India has always had more than its fair share of beggars and 'holy men', whose living, whether by misfortune or by profession, depends on the charity of others. To such men the kind-hearted chaplain soon became known, and his house became a regular rendezvous. He let it be known that once a week, on Sundays, he would distribute food and money, and they came by hundreds, 'young and old, male and female, bloated and wizened, tall and short, athletic and feeble; some clothed with abominable rags; some nearly without clothes; some plastered with mud and cow-dung; others with matted, uncombed locks streaming down to their heels; others with heads bald or scabby; every countenance being hard and fixed, as it were, by the continual indulgence of bad passions, the features having become exaggerated, and the lips blackened with tobacco, or blood-red with the juice of the henna.'

It was Sabat, Martyn's Arab assistant, who challenged him to preach to them. Martyn recoiled, but could think of no reason to refuse except shame and fear, and these he could not recognize. So 'I determined to preach to them, though I felt as if I were leading to execution'. And regularly, for most of his time in Cawnpore, except when his illness made it physically impossible, he tried every Sunday to bring the gospel of the true God to this motley crowd.

Their reactions were varied, but always lively and uninhibited. He spoke of God as Creator of all things, and every sentence was punctuated by loud applause. He spoke of the folly of worshipping the sun and moon, mere created things, and the Muslims applauded, while the Hindus groaned and hissed. Week by week their numbers increased, and their attention became closer, and when he spoke of the destruction of Sodom, and the need for men to repent and turn to God, the impression was deep and obvious.

But from this, as from so much of his work, Martyn saw no lasting results. He feared the whole enterprise had been useless, but in this he was wrong. As he preached to his beggars one day, a group of young Muslims came to see what was happening, stood in a row in front of the preacher, and made their disdain for such heretical nonsense quite clear. But one of the group was impressed: Sheikh Saleh, a zealous and influential Muslim, keeper of the jewels of the King of Oudh, was struck by a gospel which could be preached to such people, and lost no time in finding out more. He got a job among Martyn's translating staff, and when he was entrusted with the Persian New Testament to take to the binder, he first read it through from Matthew to Revelation. The Word of God fell on prepared ground, and Sheikh Saleh became a Christian. Later baptized as Abdul Masih, 'Slave of Christ', he proved a great force for his new Master in India.

But of all this Martyn as yet knew nothing. 'Without the work of translation', he wrote to David Brown, 'I should fear my presence in India were useless.' This is, of course, an overstatement, but there is no doubt that by far the major part of Martyn's contribution to the work of God in India, and indeed throughout the Middle East, was his translation work. It was this which, at Dinapore and at Cawnpore, occupied most of his time, and it is for this that he must be remembered. The one-time mathematician and classical scholar emerges ever more clearly as a natural linguist, a man prepared by God to make the definitive translations of the New Testament into two languages, and to do much valuable work in several others, and all by the age of thirty-one.

* * *

Even without encouragement from others, Martyn could not

keep himself away from translation and philological research. He reached Dinapore with Hindustani translations of much of the Prayer Book and of the Parables, with a brief commentary, all but completed. At the time he was working principally on Hindustani and Sanscrit, but his attention was diverted to other fields by his friends.

Claudius Buchanan, the chaplain in Calcutta, was the moving spirit behind a new burst of translation work. 'The Associated Clergy', a sort of postal link between the chaplains in India, was the medium he used, and through its members he and David Brown planned a series of Bible translations into the major languages of the East. In June, 1807, David Brown wrote to Martyn, assigning to him the translation of the New Testament into Hindustani (as Urdu was then called) and the supervision of translations into Persian and Arabic, to be done by two experts, Mirzu Fitrut and Nathaniel Sabat, under his direction.

The Sanscrit grammar was laid aside, and Persian and Arabic took its place, together with a more intensive study of Hebrew, which he felt to be an essential background. Indeed, from now until the end of his life, Hebrew more and more enthralled him. In those days it was fashionable to see in Sanscrit the root of the Asian and European languages, but Martyn began to believe that Hebrew was the more basic. The more he worked on it, the more he became convinced of his theory. His friends were regaled in conversation and in letters with details of Hebrew grammar, which fascinated him so much that he could not imagine anyone would find them boring.

Philology so gripped him that often he could not sleep for following up some connection between Hebrew and Persian word-forms: 'I made some discovery respecting the Hebrew verb, but was unfortunately so much delighted that I could not sleep, in consequence of which I have had a head-ache ever since.' 'One night I did not sleep a wink. Knowing what would be the consequences the next day, I struggled hard, and turned every way, that my mind might be diverted from what was before it, but all in vain. One discovery succeeded another, in Hebrew, Arabic, and Greek, so rapidly that I was sometimes almost in an ecstasy.' He saw this preoccupation as the mark of an unspiritual mind, and prayed to be delivered from it. 'Truly love is better than knowledge. Much as I long to know what I seek after, I would rather have the smallest portion of humility and love than the knowledge of an archangel.' His love of languages was absorbing, but much more absorbing was his love of God, and God saw to it that the balance was preserved.

But more delightful even than philology in the abstract was the work of translation, when the subject of the translation was nothing less than the Word of God. 'What do I not owe to the Lord, for permitting me to take part in a translation of His Word? Never did I see such wonder and wisdom and love in the blessed book, as since I have been obliged to study every expression; and it is a delightful reflection that death can not deprive us of the pleasure of studying its mysteries.' No wonder a man with such a perception of the value of the Bible was willing to go to all lengths to produce the best possible translation, and never tired of the work! 'What a source of perpetual delight have I in the precious book of God!'

Indeed Martyn was a perfectionist in his translations. He would not begin until he had a real grasp of Hindustani, both as a living language, and also as a potential literary language. His Hindustani translation was indeed an excellent work of literature, but it was also unanimously pronounced to be idiomatic and simple enough to appeal to the least educated Indian. The first draft of the translation was followed by a minute process of revision and correction, and no sentence was allowed to pass until he was quite sure it could not be improved. He refused to hurry, even when a single chapter took two hard days' work to revise. And so effectively was it done that fifty years later it was said of Martyn's Hindustani New Testament that 'all subsequent translations have, as a matter of course, proceeded upon it as a work of excellent skill and learning, and rigid fidelity.'

The Hindustani was mainly Martyn's own work. But for the Persian and Arabic he had his experts, Mirza Fitrut and Sabat.

Mirza Fitrut was a Muslim, and Martyn had long talks with him on Islam and Christianity. After one such he recorded, 'He is, poor man, totally indifferent about all religion; he told me that I had produced great doubt in his mind, and that he had no answer to give.' Again, 'When I said that, notwithstanding his and Sabat's endeavours to identify the two religions, there is still so much difference "that if our word is true you are lost", they looked at each other almost with consternation, and said "It is true".' Mirza presents throughout a pathetic picture of doubt and uncertainty, and Martyn's efforts to win him for Christ were endless, but when they finally parted, Mirza was still in his agnostic state.

Sabat was very different. A proud and fanatical Muslim, he had once been responsible for the violent death of a friend who had become a Christian. Overcome with remorse, and haunted by the peaceful look of the martyr, Sabat started to read the New Testament; its truth entered his heart 'like a flood of light' and in Madras he sought and received Christian baptism, taking the name of Nathaniel. He was now an ardent, but very ignorant, advocate of Christianity, bringing into his Christian profession all the pride and fanaticism of his Muslim past. After working with Martyn, however, he took offence at criticisms of his translations, and published a violent attack on Christianity, declaring himself a Muslim again. Later he again professed himself a Christian, and died in a rebellion in Sumatra, proclaiming that he was a martyr for the faith.

Martyn never doubted the sincerity of Sabat's faith, though his character showed little sign of a new birth. For over three years Martyn's patience was tried by this extraordinary 'artless child of the desert'. The slightest insult, real or imagined, was enough to make him stop work and demand the dismissal of the offender. His rages were usually brief, but furious. As an Arab, he held both Indians and Europeans in supreme contempt, and offered to instruct the Senior Wrangler in the art of logic, in which he felt he was woefully deficient. In discussion he was pedantic, dogmatic, and at the same time amazingly childish. In personal relationships he was arrogant, quick to quarrel and take offence. Often Martyn was exasperated: 'Think of the keeper of a lunatic, and you see me.' But it is a striking testimony to his humility that he still loved Sabat as a Christian brother, and was so gentle with him that even the proud Arab said at last, 'He was less a man than an angel from heaven.'

Needless to say, Sabat was superbly confident in his ability as a translator. A pure Arab by birth, and having lived some years in Persia, he had seemed to the Calcutta chaplains to be the ideal man, and he himself shared their opinion. 'Another of his odd opinions is that he is so under the immediate influence and direction of the Spirit, that there will not be one single error in his whole Persian translation. You perceive a little enthusiasm in the character of our brother!' He was 'prodigiously proud' of the Persian translation, which was largely his work, and Martyn at first accepted his opinion of it. So the Persian New Testament was finished, and the Arabic was nearing completion.

*   *   *

But as the Persian and Arabic translations reached Calcutta, criticisms began to be made; Sabat's Arabic grammar was loose, and his Persian too stilted and full of Arabic words to appeal to a native Persian. Sabat, of course, was furious, but Martyn would never accept a second-best. He gradually became convinced that truly idiomatic translations could not be made except in Arabia and Persia, just as his own Hindustani translation had been done so perfectly in India. The idea of going to these countries gripped his mind. By now he was convinced that the chief purpose of God for his life lay in translation work, and the possibilities of the Arabic New Testament especially thrilled him: 'We will begin to preach to Arabia, Syria, Persia, India, Tartary, China, half of Africa, and all the south coast of the Mediterranean and Turkey, and one tongue shall suffice for them all.' The prospect was so exciting that he could even bring himself to consider leaving India, at least for a time.

There was another reason too. At Dinapore his health had deteriorated, and at Cawnpore the situation was becoming serious. A more leisurely man might have survived even there, but Martyn could not be leisurely. It was the preaching that exhausted him, four times every Sunday. Translation work was less exacting, but to raise his voice was agony. 'Study never makes me ill, scarcely ever fatigues me. But my lungs! Death is seated there; it is speaking that kills me. May it give others life!' So he wrote to Lydia in April, 1810. By this time his friends were really alarmed. Martyn himself had for some time been recording in his diary his expectation of an early death, and it now appeared very likely to be fulfilled. Every sermon left him with a burning pain in his chest, and even a heated discussion would lead to a collapse, when he could hardly speak above a whisper. During this spring the news reached him that his sister Sally had just died of the same illness, as had his elder sister earlier. Clearly he was going the same way, and sinking fast. They told him the only hope was to go to sea, but he would not hear of it.

But then came the idea of a visit to Arabia, and the two reasons together weighed more with him. He wrote to David Brown, who replied, 'But can I then bring myself to cut the string and let you go? I confess I could not, if your bodily frame were strong, and promised to last for half a century. But as you burn with the intenseness and rapid blaze of heated phosphorus, why should we not make the most of you? Your flame may last as long, and perhaps longer, in Arabia than in India.'

'Now let me burn out for God' he had wished; – 'The intenseness and rapid blaze of heated phosphorus' was the verdict.

Brown's agreement settled it, and in October, 1810, Martyn left Cawnpore, taking with him Sabat's completed Persian New Testament, and the almost completed Arabic. Arabia was his destination, and then, if the flame still burned, Persia.

*   *   *

The return after four years to the Christian fellowship of Calcutta was a delight to Martyn. He did not know it, but this was the last time he was to find himself among Christians of like mind. To them it was a mixed pleasure: they knew he was ill, but were not prepared to see him so 'much altered, thin, and sallow'.

Thomason, formerly Simeon's curate, and now following in

Martyn's steps, had just reached Calcutta. 'This bright and lovely jewel first gratified our eyes on Saturday last', he wrote of Martyn. 'He is on his way to Arabia, where he is going in pursuit of health and knowledge ... He has some great plan in mind, of which I am no competent judge, but as far as I do understand it, the object is far too grand for one short life, and much beyond his feeble and exhausted frame. Feeble it is indeed! How fallen and changed! His complaint lies in his lungs ... In all other respects he is exactly the same as he was; he shines in all the dignity of love, and seems to carry about him such a heavenly majesty as impresses the mind beyond description. But if he talks much, though in a low voice, he sinks, and you are reminded of his being "dust and ashes".'

Further consultations with the experts now led Martyn to the conclusion that the most urgent task was the revision, or even complete retranslation, of the Persian New Testament, which in Sabat's version was universally condemned. Arabia must wait, and Persia must be the first objective. After that he might hope to move west to Baghdad, or Damascus, and eventually into the heart of Arabia.

They found a ship bound for Bombay, and on January 7, 1811, embarking suddenly to avoid painful farewells, Henry Martyn left India, where he had fully intended to spend his whole life. He never returned.

V. Alone Against Islam

The Middle East, that great area stretching from Afghanistan to the Dardanelles, and from the Caucasus to the Arabian peninsula, was then, even more than it is today, the unchallenged stronghold of Islam. Since the great Muslim conquests of the seventh century, through almost the whole of that area the name of Christ was known only as one of a series of prophets far inferior to

Muhammad; the prophet of Mecca ruled supreme. Into this vast mission field Martyn was now entering, a solitary and dying man.

We can not now dwell on the details of the five months spent in reaching Persia, the inevitable sea-sickness, now combined with a more serious illness, the walks in the cinnamon groves of Ceylon, the talks with Portuguese Roman Catholics in Goa, the hospitality, conversations and discussions with the learned in Bombay, the brief visit to the 'burning, barren rocks' of Arabia when they landed at Muscat, and the slow, hot voyage up the Persian Gulf. Martyn's lively interest has left us many vivid pictures of these days, and of the strange assortment of people who always seem to have clustered round this man of God, from the African slave and the Parsee poet, to the 'high society' of the 'gate of India'. But what is even more interesting than Martyn's impressions of his acquaintances, is the impression which he made on them. We are fortunate in having from this voyage the views of three impartial observers, men of no great religious pretensions, but experienced and critical assessors of a man's character.

Mountstuart Elphinstone, on his way to be British Resident in Bombay, after a term as ambassador in Cabul, was Martyn's fellow-passenger from Calcutta to Bombay. His lively mind and classical learning made him a congenial companion, and he in turn wrote of Martyn, 'We have in Mr. Martyn an excellent scholar, and one of the mildest, cheerfullest, and pleasantest men I ever saw. He is extremely religious, and disputes about the faith with the Nakhoda, but talks on all subjects, sacred and profane, and makes others laugh as heartily as he could do if he were an infidel . . . A far better companion than I reckoned on, though my expectations were high. His zeal is unabated, but it is not troublesome, and he does not press disputes and investigate creeds. A man of good sense and taste, and simple in his manners and character, and cheerful in conversation.'

Such comments from a man of the world come as something of a revelation to the reader of Martyn's diary. The man was human after all; he had a sense of humour; he was good company, not for ever brooding over his spiritual failures, or at least not openly.

The impression is confirmed by two men to whom Elphinstone

introduced him in Bombay. Sir James Mackintosh, Recorder of Bombay, a man often cynical, and never imposed on by hypocrisy, found he rather liked Martyn. 'A mild and benevolent enthusiast', he called him, and was not so much upset as might be expected by 'the novelty of grace before and after dinner, all the company standing'. Later he was more critical: 'His meekness is excessive, and gives a disagreeable impression of effort to conceal the passions of human nature.' But further contact brought him to enjoy the company of this 'mild and ingenious man'.

Sir John Malcolm, a diplomat just returned from an embassy in Persia, wrote a letter of commendation for Martyn to Sir Gore Ouseley, the ambassador in Persia. 'Mr. Martyn expects to improve himself as an oriental scholar; he is already an excellent one. His knowledge of Arabic is superior to that of any Englishman in India. He is altogether a very learned and cheerful man, but a great enthusiast in his holy calling ... I am satisfied that if you ever see him, you will be pleased with him. He will give you grace before and after dinner, and admonish such of your party as take the Lord's name in vain; but his good sense and great learning will delight you, whilst his constant cheerfulness will add to the hilarity of your party.'

Learned, enthusiastic, and firm for the faith, yet mild, sensible, cheerful, and good company: that was how Martyn appeared to unbiased minds on what proved to be almost his last contact with Europeans. Once away from Bombay, he had little further use for his native language.

* * *

He reached Bushire, on the East side of the Persian Gulf, in May, 1811, at the hottest season in that hot, barren area. This was no place for a sick man to stay, prostrated by headaches and sunstroke, but for a week Martyn lived in Bushire, turning himself into a Persian. 'The Persian dress consists of stockings and shoes in one, next a pair of large blue trousers, or else a pair of huge red boots; then the shirt, then the tunic, and above it the coat, both of chintz, and a greatcoat. On the head is worn an enormous cone, made of the skin of the black Tartar sheep, with the wool on. If to this description of my dress I add that my beard and mustachios have been suffered to vegetate undisturbed ever since I left India, that I am sitting on a Persian carpet, in a room without tables or chairs, that I bury my hand in the pilaw, without waiting for spoon or plate, you will give me credit for being already an accomplished Oriental!'

Under this strange disguise the once precise black-gowned scholar left Bushire on a pony among a caravan of thirty horses and mules. They travelled by night. The reason for this soon became obvious, as the first day, when they had hoped to sleep, the thermometer in the tent gradually rose to 126°, which made sleep impossible, and fever almost inevitable. For three days they had to bear this heat, but Martyn found that a large wet towel wrapped round his body under his clothes would at least keep him alive. But fever, and the fear of scorpions, ruined what little hope he had of sleep, until, on the fourth night, more dead than alive, they reached the foot of the mountain plateau. They passed a foul-smelling river of oil welling out of the foot of the mountains, and began to climb up a narrow track among precipitous rocks, where their only safeguard was the surefootedness and experience of the mules.

At last they emerged on to a large plain, where the heat was little short of that on the coastal strip, but another such ascent brought them up to a plateau where the cold was so piercing that all the clothes they could muster still left them shivering. On they climbed among scenery which would have delighted Martyn if he had been in a fit state to appreciate it, over several more ranges of mountains, menaced by mosquitoes, precipices, and robbers. Sometimes Martyn had to demand a rest, as he was too ill to go on. His fever would not let him sleep, and so he found himself constantly sleepy in the saddle, and in danger of falling off, a danger which was only increased by the numbness due to cold.

For ten days the nightmare journey lasted, until at last Martyn found himself, 'gasping for life under the double pressure of an inward fire and an outward burning sun', outside the walls of the city where his name was long to be remembered, a white city surrounded by luscious gardens, and dominating its own fertile valley, Shiraz, renowned as the home of Muslim scholars and poets.

Here he had an introduction from Sir John Malcolm to an influential citizen, Jaffir Ali Khan, who immediately welcomed him with rich hospitality, and was his host for the whole of his stay in Shiraz. Jaffir Ali Khan had a brother-in-law, Mirza Said Ali, who was said to speak the purest form of Persian. As soon as he heard of Martyn's plan to produce a completely accurate Persian New Testament, Said Ali offered his help, and Jaffir Ali Khan pressed Martyn to accept his hospitality.

He had not intended to stay long in Shiraz, and wanted to press on into Arabia, but such an offer was too good to miss. Sometimes he would question the wisdom of such delay, 'but placing myself twenty years on in time, I say "Why could not I stay in Shiraz long enough to get a New Testament done there, even if I had been detained there on that account three or six years? What work of equal importance can ever come from me?".' He was right, for the Persian and Hindustani New Testaments are the most solid and abiding results of Martyn's work. He himself could conclude as he left Shiraz, 'No year of my life was ever spent more usefully.'

From June to February they worked together, sometimes in Jaffir Ali Khan's house, sometimes in a garden outside the walls where waterfalls splashed, and roses bloomed, and nightingales filled the air with their song. This was the work in which Martyn was most happy, and Said Ali proved an efficient and interested colleague. So in eight and a half months the whole Persian New Testament was finished, and a version of the Psalms well under way. Nor was this a rough, unpolished work. It was simple enough for any peasant to follow, and elegant enough to earn the praise of the Shah himself, and above all it was accurate and true to the original text, for this was Martyn's supreme concern. We shall follow the fortunes of this translation later; but the year in Shiraz was not all spent in translating.

*   *   *

Shiraz was a centre of Muslim learning. The Shia sect of Islam, which is still dominant in Persia, was there at its strongest. And it was at this time largely unchallenged by any Christian witness. Martyn's passionate concern to bring the gospel of Christ to the Muslim world was as yet shared by a pathetic few in the Christian church; even today the challenge of Islam is not being squarely faced: then it was virgin soil.

The arrival of the foreign scholar in the city was inevitably the cause of comment. Some said he had come to learn from the mullahs, and to become a Muslim. Others thought it was a trick, and he would come back with an army to take the city. The boys threw stones at him as he rode around, and his outspoken defence of the gospel drew from the Prince's nephew the remark that the proper answer was the sword.

But the general reaction was one of curiosity, and of frantic defence of the religion of the Quran as the Christian's arguments and attacks on Islam began to be rumoured around the city. They came to see him one after another, and often a whole day's translation work would be lost as he argued and reasoned with the learned and the fanatical. Jaffir Ali Khan's house became the centre of a discussion which began to alarm the highest authorities, and before long Mirza Ibrahim, 'the Preceptor of all the Mullahs', prepared and published a defence of Islam, intended 'to silence me for ever'. It consisted of arguments, mostly familiar, from the miracles of Muhammad, especially the miracle of the incomparable splendour of the Quran. Mirza Ibrahim moreover declared publicly that 'if I really confuted his arguments, he should be bound in conscience to become a Christian'.

Martyn had little hope of such honesty, but he drafted a reply in three tracts in which he dealt with the whole question of miracles, pointed out the less commendable sides of the life of Muhammad, and contrasted the Quran's ineffective way of salvation with the atonement wrought by Christ. Privately Ibrahim confessed the force of the arguments; publicly he stood his ground. How truly Martyn had written as he prepared his reply, 'How powerless are the best directed arguments till the Holy Ghost renders them effectual!'

Even less encouraging was his interview with the highest doctrinal authority of Shiraz, the Mujtahid. The account is pathetic: it shows a proud, self-important man trying by bluff and high-sounding words to impress the audience, and Martyn too good-mannered to bring him to close quarters. Again and again the same story recurs: Martyn's clear arguments and declarations from Scripture are met by long, involved, metaphysical dissertations, very likely as meaningless to their authors as to the reader, but impressive to what was hardly an unbiased audience. Islam, which could not commend itself in plain words to mind or conscience, held itself disdainfully aloof from this solitary attacker.

But not all the men of Shiraz were satisfied with the empty sophistry of the Shia sages. Ibrahim himself never appeared in the mosque, and though others attributed this to his extraordinary piety which made public worship unnecessary, Martyn had other ideas. And if, among the orthodox Shia, Islam was losing its grip, there were many who had openly renounced it, including the son of the Mujtahid himself. Many such 'heretics' crowded to another house, where Mirza Abul Casim, a little old man with a silver beard, led his disciples in silent meditation.

These were the Sufi mystics, still a strong force in Persia. Their doctrine is that of mystics everywhere, that all is one – God and man, heaven and hell, pleasure and pain, all are one, and man's search is to find mystic absorption into the consciousness of this oneness. Martyn's colleague, Said Ali, formerly a Shia Muslim, was now attached to the Sufi group, and introduced Martyn to the master, Abul Casim. Discussion was useless, however, and clearly distasteful to the old man, and Martyn's visit ended in the inevitable silence of meditation. Some time later Martyn saw the true character of this religion, when he was surprised by a secret visit from Abul Casim himself, now no longer the admired sage, but a pathetic old man, breaking the fast by begging for a little wine, after which he refused discussion, and curled up to sleep on Martyn's floor, only to be awakened by a visit from some of his pupils, whereupon he resumed his stately poise.

Among such futile attempts of men to work out their own salvation, Martyn more and more saw the glory of the gospel of Christ, and tried by all means to bring it to those around him. Many of them were willing to argue, some too willing, but they were perplexed, and a little annoyed, when he inevitably brought the discussion down to the words of Scripture, and it was here that the arguments usually ended.

It was the divinity of Christ which particularly divided them. 'It is this doctrine which exposes me to the contempt of the learned Mahometans, in whom it is difficult to say whether pride or ignorance predominates. Their sneers are more difficult to bear than the brickbats which the boys sometimes throw at me; however, both are an honour of which I am not worthy. The more they wish me to give up one point, the divinity of Christ, the more I seem to feel the necessity of it, and rejoice and glory in it. Indeed, I trust I would sooner give up my life than surrender it.'

The man with whom Martyn talked most of all, and with most hope, was Said Ali. He confessed he had always been in search of a religion, and was still undecided. He listened avidly to all Martyn had to say, discussed eagerly the passages they were translating, and spent hours reading the New Testament. He had a high respect for it, especially the epistles, which he read proudly to his friends. Patiently Martyn explained and pleaded with him. He was willing enough to confess his ignorance: 'The truth is,' he remarked, 'we are in a state of compound ignorance, ignorant, yet ignorant of our ignorance.' Martyn told him he must humbly receive the truth as a child: 'True', he replied, 'I have no humility.' 'He said he did not know what to do to have his mind made up about religion. Of all the religions Christ's was the best, but whether to prefer this to Sufiism he could not tell. In these doubts he is tossed to and fro, and is often kept awake the whole night in tears. He and his brother talk together on these things till they are almost crazed.' So he continued, sometimes seriously concerned, sometimes with little more than a dilettante interest, and when Martyn left, he left him still undecided.

There is no doubt that the arguments of the young scholar had gone far to produce this considerable stir in the religious life of Shiraz, but it is hardly too much to say that his life and character were as strong a force. Among threats, abuse, and disdain, he persevered, calm, unwavering, fearless, always eager to testify to the reality of his faith, always absorbed in the services of his Lord. When a packet of letters arrived from India, one of them curiously asked to hear what sort of letters these Christians wrote. 'He took care to let his friends know that we wrote nothing about our own affairs; it was all about translations and the cause of Christ. With this he was highly delighted.' How typical of the man! It is little wonder these Muslims, whose lives Martyn found disgusting even in comparison with India, took notice of his religion. And there was one at least who went beyond an intellectual interest.

He was Muhammad Rahim, a 'decided enemy to infidels', who (as he narrates) 'visited this teacher of the despised sect, for the purpose of treating him with scorn, and exposing his doctrines to contempt. Although I persevered in this conduct for some time, I found that every interview not only increased my respect for the individual, but diminished my confidence in the faith in which I was educated. His extreme forbearance towards the violence of his opponents, the calm and yet convincing manner in which he exposed the fallacies and sophistries by which he was assailed, gradually inclined me to listen to his arguments, to inquire dispassionately into the subject of them, and finally to read a tract which he had written in reply to *A Defence of Islam*, by our chief mullahs. The result of my examination was a conviction that the young disputant was right.' He was afraid to confess this conviction until Martyn was about to leave Shiraz; he never forgot that last conversation, nor did he cease to read the book which the 'beardless youth' gave him, a Persian New Testament. On a blank leaf was written, 'There is joy in heaven over one sinner that repenteth. HENRY MARTYN.'

But it was the Persian New Testament which was Martyn's chief concern. He knew he was a dying man, and that it must be completed while he lived. Not only must it be completed: if it was to have a wide effect it must, like all books in Persia at that time, be personally presented to the Shah for his commendation. So when, in February, 1812, the work was finished, it was handed to the most skilful artists in Shiraz to produce two copies in the exquisite penmanship in which Persia excels, to be presented to the Shah and his son. This took nearly three months, which Martyn spent in endless conversations, and in his work on the Persian Psalms.

At last the copies were ready, and on May 11 he set out for Tabriz, seven hundred miles away in the far north of Persia, where he hoped to find the British ambassador, Sir Gore Ouseley, through whom alone he could gain an audience with the Shah.

He left behind him at Shiraz a small group of serious enquirers. For days they made him read them stories from the Old Testament. 'Their attention to the Word, and their love and attention to me, seemed to increase as the time of my departure approached. Aga Baba, who had been reading St. Matthew, related very circumstantially to the company the particulars of the death of Christ. The bed of roses on which we sat, and the notes of the nightingales warbling around us, were not so sweet to me as this discourse from the Persian.' He left them, reading and praying, to the care of the God in whose power to change men's hearts he most fervently believed; and who knows what was the result?

*   *   *

The first half of the journey, from Shiraz to Teheran, was covered without undue trouble, and Martyn's health is not even mentioned in his diary; indeed, the settled year at Shiraz seems to have restored him considerably, though the underlying chest trouble was always there, and sometimes made itself felt. The journey took less than a month, over cool, high mountain passes, where even in mid-summer there was ice on the pools, and along valleys green with woods and cornfields, 'the first place in Asia I have seen exhibiting anything of the scenery of England.' As usual, he took all opportunities to meet Muslims on the way, and also the Armenian Christian community at Ispahan, whose empty formalism in worship, and ignorance of the faith distressed him.

Teheran was half-way to Tabriz. But here, only a few miles from the city, was the Shah himself, at his summer camping-ground. Martyn could not bear the delay involved in reaching the ambassador, and decided to try a more direct course.

He had letters of introduction from Jaffir Ali Khan, and armed with these he approached the Shah's vizier, who in turn could present him to the Shah. The first interview was encouraging, when for two hours he discussed religious questions with two Secretaries of State; they ranged over the usual ground of miracles, the Quran, the Trinity, and the divinity of Christ. The discussion was inconclusive, but Martyn felt he had made a good first impression.

It was three days later that the invitation to the vizier's levée came. There, with his beautiful Persian New Testament, the Christian scholar faced a group of the most influential Muslims in Persia. The vizier listened for an hour or two to a heated discussion, when 'two mullahs, the most ignorant of any I have yet met with', threw at Martyn a mixture of abuse and 'impudent assertions about the law and the gospel, neither of which they had ever seen in their lives', which 'moved my indignation a little'.

Finally the vizier delivered an ultimatum: 'You had better say "God is God, and Muhammad is the prophet of God".'

It was a straight challenge to accept the Muslim creed; there could be only one answer, however disastrous the consequences to his mission. 'I said, "God is God", but, instead of adding "Muhammad is the prophet of God", I said, "and Jesus is the Son of God". They had no sooner heard this, which I had avoided mentioning until then, than they all exclaimed, in contempt and anger, "He is neither born nor begets", and rose up, as if they would have torn me in pieces. One of them said, "What will you say when your tongue is burned out for this blasphemy?" My book, which I had brought, expecting to present it to the King, lay before Mirza Shufi. As they all rose up, I was afraid they would trample upon the book, so I went in among them to take it up, and wrapped it in a towel before them, while they looked at it and me with supreme contempt. Thus I walked away alone to my tent, to pass the rest of the day in heat and dirt. What have I done, thought I, to merit all this scorn? Nothing, I trust, but bearing testimony to Jesus. I thought over these things in prayer, and my troubled heart found that peace which Christ hath promised to His disciples.'

A message followed that he could only approach the Shah through the ambassador: to Tabriz he must go.

This journey again took a month, but a far less pleasant month than the previous one. The country was generally mountainous and barren; accommodation was hard to find, as all the villages were busy preparing for the imminent journey of the Shah along the same road; food was scarce, and money began to run out. But far worse was the weather: piercing cold alternating with long hours of exposure to the sun, soon brought on fever for most of the party. Martyn was in no state to resist a fever, and day after day with a splitting head, too ill to move, or ride on in such a delirious state that the whole experience was as unreal as a nightmare. But he had to reach Tabriz, and day after day they toiled on until 'at last I reached the gate, and feebly asked for a man to show me the way to the ambassador's'.

He was not far from death, but he could not have come to a better place: the healthy climate of Tabriz earned for it the name of 'fever-dispeller', and so it proved. For weeks Martyn lay weak and often delirious, reduced to a 'mere skeleton', but the constant care of Sir Gore Ouseley and his wife, together with the climate, had its effect, and in less than two months he was, if not fully restored, well enough to travel.

But Sir Gore persuaded him that he was not yet well enough to attempt a second visit to the Shah. Instead the ambassador promised to present the volume himself, with all the dignity at his command, and this he did.

The response, which Martyn never saw, would have exceeded all his expectations, and amply justified the trouble he had taken to reach the Shah. 'The copy of the gospel, which was translated into Persian by the learned exertions of the late Rev. Henry Martyn, has proved highly acceptable to our august mind. It has been translated in a style most befitting sacred books, that is, in an easy and simple diction. The whole of the New Testament is completed in a most excellent manner, and this circumstance has been an additional source of pleasure to our enlightened and august mind. If it please the most merciful God, we shall command the Select Servants, who are admitted to our presence, to read to us the above-mentioned book from the beginning to the end, that we may, in the most minute manner, hear and comprehend its contents.'

The Shah's judgement was echoed by voices all over the world, and soon five editions were in print, the first, at St. Petersburg, under the personal supervision of Sir Gore Ouseley himself.

But meanwhile, the translator, his work done, was forming other ideas. He could not hope, as he was, to proceed to Arabia, but there was a hope, even if only a faint one, that he might reach England – and Lydia. Once thought of, the idea would not leave him; he wrote to India for permission, wrote to Lydia and to Simeon to tell them he was coming, though he had little hope of reaching them alive, ignored Sir Gore's warning of his dangerous condition, and on September 2, 1812, set out from Tabriz on his last journey, bound for Constantinople.

*   *   *

The route lay through the mountainous country of the far north of Persia, and then right across the whole length of Turkey, a distance of over 1,300 miles. Scarcely even convalescent as he was, Martyn was still wide awake to the grandeur of the plain of Tabriz, with its distant blue mountains, and the fine valleys further north. Here he was far out of the usual haunts of Europeans, and people stared at him. Accommodation was bad: smelly, public, and infested with lice and mosquitoes, but the sick man's diary contains more of lively interest than of complaint. The approach to Mount Ararat gave rise to meditation on the salvation of Noah, and the great work of God since his time. 'On the peak of that hill the whole church was contained; it has now spread far and wide, even to the ends of the earth, but the ancient vicinity of it knows it no more. I fancied many a spot where Noah perhaps offered his sacrifices.' At the same time he found his interest in philology reviving, and scarcely noticed the distance they covered as his brain raced from a problem in the translation of Psalm 16 to speculations on the eighth conjugation of the Arabic verb.

From Erivan, in the extreme north, while he waited for new

horses, Martyn rode out to visit the monastery of Etch-miazin, the metropolis of the Armenian church, where he found a young and talented monk intent on introducing a reformation in the church. Martyn advised and encouraged him, and so much enjoyed his visit that he told the Patriarch, 'I could be almost willing to become a monk with them.' They gave him new equipment for the journey, and a sword to guard against the Turkish robbers, and sent him on his way.

So began the last, fatal stage of the journey. From Tabriz to Erivan there is little mention of his health, but now again, as he enters Turkey, the subject begins to recur. Over fast-flowing rivers and mountain passes the little heavily-armed cavalcade made its way long the Royal Road for Constantinople, through the territory of the robber chief, Cara Beg, 'through the midst of danger', while a 'gracious Providence kept all mischief at a distance'. Leading the party now was a Tartar, Hasan, who, as Martyn became gradually more ill and feeble, took control, and ruled even the Englishman with a rod of iron. His word became law. In the inns Hasan was given a dinner of four or five dishes, while Martyn had rotten eggs. Hasan's will determined the time-table: when Martyn was well enough, and wanted to hurry, Hasan 'was riveted to his bed'; when Martyn was too ill to move as the fever again gripped him, Hasan hurried him on, and abused him for holding the party up.

After a furious ride all day and all night, when 'I hardly knew how to keep my life in me', and a rest of three or four hours, Hasan again hurried Martyn on, as he was afraid of arrest for an offence previously committed in that neighbourhood, and 'galloped furiously towards a village which, he said, was four hours distant, which was all I could undertake in my present weak state; but village after village did he pass, till night coming on, and no signs of another, I got off my horse, and sat upon the ground, and told him I neither could nor would go any further. He stormed, but I was immovable, till a light appearing at a distance, I mounted my horse and made towards it, leaving him to follow or not, as he pleased'. With difficulty Martyn got himself a stable-room to sleep in. Here the rest of the party imposed themselves on him.

'My fever here increased to a violent degree; the heat in my eyes and forehead was so great, that the fire almost made me frantic.' They ignored his appeals to them to put it out, or else to move him outside, so 'at last I pushed my head in among the luggage, and lodged it on the damp ground, and slept'.

The next night 'the ague came on with a violence I never before experienced. I felt as if in a palsy, my teeth chattering, and my whole frame violently shaken. Hasan sat with perfect indifference, ruminating on the further delay this was likely to occasion'.

Next day, 'no horses being to be had, I had an unexpected repose. I sat in the orchard and thought, with sweet comfort and peace, of my God; in solitude my company, my friend, and comforter. O when shall time give place to eternity? When shall appear that new heaven and new earth wherein dwelleth righteousness? There, there shall in no wise enter in anything that defileth: none of that wickedness that has made men worse than wild beasts, none of those corruptions that add still more to the miseries of mortality, shall be seen or heard of any more.'

It was not to be long. These were the last words he wrote, and the Tartar hustled a dying man over the mountain road to Tokat, where the plague was raging. Half-way to Constantinople, far from England and Lydia, Henry Martyn's journey ended.

'If He has work for me to do', he had written in Shiraz, 'I can not die.' But now the work was finished, and there, in an obscure corner of the Muslim world, the Armenian Christians buried an unknown English clergyman, 'of whom the world was not worthy'.

VI. 'I Know Whom I Have Believed'

'Praise is exceedingly unpleasant to me', wrote Martyn when they praised his sermon at Cambridge. He would not want a glowing record of his virtues and achievements, and that is not the purpose of this chapter. Rather it is to ask, what is the message of Henry Martyn to the church today? What has he left to us?

He left behind him a few, only a few, whose spiritual lives

stemmed from his work. He left a larger number on whom the brief presence of this man of God made an unforgettable impact: the people of Lolworth, the fellows of St. John's, the crew of the *Union*, the people of Calcutta, Dinapore, and Cawnpore, and the Muslim stronghold of Shiraz, none could ever look on Christianity in quite the same light again. He left two of the most perfect and most influential translations of the New Testament the East had yet seen. But perhaps he himself best summed up the importance of his life when he wrote, 'Even if I never should see a native converted, God may design, by my patience and continuance in the work, to encourage future missionaries'; and, we may add, not only missionaries, but Christian people of every calling. Above all, Henry Martyn has left us an example, not an example of the perfect man, but of what God can do with a very imperfect man who takes God seriously.

Sir James Stephen referred to Henry Martyn as 'the one heroic name which adorns the annals of the Church of England from the days of Elizabeth to our own'. But hero-worship can be dangerous: it can blind us to the facts. Heroic, Martyn may have been; perfect he certainly was not. Again and again a very human weakness appears, and again and again we are amazed that a man so like ourselves could have been used to such effect. 'It is consoling to a poor sinner like myself', wrote Bishop Daniel Wilson, 'to see how the soul even of a saint like Henry Martyn faints and is discouraged, laments over defects of love, and finds an evil nature still struggling against the law of his mind.'

Who has not known times when he was afraid to speak out in the cause of Christ? So did Martyn, and rebuked himself for his fear of man, but it was with him to the end, a fear usually conquered, but nonetheless truly fought. Who has not said and done things he would give anything to recall? So did the impetuous Martyn. Who has not known his love for God dimmed by too great a love for the pleasures of the world, or gone through long periods of spiritual barrenness, when all joy in religion seemed impossible, God seemed far off, and doubts arose incessantly? So did Martyn, and cried out in despair. No one was more keenly aware of his weakness than Martyn himself, whose diary some have labelled morbid, but which bears rather the stamp of a stark realism.

But the example of Martyn is of one of those who 'out of weakness were made strong'. 'I devoted myself unreservedly to the service of the Lord', he wrote in 1804, 'to Him, as to one who knew the great conflict within, and my firm resolve, through His grace, of being His, though it should be with much tribulation.' He brought to the service of God the perseverance that had won him his academic triumphs, and not even the delights of philology were allowed to distract him from his one end, the pursuance of the will of God. 'Every wheel of the chariot must be in motion to gain the race', he wrote, and he so put it into practice that at the close of his work in India a colleague said, 'If ever man, since St. Paul, could use these words, he may: "This one thing I do".' Alone against British indifference, Indian apathy, and Muslim hostility, he stood his ground; not that he enjoyed being alone, or revelled in argument, but his aim did not waver.

So much we have already seen; but the question we must ask is, What enabled this sensitive, retiring scholar to persevere in circumstances which might have conquered a stronger man? What was the mainspring of this remarkable life?

The answer stands out in his diary with startling clarity: Henry Martyn believed in God.

*   *   *

How often those words in the Creed are used so lightly that they slip off the tongue without a thought: 'I believe in God, the Father Almighty.' But Martyn's diary gives to them a new meaning. God was to him vividly real, 'nearer than father or mother or sister, a nearer relation, a more affectionate friend.' And what a God! Not the God of so much debased twentieth-century thought, the benevolent but frustrated spectator on a world run riot; but the God of the Bible, the God of Abraham, Isaac, and Jacob, the God of Moses and Elijah, the God of Peter and Paul, the God and Father of our Lord Jesus Christ; the mighty God in whose hands are all the corners of the earth, the King of kings and Lord of lords, who knows the end from the beginning, and accomplishes all things according to the counsel of His will; the God who knows and cares for the least of all His creatures, and will not let a hair of His servants' heads perish; God, the Father Almighty.

To know and love and serve such a God was the one concern and delight of Martyn's life. 'Oh how is every hour lost', he wrote, 'that is not spent in the love and contemplation of God, my God'; and again, 'In prayer at night my soul panted after God, and longed to be entirely conformed to His image.' 'I do not know that anything would be a heaven to me, but the service of Christ, and the enjoyment of His presence.' 'As for self, contemptible self, I feel myself saying, let it be forgotten for ever; henceforth let Christ live, let Christ reign, let Him be glorified for ever.'

It is no wonder that a soul so much in love with God found constant delight in prayer and in the reading of His Word. It was not always easy, and times of barrenness did come, but he could not be content with such a state, and cried to God for help, until he found himself wondering how prayer could ever have lost its appeal: 'How sweet is prayer to my soul at this time. I seem as if I could never be tired, not only of spiritual joys, but of spiritual employments, since these are now the same.' At the end of that fearful journey to Shiraz, he wrote, 'I enjoyed much comfort in prayer. What a privilege to have a God to go to, in such a place, and in such company! To read and pray at leisure seemed like coming home after being long abroad.'

And if to meet God in this less direct way was like returning home, what would it be to meet Him face to face? As a steady refrain through the diary comes the cry of the exile, longing for his true home in heaven, longing to be free of the evil of the world, and at home with God.

Meanwhile, he could not doubt the God who was so real to him. If God sent illness, or even death, Martyn could not complain. 'While there is work which we must do', he affirmed, 'we shall live,' but God, not Martyn, knew when that work was complete, and the servant gladly accepted his Master's verdict. 'God, who keeps me here awhile, arranges every part of His plans in unerring wisdom, and if I should be cut off in the midst of my plans, I shall still, I trust, through mercy, behold His works in heaven, and be everlastingly happy in the never-ceasing admiration of His works and nature.' This is not fatalism, or even an irrational optimism; it is the inevitable confidence of one who lives close to a God whom he knows to be perfect both in wisdom and power.

Perhaps it might not be God's purpose that he should see any results to his work; even so, he was 'contented to be left without fruit if such were the will of God'. All the time it is on God that his eyes are fixed; illness and failure seem to take their place naturally within the scheme of God's purpose; and in circumstances which ought to have damped his enthusiasm, he found himself 'happy all day in the love of God'. When the Indians at Dinapore regarded him as an enemy, and the British opposed his plans, he looked to a higher authority: 'Though the heathen rage, and the English people "imagine a vain thing", the Lord Jesus, who controls all events, is my Friend, my Master, my God, my All. On this Rock of Ages, on which I feel my foot to rest, my head is lifted up above all mine enemies round about me, and I sing, yea, I will sing praises unto the Lord.'

What was it then that made this weak man strong, strong enough to face with undying confidence a life from which the strongest might have shrunk? Simply this, that Henry Martyn believed in God.

* * *

But Martyn knew that he was not the only object of God's concern. The same wise and loving providence of God on which he relied for his daily life, was wide enough to cover the whole world; the God who was working out His plans with unerring wisdom in this one life, was also working out His eternal purpose in the world, and it was within this purpose that Martyn's missionary work had its place. God Himself was at work: Martyn was not alone. 'I am going upon a work immediately according to the mind of Christ, and my glorious Lord, whose power is uncontrollable, can easily open a way for His feeble follower through the thickest ranks of his enemies. And now, on let me go, smiling at my foes; how small are human obstacles before this mighty

Lord! How easy is it for God to effect His purposes in a moment! What are inveterate prejudices when once the Lord shall set to His hand?'

If there had been any doubt in Martyn's mind, the plain teaching of the Bible would have settled it: 'The Word of God is more precious to me at this time', he wrote in Shiraz, 'than I ever remember it to have been; and of all the promises in it none is more sweet to me than this, "He shall reign till He hath put all enemies under His feet".' He was engaged in the invincible purpose of the sovereign Lord. 'I want to keep in view that our God is the God of the whole earth, and that the heathen are given to His exalted Son, the uttermost parts of the earth for a possession.'

It was this knowledge that gave him what to many would seem a hopelessly optimistic view of the future of missionary work in Asia. The vision recurs of the nations of the East bowing before their God. As he approached India he read Isaiah 42. 8: 'I am the Lord, that is my name, and my glory will I not give to another, neither my praise to graven images;' and he meditated, 'Who knows whether even the present generation may not see Satan's throne shaken to its base in India?' Later, 'Surely good is intended for this country.' Is this just vain optimism? To the man who read the Word of God, and knew the God whom he served, it was sober realism. So too when he was in Shiraz: 'The Word of God has found its way into Persia, and it is not in Satan's power to oppose its progress, if the Lord have sent it.'

Not only over nations did Martyn recognize God's sovereignty, but over individual men as well, and often, when talking with someone, Martyn would see his complete inability to make any impression, and would cry to God to do what man could not do. The finest of words and arguments, without the power of the Holy Spirit, were so much wasted breath. Only God could give a man new life, and to His almighty touch even the most hardened must respond.

As he watched a Brahmin performing his devotions to the sacred river, he recognized that it was the sheer grace of the sovereign God that had made a difference between them. Like so many of the great missionaries of his day, Martyn believed in

God's election of His people, not as a mere theological quibble, but as an obvious fact of experience. And like them he saw no inconsistency between this belief and a zeal to win men for God; indeed, far from being a barrier to evangelism, it provided the strongest of incentives, to know that he was an instrument in the hand of the almighty God. The missionaries of Serampore summed up their attitude: 'We are sure that only those ordained to eternal life will believe, and that God alone can add to the church such as shall be saved. Nevertheless, we can not but observe with admiration that Paul, the great champion for the glorious doctrines of free and sovereign grace, was the most conspicuous for his personal zeal in the work of persuading men to be reconciled to God. In this respect he is a noble example for our imitation.'

And Martyn did imitate him. It needs no further quotation to prove his zeal and agonizing longing to persuade men and women to be reconciled to God: his life demonstrates it. The man who slaved away his life among people whom the lowest clerk of the East India Company despised, and who dragged his dying body over many hundreds of miles of sea and mountains, did it for this purpose: to do the will of God, and to save men and women from destruction.

Sometimes he saw their sin and their squalor, their misery of body and soul, and he pitied them. Sometimes he was indignant at their blasphemy and contempt for the true God. Often he seemed to see the reproachful look which the lost at the last day will cast upon the watchman who had failed to warn them of their danger. But above all he knew that the God whom he knew and loved was calling them to repentance, proclaiming salvation to them through faith in His Son; and he knew that God had called him to be the messenger.

That is the message of Henry Martyn for today. He believed in God, the sovereign God of the Bible, and on that belief he acted.

God has not changed.

*   *   *

Over the fire-place in Simeon's dining-room hung a portrait. It was of Henry Martyn, painted in Calcutta just before he left

[301]

India for Persia. Simeon used to show it to his friends and say, 'There, see that blessed man. What an expression of countenance! No one looks at me as he does; he never takes his eyes off me. and seems always to be saying, "Be serious; be in earnest; don't trifle, don't trifle".'

Simeon smiled, and added, 'And I won't trifle; I won't trifle'.

JOHN G. PATON

Missionary of the Cross
(New Hebrides)

by

JOHN D. LEGG, B.A., B.D.

I.   Preparation (1824–58)

'The Cannibals! You will be eaten by the Cannibals!' This was the old Christian's final argument why the young man should not go to the South Seas as a missionary. The reply of thirty-two-year-old John Paton was characteristic: 'Mr. Dickson, you are advanced in years now, and your own prospect is soon to be laid in the grave, there to be eaten by worms; I confess to you, that if I can but live and die serving and honouring the Lord Jesus, it will make no difference to me whether I am eaten by Cannibals or worms; and in the Great Day my resurrection body will arise as fair as yours in the likeness of our risen Redeemer.' This single-minded purpose endured throughout fifty years of missionary service – despite the cannibals and many another trial. We must, therefore, begin by tracing the origins not only of this purpose, but of everything which went into the making of a great missionary.

John Gibson Paton was born on May 24, 1824, on a small farm near Dumfries in southern Scotland, the eldest son of James and Janet Paton. Five years later the family moved to the village of Torthorwald, still only four or five miles from Dumfries. The influence of the Covenanters thus surrounded Paton from his earliest days, as he grew up among the memorials of those who had fought and suffered in that very region for the crown-rights of Jesus Christ, among whom were the ancestors of his father's mother. Furthermore, his parents were themselves cast in the same mould as their godly forbears. James Paton, by trade a stocking-maker, was no ordinary man; he belonged to the Reformed Presbyterian Church, which represented the purest stream of Covenanting tradition, and in addition established his own house as a nursery of true godliness. After his conversion at the age of seventeen, he introduced family prayers to his parents' home, and later continued in the doctrine and spirit of the Covenanters in the cottage at Torthorwald. He made the deepest and best of impressions on his children, especially John, who bears witness to the influence upon him of his father's godliness and habitual communion with God. Tradition had it that James Paton had only three times missed public worship in Dumfries, twice owing to exceptionally bad weather, and on one occasion to a cholera attack. Family prayers began and ended every day, and an immoral woman of the village later revealed that on winter nights she had crept up to the window and had heard the good man praying that God would convert sinners. This alone had kept her from suicide and at last brought her to Christ. The Sabbath, with church attendance, Bible-reading, catechizing and instruction was 'a holy, happy, entirely human day'. Paton tells us that the continual study of the Westminster Shorter Catechism 'laid the solid rock-foundations of our religious life'. In later days he never departed from the Covenanting faith of his fathers, although he lived well into the days of scepticism, when even evangelicalism became a very diluted thing.

Young John had a great desire to learn, and though before he was twelve he left school and began learning his father's trade, he used every spare moment to study Latin and Greek. (These 'spare moments' were snatched during the one-and-a-half-hour meal breaks in a working day lasting from six in the morning to ten at night.) The reason for this study must be given in his own words: 'I had given my soul to God and was resolved to aim at being a Missionary of the Cross or a Minister of the Gospel . . . How much my father's prayers at this time impressed me I can never explain nor could any stranger understand. When, on his knees and all of us kneeling around him in Family Worship, he poured out his whole soul with tears for the conversion of the heathen world to the service of Jesus, and for every personal and domestic need, we all felt as if in the presence of the living Saviour and learned to know and love him as our Divine Friend. As we rose from our knees, I used to look at the light on my father's face, and wish I were like him in spirit – hoping that, in answer to his prayers, I might be privileged and prepared to carry the blessed Gospel to some portion of the heathen world.'

It was in these days too that he learned an all-important lesson concerning God's providential care over His children. During a very bad time the Paton family were caused much distress, and on one occasion while James Paton was away overnight selling his work, they ran out of food. The hard-pressed mother told her children that she had told God everything, and that He would send them food in the morning. Next day a present of food from her father arrived, for which thanks were duly given, and the lesson, which Paton never forgot, impressed upon them.

Paton furthered his education by saving enough to spend six weeks at Dumfries Academy, and then took a post as visitor and tract-distributor with a congregation in Glasgow, which gave him a free year at the Free Church Seminary. This, of course, meant that he had to leave home, and his father walked with him the first six miles of the way. 'His counsels and tears and heavenly conversation on that parting journey', wrote Paton many years later, 'are fresh in my heart as if it had been but yesterday . . . We halted on reaching the appointed parting place; he grasped my hand firmly for a minute in silence, and then solemnly and affectionately said: "God bless you, my son! Your father's God prosper you and keep you from all evil!" Unable to say more, his lips kept moving in silent prayer: in tears we embraced and parted . . . I watched through blinding tears, till his form faded from my gaze; and then, hastening on my way, vowed deeply and oft, by the help of God, to live and act so as never to grieve or dishonour such a father and mother as He had given me . . . It is no Pharisaism, but deep gratitude, which makes me here testify that the memory of that scene not only helped, by God's grace, to keep me pure from the prevailing sins, but also stimulated me in all my studies, that I might not fall short of his hopes, and in all my Christian duties, that I might faithfully follow his shining example.'

Ill-health cut short this year, but after convalescence and a period teaching and saving he returned to the college, only to run short of money once again. He was on the point of giving up once more, when in God's providence an advertisement for a teacher caught his eye. He applied for and gained the post. Here he prospered until his very success in taming ruffians and increasing the number on the roll, led to his replacement by a better-qualified teacher. Again it seemed as if Paton would have to give up his studies, but once more God opened the next stage of his preparation. A previously-written application to become a Glasgow City Missionary now brought an acceptance and appointment to a degraded area around Green Street in the Calton district of the city.

Paton began visiting and preaching, but the only place for a Sunday service was in a hay-loft – with the cows underneath. After a year's hard work he had six or seven regularly attending this meeting and another held in a house on a week night. The Mission directors, judging the inhabitants 'unassailable by ordinary means', proposed to move Paton to another district, but he pleaded for another six-months' trial, during which great progress was made and after which the work never looked back. As the converts multiplied so did his meetings and after a short while we find five or six hundred attending regularly. Apart from Sunday meetings (which began at seven in the morning) he held Bible classes, prayer-meetings where he expounded the Scriptures systematically, and a communicants' class based on 'Paterson on the Shorter Catechism'. So Paton led many of the inhabitants of this degraded area into the riches of Covenanting Christianity.

Paton was always a vigorous advocate of total abstinence and he encountered much opposition from the publicans of the area, who organized disturbances at his meetings and endeavoured to get him into trouble with the police. He had friendly relations with the many Roman Catholics in the district as he visited and talked with them, but when some were converted the priests were roused and caused much trouble. Matters came to a head when Paton tried to prevent an ex-Catholic from being abducted by her former spiritual guides. He was assailed in the press, received anonymous letters threatening his life, and was publicly cursed from the altar by the priests. Stones were thrown at him, pails of boiling water emptied above him, but, apart from one stone which found its target, he was unscathed, and as he refused to run away, or to allow himself to be given a short 'holiday', he was eventually left at peace.

Although there were many social and moral results of his work, his chief emphasis was on evangelism. Among his converts were the Irish woman and her drunken husband who had allowed him to hold meetings in their house, an infidel lecturer who burned his former 'Circulating Library' and turned to the Bible on his supposed death-bed and found Christ, and a doctor who was both an unbeliever and a drunkard until Paton persevered with him. Children too were among the converts, such as a lad named John Sim who, on his death-bed, pleaded with Paton, 'Oh, do tell me everything you know or have ever heard about Jesus, the spotless Lamb of God'. A friend of these early days, Thomas Binnie, declared later, 'Dr. Paton realized, as no other man I ever met did, the awful danger of the unsaved. He realized that salvation was possible, and that he might be the means of bringing the perishing to the Saviour, and that he must live for that and that alone.' This applied in Glasgow first of all, but Paton tells us that, though happy and successful there, he 'continually heard . . . the wail of the perishing heathen in the South Seas; and I saw that few were caring for them, while I knew well that many would be ready to take up my work in Calton . . . Without revealing the state of my mind to any person, this was the supreme subject of my daily meditation and prayer'.

Throughout these ten years Paton struggled on with his studies at Glasgow University, at the Reformed Presbyterian Divinity Hall, and also in unfinished medical studies. 'I was sustained', he says, 'by the lofty aim which burned all these years bright within my soul, namely to be owned and used by Him for the salvation of perishing men.' At this time the Synod of Paton's church was deeply concerned to find another missionary for the South Seas, and Paton was grieved at the lack of response. His own response was as follows: 'The Lord kept saying within me, "Since none better-qualified can be got, rise and offer yourself." Almost overpowering was the impulse to answer aloud, "Here am I, send me." But I was dreadfully afraid of mistaking my mere human emotions for the will of God, so I resolved to make it a subject of close deliberation and prayer for a few days longer and to look at the proposal from every angle . . . I felt a growing assurance that this was the call of God to His servant. The wail and claims of the heathen were constantly sounding in my ears. I saw them perishing for lack of the knowledge of the true God and His Son Jesus, while my Green Street people had the open Bible and all the means of grace within easy reach ; . . . from every aspect at which I could look the whole facts in the face, the voice within me sounded like a voice from God.' Would that all missionaries so tested their call and had such a clear vision of the perishing heathen!

When Paton and a fellow student offered themselves and were accepted for the New Hebrides Mission there was opposition from nearly everybody. 'Some retorted upon me, 'There are heathen at home; let us seek and save, first of all, the lost ones perishing at our doors". This I felt to be most true, and an appalling fact; but I unfailingly observed that those who made this retort neglected those home heathen themselves . . . They would ungrudgingly spend more on a fashionable party at dinner or tea, on concert or ball or theatre, or on some ostentatious display, or worldly or selfish indulgence, ten times more, perhaps in a single day, than they would give in a year, or in half a lifetime, for the conversion of the whole heathen world, either at home or abroad.' This reaction only increased Paton's determination, and the matter was finally settled by seeking his parents' opinions. They assured him that they had long ago given him to the Lord, and that their prayers had been that, if the Lord saw fit, He would call and prepare him to be a missionary of the Cross.

We have lingered over these early days because it is here that we see God's hand upon His servant leading and preparing him for a great work. We can trace the work of preparation in his background, in his parents' training and example, in his struggles and self-discipline, in his battles for the Lord, in his work in heathen Glasgow, and not least in the increasing conviction and widening experience of his Father's providential care. Well might he remember his mother's words, 'O my children, love your heavenly Father, tell Him in faith and prayer all your needs, and He will supply your wants so far as it shall be for your good and His glory.' The God of Abraham, Isaac and Jacob, the God of the Covenanters, the God of his father, and the God who had kept him in every situation would go with him. 'I saw the hand of God very visibly, not only preparing me for, but now leading me to, the foreign mission field.'

II. Tanna (1858–62)

The New Hebrides group in the South Seas consists of thirty or more islands spread over four hundred miles, lying about a thousand miles from New Zealand and rather more from Sydney, Australia. Paton and his young wife, together with his colleague, the Rev. Joseph Copeland, set sail in April, 1858. Their immediate destination was Aneityum, the most southerly of the islands, where missionaries were already established, notably John Geddie of Nova Scotia and John Inglis of Scotland, who would help them to settle on the nearby island of Tanna. On the voyage Paton conducted Bible classes both among crew and passengers, it would appear with some success. On arrival at Aneityum, the new missionaries boarded the small mission schooner, 'John Knox'. A collision with the vessel that had brought the Patons left the 'John Knox' dismasted and helpless. The other ship sailed away and left them to drift towards Tanna, where the boat would have been wrecked and their lives endangered. However, from the very beginning God's hand was upon them for good and help came in time to avert disaster. Paton proceeded to Tanna thus reassured that God was with him as he ventured forth with the great good news. Dr. Inglis of Aneityum accompanied them to Tanna and helped in the purchase of a site for a house at Port Resolution on the island's east coast.

Paton was not long left in ignorance of the true nature of the heathenism into which he had come. 'The depths of Satan', he writes, 'outlined in the first chapter of the Romans, were uncovered there before our eyes in the daily life of the people, without veil and without excuse.' Even while they were building the house, the local "Harbour People" and the "Inland People", faces painted, feathers in their hair, pursued their bitter feuds around them. One morning their Aneityumese cook informed them that those slain in the battle had been cooked and feasted upon at the boiling spring, the only source of fresh water on the island. Not only had they washed the blood into the water, they had also bathed there, polluting all the water. Even he seemed to think it far worse that Paton's tea should be spoilt than that men should be killed! Cannibalism face to face was far different from that coolly conceived in Scotland . . . but worse was to come. Next evening he was told that one of the wounded had died and that the widow had just been strangled so that she might accompany him to the other world and continue as his servant. Not only widows, but unwanted wives, infants and aged parents were thus killed as convenient. Paton's heart was filled with horror. Could it be possible to teach such men the faith of Christ, or even to civilize them? Horror was, however, accompanied by pity and he longed for the day when he could speak to them in their own language of the only true God and the Saviour through whom forgiveness, even for such sins as these, could be obtained. The missionaries were left alone on Tanna in November and soon began to pick up the language and to discover the islanders' religion. This was controlled by the Sacred Men, who were supposed to influence the gods and evil spirits, and to cause or remove sickness and death by Nahak, a form of black magic.

Missionaries had never fared well on Tanna. Indeed, the Patons' house was on the same site as that of two missionaries of the London Missionary Society who had been driven from the island by the natives sixteen years earlier. Moreover, several Samoan teachers had been persecuted and one murdered. Paton's own troubles began almost immediately. They discovered soon, but too late, that the site of the house was most unhealthy, and fever attacked them. In the February of 1859, Mrs. Paton gave birth to a son, but within five weeks both she and the baby were dead. Paton was left alone. Although suffering from the fever himself, he had to do almost all that was necessary for their burial with his own hands, yet the Lord sustained him. He records: 'I built the grave round and round with coral blocks, and covered the top with beautiful white coral, broken small as gravel; and that spot became my sacred and much-frequented shrine, during all the following months and years when I laboured on for the salvation of these savage Islanders amidst difficulties, dangers and deaths.

Whensoever Tanna turns to the Lord and is won for Christ, men in after-days will find the memory of that spot still green, where with ceaseless prayers and tears I claimed that land for God in which I had "buried my dead" with faith and hope. But for Jesus and the fellowship He vouchsafed me there, I must have gone mad and died beside that lonely grave!'

The loss of his godly young wife was perhaps Paton's bitterest trial but it was by no means his last. The Tannese showed greed and deceit in every possible way, begging, stealing or 'tabooing', as they felt they could profit best. A drought was immediately blamed on the missionaries and their God, as also were the ill-nesses produced by the succeeding hurricanes and heavy rains. The white people from a ship wrecked on the beach brought more trouble to Paton by their ill-treatment of the Tannese. An Aneit-yumese teacher died; Mr. Mathieson, in another part of the island, was taken ill; and all the while inter-tribal warfare raged about them. When an aged chief died, the whole island united (a most unusual event) in seeking the missionaries' death. So it continued for the whole of Paton's stay on the island. Sometimes one chief, then another would defend him, often in hope of gain or jealousy of a rival. Nevertheless, in general all were against him. Fever attacked him almost continuously and again he nearly died before he could move his dwelling to higher and more healthy ground, being nursed back to health by Abraham, a faithful Aneityumese teacher.

'The prejudices and persecutions of Heathens were a sore enough trial, but sorer and more hopeless was the wicked and contaminating influence of, alas, my fellow-countrymen.' These were traders who treated the missionaries with violent contempt, thus encouraging the Tannese to treat them as they pleased. Some lived among the islanders, inciting them to fight among them-selves, so that they could sell them weapons and ammunition. Others were engaged in the sandal-wood trade, often murdering the natives as they stole the wood, and killing one another in their drunken quarrels. Such conduct led the Tannese to suspect and hate all white men. All in all, Paton had as much trouble with these 'white-skinned savages' as with the islanders. Eventually, they deliberately spread measles among the Tannese – for them a deadly disease – which killed over a third of the island's population, including many of Paton's Aneityumese teachers. One white man was, of course, the same as another to the Tannese and all their rage fell upon Paton, living in their midst. Among all these trials and sorrows Paton patiently persisted in his work, never thinking of revenge or shooting even in self-defence. He trusted only in the Lord who had placed him there and to whom had been given all power in heaven and in earth. Several times, as he worked, he was surrounded by Tannese with levelled muskets, but as he prayed to Christ 'either Himself to protect me, or to take me home to His glory', they withdrew, leaving him unharmed. So the Lord preserved him, as he persevered in faith and common-sense.

Soon Paton was able to speak to them of 'sin and salvation', and this he did unceasingly. Attendance at 'the Worship' at the mission-centre rose to about forty, but Paton would hold services anywhere, sometimes journeying miles inland to pray and preach on the battle-ground between the opposing tribal armies. With the help now of Abraham only (Mr. Copeland having had to go elsewhere) Paton continued his instruction for three and a half years. Sometimes his hearers were sixty in number, at other times but a handful. He had some enquirers by night and these he instructed in more detail.

Three or four Tannese, including a chief called Nowar, professed to have become Christians, and Paton alternately mourned and hoped over his 'converts'. Their knowledge was very limited, their conduct most inconsistent; Nowar in particular vacillated between loyalty to God and Paton, and to the old ways of Tanna. How must Paton have grieved, as he fled from his enemies, to hear Nowar say, 'When so many children are being killed, why do they not send one for food to me and my family? They are as tender and good as the young fowls.' Yet Nowar, with two others, lived to be a very old man, all the while claiming to believe in Christ, in spite of much hatred and persecution. One Tannese who was most certainly born again was Kowia, a chief who had come to a knowledge of Christ on neighbouring Aneityum and returned to his own island as a teacher. He was one of the victims of the measles epidemic and died with these words on his lips, 'I fear God is taking us all away from Tanna, and will leave my poor people dark and benighted as before, for they hate Jesus and the worship of Jehovah . . . Farewell, Missi', (their name for Paton) 'I am very near death now; we will meet again in Jesus and with Jesus.' On all this Paton comments, 'Thus died a man who had been a cannibal chief, but by the grace of God and the love of Jesus changed and transfigured into a character of light and beauty. What think ye of this, ye scoffers at Missions? What think ye of this, ye sceptics as to the reality of conversion?'

With most, however, it was hatred and persecution. Though doubtless not perfect, yet Paton had given them no cause for offence by his own behaviour; his message had not been false or inadequate, but God's time to save Tanna had not yet come and sin continued to hold its slaves fast. One morning, after he had preached to assembled tribes, (assembled, that is, for war) three Sacred Men stood up, declaring their unbelief in Jehovah. They said, further, that if they could obtain a scrap of any fruit or food Paton had eaten, they had power to kill him. Since this Nahak, or witchcraft, was the source of most of the terror on the island, Paton determined, having thus received a challenge, to take it up with God's aid. So he deliberately and publicly took a bite from each of three fruits and gave one to each of the Sacred Men, denying openly their power over him. The other Tannese fled in terror, but Paton stayed to watch the wavings and incantations. Eventually the priests decided that they needed the help of the other Sacred Men, but would certainly kill him before the following Sunday. On that day Paton, still in perfect health, went to the public ground to preach again and there the Sacred Men had to admit their failure. Paton gathered the people round him to tell them of the love and mercy of God, and though one of the Sacred Men tried to kill him with a spear, the other two became his firm friends, even if not truly converted.

Miaki, the war-chief, said to Paton near the end of his time on Tanna: 'We hate the Worship; it causes all our diseases and deaths, it goes against our customs, and' (most revealingly) 'it condemns the things we delight in.' How typical of the natural man's rejection of the Gospel, whether in Tanna or Britain – trying to find or make excuses, but basically showing a hatred of God's law and Word!

So came the end of Paton's work on Tanna amid war and ever-increasing trials, some chiefs protecting him (when it suited them) but most seeking his death. The tale of Paton's hiding and fleeing, and his escape in an open boat, only to be driven back to the same place by the storm, would take too long to tell, but we must notice some of the incidents which best illustrate God's dealings with His servant during the last struggle before leaving Tanna. When Paton's home was broken into and ransacked, he took refuge with Nowar, who at this time was friendly. The united enemy tribes soon approached and Nowar sat where he could see them, saying, 'Pray and I will watch'. 'We prayed', says Paton, 'as one can only pray when in the jaws of death and on the brink of eternity.' Nowar's people had all scattered in terror and if the warriors had advanced they would have met no opposition. Suddenly, however, the entire army turned and marched in silence back into the bush. Jehovah had heard and delivered 'His trusting and defenceless children'.

Nothing is more characteristic of Paton than his emphasis, in the midst of all these dangers, upon his experience of the presence of Christ. It is in these adverse circumstances that we find revealed, more clearly than in later success, the fellowship which Paton enjoyed with his living Lord. Once he was followed about by a wild chief bearing a loaded musket, for four hours. Of that time he records: 'Without that abiding consciousness of the presence and power of my dear Lord and Saviour, nothing else in the world could have preserved me from losing my reason and perishing miserably. It is the sober truth that I had my nearest and dearest glimpses of the face and smile of my blessed Lord in those dread moments when musket, club or spear was being levelled at my life.' Once Nowar insisted that Paton must spend the night hidden in a tree, and again his emphasis is the same: 'Never in all my sorrows did my Lord draw nearer to me, and speak more soothingly to my soul, than when the moonlight flickered among those chestnut leaves and the night air played on my throbbing brow, as I told all my heart to Jesus.' He always remembered those hours in the tree, describing them as 'the most precious I have spent on earth' and 'a foretaste of heaven'. Here, in the communion with his Lord, habitual as well as exceptional, which Paton enjoyed, we find the strength which enabled him to dare and to endure as few other men have done.

After many more exhausting and dangerous experiences Paton arrived at the Mathiesons' station in a distant part of the island. Even there his enemies followed, and set fire to the fence and the church. This fire would very soon have spread to the house where the missionaries were hiding, but Paton, uniting prayer and courage, went out to cut down the fence, while the Tannese yelled in anger – and urged one another to strike the first blow! Just then a tornado of wind came, blowing in the opposite direction from before and thus saving the house and its occupants. This was followed by rain which put out the fire. The Tannese spoke truly: 'That is Jehovah's rain!' In the days immediately preceding this, Paton had preached in many of the surrounding villages – an amazing achievement – but now he realized that he must leave Tanna, and this he did, not without immense difficulties. He took with him nothing except his Bible, his translations and the clothes on his back.

We have noted in passing not only Paton's courage but also his sure faith in his sovereign God's control over the hand and heart of the intending murderer. Paton lived, however, not only in trust but also in careful obedience. It was his firm belief 'that only when we use every lawful and possible means for the preservation of our life . . . can we expect God to protect us, or have we the right to plead His precious promises.' Again he wrote: 'Though I am by conviction a strong Calvinist, I am no Fatalist. I held on while one gleam of hope remained. Escape for life was now the only path of duty.' In spite of this Paton was criticized for leaving Tanna, even by his friends. He, however, was sure that it is better to live and work for Christ, than to be a self-made martyr, and God's work through His servant in the many succeeding years shows that Paton was right. He could still speak of the Tannese as his 'dear Islanders', and his only consolation, as he left Aneityum for Australia to seek support for and interest in the New Hebrides Mission, was the prospect of returning to them better able to help them then.

Thus far Paton's work on Tanna seemed to be fruitless, the Mission was broken up, and the Tannese were left without a preacher of the Gospel. Nevertheless, it was the record of these dreadful experiences, and especially of God's dealings with Paton himself, that was used to arouse interest in the Mission, provide funds for the work, and turn the thoughts of many to the mission field. It was the first volume of his 'Autobiography', containing the record of 'failure', not of success, that made Paton a 'household word in every Christian land'. We should not pass too quickly from the record of defeat, for thus was a great missionary moulded for a great work. God, whose purposes do not know the word 'failure', was laying the foundation of a wonderful work of grace, not only where Paton was yet to go, but also, at a future date, on this same dark island of Tanna.

III. The *Dayspring* (1862–66)

After being driven out of Tanna, Paton, now nearing the age of forty, became a world-traveller in the name of the Lord on behalf of the New Hebrides Mission. His first errand was to the Presbyterian churches of Australia, to arouse interest in missionary work and to labour for the provision of both missionaries and money for the work, but pre-eminently to raise funds for a mission ship. Before we look at the success of his mission, it ought to be made clear that Paton was not a 'beggar'. He stubbornly and successfully resisted all attempts to introduce him where he might ask for subscriptions. He went to those who had a responsibility for the Mission he served, seeking to arouse in them a realization of their duty to support those who were doing their work. Money was in fact always secondary with Paton, although he realized its importance. His chief concern was not to give an interesting talk about the life and customs of his islanders, nor to raise money for his projects, but to show to Christian people who would listen the overwhelming need of the heathen. Once the true state of affairs was appreciated, he knew that prayer, money, and, by the call of God, missionaries would follow.

As Paton started his new venture in Sydney, he had one name given him, that of a minister, who, it was hoped, would be able to introduce him to others so that he might have opportunities to speak. This man, because of his bad relations with the godly ministers in Sydney, proved more of a hindrance than a help and Paton was unable to gain access to any pulpit or Sunday School. On his second Sunday there, in frustration and with a great yearning to tell his message, he wandered out into the streets in the afternoon. Seeing children flocking into a church (Chalmers Presbyterian Church), he followed them in and after they had been addressed by the minister, Paton went to the front and pleaded to be allowed ten minutes to speak to them. He was, hesitantly, granted fifteen, but was afterwards invited to preach at the evening service and, on the Monday, he was introduced to most of the Presbyterian and Independent ministers in the town. Now opportunities poured in upon him and soon he was able to pass from New South Wales to Victoria and the rest of Australia. Everywhere he was careful to form Committees of Advice and to have respected treasurers appointed. The Lord's hand was truly upon him for good, and soon, instead of the three thousand pounds considered essential for the ship, he had five thousand.

Paton increasingly felt that more missionaries were required, as well as money, and with the approval and encouragement of the committees in Australia he returned to Scotland for a period with this very much in his mind and heart. Here, of course, there were moving meetings with his own parents and those of his dead wife. In Edinburgh he met with the Foreign Missions Committee of his own church, who welcomed him warmly and agreed to his visiting every one of their congregations and the Divinity Hall, where he spoke to the ministerial students. His address at the Divinity Hall was printed under the title 'Come over and help us' and proved most useful in deepening interest in the Mission. By the influence of the Foreign Missions Committee he was made Moderator of the Church's Synod in 1864, an honour from which he shrank, but which he finally accepted in the hope of its being useful for promoting his work on behalf of the heathen. The Reformed Presbyterian Church, soon to unite with the larger Free Church of Scotland, was at that time small and poor. However, she shared with the larger body a great missionary zeal, and it is noteworthy that as the people were aroused to give for missionary work, so also many church debts at home were removed.

Four men gave themselves for work in the islands, but Paton, in haste to return to his people, did not wait to take them with him. Nevertheless, he did not return alone to the southern hemisphere, for God had given him a new wife. Margaret Whitecross was a godly woman from a godly family. Her brother had died in his youth as a missionary abroad, while her sister was married to a minister in Australia, both husband and wife being ardent supporters of Paton's work. We must not linger over the last farewell to Paton's parents, as the patriarch of Torthorwald commended them once again to 'the care and keeping of the Lord God of the families of Israel', but hasten with Paton back to Australia. There, within an hour of landing, he had new problems to face. The new ship, the *Dayspring*, built in Nova Scotia, had arrived safely ('a white-winged angel' Paton called her) but money for current expenses was entirely lacking. Paton's search for the necessary funds was met with coldness and cruel remarks. Some advised selling the ship God had so wonderfully provided; others made it quite clear that, having paid for the ship, they expected the missionaries to pay for its upkeep – from their meagre allowances! Once again Paton was thrown entirely on his God, and how the money was found is a typical Paton story.

On the next day, Sunday, he was to preach in a church which, being the mission of a larger church, was unable even to give him the offering towards his needs. Paton continues his story: 'At the morning service I informed the congregation how we were situated, and expressed the hope that under God and their devoted pastor they would greatly prosper, and would yet be able to help in supporting our Mission to their South Sea neighbours. Returning to the vestry, a lady and gentleman waited to be introduced to me. They were from Launceston, Tasmania. "I am", said he, "Captain and owner of that vessel lying at anchor opposite the *Dayspring*. My wife and I, being too late to get on shore to attend any church in the city, heard this little chapel bell ringing and followed when we saw you going up the hill. We have so enjoyed the service. We do heartily sympathize with you. This cheque for £50 will be a beginning to help you out of your difficulties".' Within four days of this providential occurrence, £456 had been received and when the *Dayspring* sailed she was free from debt.

In his travels Paton was not concerned only to advocate the cause of missions. He always combined with the missionary's story the preaching of the Gospel, believing rightly that only those who own the Saviour as their Lord and see their duty to Him will understand truly the claims of the heathen. On one journey through Australia he found that an expected mail-coach would not be leaving for a few days and that he must reconcile himself to several days' delay. Observing a man, drunk at all hours of the day, followed about by his three small daughters whose mother had recently died, Paton sought him out day after day, appealing to him to give up his foolish ways. At last he succeeded and the man became not only an abstainer but also a Christian, later holding the office of elder in a church. Paton also took an interest in the aborigines, who were widely regarded as being more like brutes than men and utterly beyond the reach of the Gospel. He took some trouble, not only to prove that they were rational beings, capable of knowing God, but also to induce the Australian Christians to put forth greater efforts to send the Gospel among them.

After five years Paton was able to return to the islands, but almost at once he was urged by his fellow-missionaries to go back to Australia, to make provision for the continued support of the *Dayspring*, which had taken him to the islands. He returned by other vessels and while on the island of Maré (in the Loyalty Islands), awaiting a boat to Sydney, he saw to his great grief the work of British missionaries being undone by Roman Catholics (the island having come under French control) 'presenting to the natives', says Paton, 'as many objects of idolatry as their own'. Detained again on New Caledonia, he baptized the children of a number of Protestant parents in defiance of the French military authorities. When the Governor's private secretary arrived to enquire as to his authority for doing this, he replied, 'On the authority of my great Master', and a later interview with the Governor himself terminated with a conducted tour of the island, with no mention of the baptisms.

Paton's long overland journeys brought him many trials, for travel by train was rarely possible. More often he went by coach, or walked, and, on one occasion, ventured on horseback. The horse, in fact, ran away with him, and although he arrived at his destination safely he was so shaken and giddy that he could not stand and sounded, when he tried to speak, as if he, a life-long total abstainer, were drunk! Several times he was lost in the bush and was once rescued in the nick of time from a deadly swamp. Even in Scotland he was not exempt from hardship, suffering a severe attack of frostbite in one foot as a result of a visit to the Orkneys. The effects of this remained with him for the rest of his life. Worse trials, however, befell Paton in the form of conflicts with men, in which his reputation and character and the whole future of his work were concerned.

When he returned to Sydney in the year 1865, Paton was engulfed in his worst conflict so far. *H.M.S. Curaçoa* had been sent to punish the islanders for their treatment of the missionaries, including the murder of two on the island of Erromanga. Tanna was also visited and, failing to find those who had persecuted Paton, the Commodore shelled and destroyed two villages, the inhabitants having been warned of this the previous day. The missionaries had been asked to go as interpreters, which they did, using their influence on the side of mercy and peace. A certain newspaper, however, printed some sensational articles describing the alleged slaughter of the Tannese, with pictures showing the Tannese being blown to bits, and the *Dayspring* lying safely in the lee of the *Curaçoa*, with the missionaries supposedly gloating over their revenge. Everyone immediately assumed the missionaries' guilt, and the 'news' spread to Britain and America, filling friends of the Mission with dismay. Paton records, 'As I stepped ashore at Sydney, I found myself probably the best-abused man in all Australia, and the very name of the New Hebrides Mission stinking in the nostrils of the people.' Immediately he went into battle, demanding and receiving an unequivocal withdrawal and printed apology from the newspaper. In spite of this and a written statement from the captain of the *Curaçoa*, Paton's work in Sydney was for a time rendered almost impossible.

Worse was to come, however. Dr. Geddie of Aneityum attacked his fellow-missionaries before the Sydney presbytery, saying that rather than have anything to do with the *Curaçoa*'s visit, he would have had his hand burned off. This melodramatic but popular statement Paton countered by reminding them that he had lost all on Tanna and sought no redress, not even presenting to the Governor of Sydney a petition sent by friendly chiefs on Tanna. The *Curaçoa*'s visit had been brought about by a different petition. Dr. Geddie had to admit that he had written and signed this petition. On the whole the churches of Australia and the world supported Paton, but much harm had been done and more than one personal friend was lost to him over this affair. Paton endured many other griefs from both Christians and non-Christians as he travelled in the service of his Master and the Mission; nevertheless, possibly the bitterest trial of all at this time was not to be able to return to Tanna. There he would almost certainly have been killed, so instead he went to the island of Aniwa, where he spent the next fifteen years.

IV. Aniwa (1866–81)

Aniwa lies about twenty miles to the north-east of the much larger island of Tanna. Indeed, when the *Dayspring* took Paton to Aniwa, she called first at his old island-home. The old chief Nowar, unstable but friendly, came aboard and tried to persuade Paton to stay. He took the missionaries ashore and, leading Mrs.

Paton by the hand, showed her the tree where her husband had hidden, saying, 'The God who protected Missi there will always protect you'. His pleas were all in vain, but, before they left, he made a visiting Aniwan chief, a Sacred Man, promise to protect the missionary and his wife. So Paton came to Aniwa, where at the age of forty-two he began his work again. Everything had to be learned afresh, except the mature and proved trust in his God which led him on.

When they sought a site for a house, the one which they chose was refused them and the Aniwans compelled them to have another. Strangely enough this proved to be a better site, although the mounds on it consisted of the bones and refuse of centuries of cannibal feasts. Years later an old chief revealed their reasons. 'When Missi came, we saw his boxes. We knew he had blankets and calico, axes and knives, fish-hooks and all such things. We said, "Don't drive him off, else we will lose all these things. We will let him land, but we will force him to live on the Sacred Plot. Our gods will kill him and we will divide all he has amongst the men of Aniwa".' They watched Paton build, and nothing happened; he planted bananas and they felt sure he would be killed, but he ate the bananas and still no one died. So they came to the conclusion that Jehovah God was stronger than the gods of Aniwa.

Once again Paton began to treat illness as best he could, in spite of their superstitious fears of medicine; once again he learned a new language, helped in some measure by the ability of some to understand his Tannese. One day he needed some materials from the house and sent a message to Mrs. Paton by a friendly old chief. He wrote the message on a piece of planed wood, assuring the chief that, if he would take it to her, she would send what he needed. He was amazed to see Mrs. Paton look at the wood and fetch the required articles. Paton explained how the wood could speak and improved the occasion to show how God speaks to us through His book. A great desire was awakened in the old chief to see and read God's Word and he became an invaluable help to Paton in learning the language and later in Bible translation.

Very few, however, were so friendly and all the dangers of Tanna were repeated on Aniwa. Paton was once again in frequent danger of death. Accidents and illnesses were attributed to the missionaries, leading to threats and attempts to set their house on fire. For ten days a savage Erromangan lurked around, waiting for his opportunity with tomahawk and musket. The situation into which the Patons came was fraught with difficulties, and causes for offence soon appeared. Two Aneityumese teachers, who had arrived shortly before the missionaries, had been virtually enslaved, being compelled to work all Friday and Saturday to prepare food for the feast with which the Aniwans followed the Sunday 'service'. When Paton stopped this and also refused to pay them for attending 'the Worship', the Aniwans became angry and revengeful. 'Often', writes Paton, 'have I had to run into the arms of some savage when his club was swung or his musket levelled at my head and, praying to Jesus, so clung round him that he could neither strike nor shoot me till his wrath cooled down and I was able to slip away . . . At other times nothing could be said, nothing done, but stand still in silent prayer, asking God to protect us or to prepare us for going home to His Glory.'

Amid all this the Word of God took effect. Paton's first Aniwan convert was the old, friendly chief, Namakei. Namakei, whose brother had tried to shoot Paton, came to a knowledge of Christ as his Saviour together with another chief and his wife, and thus the church on Aniwa began. Both Namakei's daughter Litsi Soré (the Great), and her cousin, Litsi Sisi (the Less), whose father had intended Paton's death, were motherless and their fathers entrusted them to the Patons. Namakei and his brother thus became more and more deeply interested in the missionaries and their work. Other orphans were placed in Paton's care and when troubles increased, as a few men openly put away their idols, it was the orphans, the self-appointed guardians of the missionaries, who warned and saved them. Paton bore a bold testimony to the sinfulness of many Aniwan practices, finding as he did so that the Word of God brought conviction of sin and begot faith, and this faith brought forth 'works meet for repentance'. He gives details of three murderers of their own children (two fathers, one mother) and records how each was converted and later adopted an orphan. Another man murdered his wife so that he could take another.

This produced no critical reaction from his village, but his second wife led him and their children to church and to Christ. Murderers were often honoured among the heathen and one lad lamented the fact that, now he was a Christian, he would always have to remain a common man, without fame and honour. Later he learnt the way of Christian greatness, becoming a teacher, first in his own village and then on a heathen island.

The work was thus going reasonably well, if slowly, but it was the sinking of the well that gave finality to the victory of Christ and His Spirit on Aniwa. The island had no permanent fresh-water supply, only a somewhat temperamental water-hole on the ground of two Sacred Men, who claimed to control it – and, of course, demanded money for so doing. This Paton refused to encourage and he determined, by the help of God, to sink a well near his own house. He was completely ignorant of such matters, but trusted that God in His providence would guide him aright. He reckoned on having to dig through earth and coral for about thirty feet, but had always the fear that his well would pro-duce only salt-water. When he announced his plan to Namakei and his co-chief they thought that he was going mad (and said so) and appointed men in relays to watch him lest he took his own life. Soon Paton became exhausted, but induced the young Aniwans to help by offering them English fish-hooks as rewards. When the hole was twelve feet deep, however, the sides caved in and, although Paton continued, not a single Aniwan would enter the hole. The friendly chief devised ingenious arguments to dissuade Paton from persisting in the work. 'Now', said he, 'had you been in that hole last night you would have been buried, and a man-of-war would have come from Queen 'Toria to ask for the Missi that lived here. We would have to say, "He is in that hole". The Captain would ask, "Who killed him and put him down there?" We would have to say, "He went down there himself". The Captain would answer, "Nonsense! Who ever heard of a white man going down into the earth to bury himself? You killed him, you put him there; don't hide your bad conduct with lies!" Then he would bring out his big guns and shoot us . . . Give up this mad freak, for no rain will be found by going downwards on Aniwa.'

Nevertheless the work of excavation went on. Paton did all the digging himself, having rigged up a pulley-system for emptying his buckets with the help of one of the teachers. As he neared thirty feet the earth began to be damp, but although he had faith that God would provide a spring, the fear of finding salt-water after all was always there. He announced his hope of finding water on the morrow to the old chief, who replied, 'We expect daily, if you reach water, to see you drop through into the sea and the sharks will eat you!' Sharks, however, were more remote than cannibals and next day he sank a narrow shaft in the centre of his pit. Thus he found water in 'Jehovah's well', brackish but fresh. The chiefs had gathered nearby, but when Paton took up a jugful of water for them to see and taste they hardly dared approach the fearsome spot. Strange to say, the level of water in the well rose and fell with the tide, but the water was fresh nevertheless. Later, during a drought, the well saved the islanders from death. The lesson of Jehovah's well was enforced when six or seven others tried to sink wells in different places, only to meet with either coral rock or salt-water. 'Missi not only used pick and spade, but he prayed and cried to his God', was their discerning comment.

On the next Sunday Namakei asked permission to preach, and gave them a sermon on the well, ending: 'The Jehovah God has sent us rain from the earth. Why should He not also send us His Son from Heaven? Namakei stands up for Jehovah.' That very afternoon he and several others brought their idols to Paton and during the days that followed the missionaries 'stood still and saw the salvation of the Lord'. Idols were burned, or buried, or sunk in the depths of the sea. Thus in time, every inhabitant of Aniwa became an avowed worshipper of Jehovah, only two remaining unbaptized – both of whom manifested clearly that they had new hearts, shyness and infirmity alone holding them back. A change so sudden and so complete may lead some to question whether this was a real work of the Holy Spirit, and not a merely external turning from idolatry to nominal Christianity. However, the evidence is quite plain; the entire life of Aniwa was influenced by the new faith. They unitedly resolved to ask God's blessing on every meal and, by some sort of common consent, family prayer began to be offered morning and evening, not to gods of stone, but to the Heavenly Father. The Lord's Day was immediately recognized and observed and soon the chiefs met to improve discipline and law on the island. We have already seen some evidence of a true work of God in the lives of the converted murderers; more will appear as we trace the progress of the Gospel on the island.

Paton was careful to train the Aniwans to do things for themselves, including the construction of their church. They decided what was needed, divided the responsibility, and set to work. Soon the building was completed. That same year a hurricane razed it to the ground, but immediately they commenced rebuilding. Shortly, the work was halted through the lack of a large tree, none big enough remaining on the island. At this point, a chief whom Paton had only just persuaded to take his share of the work supplied the need, giving the central roof-tree from his own house.

It was in 1869, nearly three years after settling on the island, that Paton held his first Aniwan communion. It was preceded by the baptism of the twelve Aniwans who were to partake of the Lord's Supper with the missionaries and the six Aneityumese teachers. These twelve had been approved for baptism out of the original twenty who had been allowed to attend the communicants' classes; they were headed by the old chief Namakei. Paton's heart was full to overflowing as the islanders, in unusual silence, watched the service. 'At the moment when I put the bread and wine into those dark hands, once stained with the blood of cannibalism, but now stretched out to receive and partake the emblems and seals of the Redeemer's love, I had a foretaste of the joy of Glory that well nigh broke my heart to pieces. I shall never taste a deeper bliss, till I gaze on the glorified face of Jesus Himself.' In the afternoon an open-air prayer-meeting was held, in which seven of the new church-members led the people in prayer.

Instruction went on throughout the island, by the roadside, under a tree, or anywhere else where the people would listen. Reading, naturally occupied first place, with sewing, dressmaking and singing also receiving attention. Each village later built its own school, which served as church on Sundays, and to these schools Paton sent his Aneityumese teachers or the best of the Aniwan teachers trained in his own school. Thus the Gospel produced a new society, based on Scriptural principles, applied, as closely as the chiefs could manage, to their own circumstances. Paton translated, printed, and, above all, expounded the Scriptures – and the work progressed.

Later on, a Sabbath would be spent as follows: services would begin soon after dawn, the worshippers being summoned by the church bell; in each service an elder or one of the members would lead in prayer. Immediately after the second service comes Paton's communicants' class, based on the Shorter Catechism, proved from Scripture and applied to conscience and life. At the same time an informal prayer-meeting is being held by the church-members – their own idea. After Sunday School come the village tours, with Paton and an experienced elder each taking half the island. As the day closes the people in every village assemble for evening prayers, together with hymns. Paton comments: 'When I returned to so-called civilization and saw how the Lord's Day is abused in white Christendom, my soul longed after the holy Sabbaths of Aniwa.'

The converts rejoiced in the newly-discovered love of God, their lives shining by contrast with their former state. Many showed amazing zeal to spread the Gospel and so it penetrated to every part of Aniwa and to many of the neighbouring islands. Some of them wanted to preach the Gospel to an inland tribe and sent a message that they would come and do so on the following Sunday. The reply was: 'If you come, you will be killed.' They went, unarmed. Spears began to be thrown at them, which they dodged or struck aside, not even throwing them back. The inland people stopped their attack out of sheer surprise and listened in awe to the believers' message. Chief and tribe later confessed Christ for themselves. Such sacrificial efforts for the salvation of others argue well for the reality of Paton's achievements. Another evidence that the Holy Spirit made the change is the way in which the converted Aniwans died. Naswai, an inland chief, who was both teacher in his own village school and an elder in the church, died during Paton's absence. Before his death he pleaded with his own people, many of whom had long resisted the Gospel, to love and serve Christ, assuring them with his last breath that he had been a new creature since he gave his heart to Christ and that he was perfectly happy in going to be with his Saviour.

After 1881 Paton visited the island only rarely, but the Aniwan elders carried on the work faithfully, for here was a truly indigenous church, notwithstanding their love and reverence for their Missi. Visiting them in 1886, he was awakened early on the Sunday by the sound of singing. He jumped up and enquired what was happening, receiving this reply: 'Missi, since you left, we have found it very hard to live near to God, so the Chief and the teachers and a few others meet when daylight comes on every Sabbath morning and spend the first hour of every Lord's Day in prayer and praise. They are met to pray for you now, that God may help you in your preaching, and that all hearts may bear fruit to the glory of Jesus this day.' The same elders had conducted communicants' classes and presented to Paton many candidates for church membership. Paton was moved to compare the faithfulness of these Aniwan elders with that of those in lands long supposed to be Christian. If we do the same, we shall surely be humbled. Here was a true church, in which elders and people all played their part, a church ruled by the Holy Spirit. Paton could well be satisfied with the results of his labours, but his service was by no means finished yet.

V. The World (1881–1905)

Paton's last twenty-five years were spent in a multiplicity of activities which took him into many countries and allowed him only a few months in his beloved islands. We shall gain a clearer picture of his varied interests and, indeed, of his greatness, if we abandon chronology and look at some of the directions in which his energy was turned. His journeys seem amazing when we consider, not only the slow means of travel, but also his advancing years. These travels were not sightseeing tours but full of hard work; the older he became, the harder he seemed to work. Indeed, when the doctor ordered a rest for the ill and old man, he grew more impatient as the days passed, saying, 'I will be no more a loafer. If I cannot work here I must go home to Victoria and off to the islands where I can live and die among my dear Aniwans.' These later travels began with a visit to Britain and a period of six years spent in visiting the various colonies of Australasia, but then in 1892 he was sent on a tour round the world with various commissions, visiting America, Canada and Britain before resuming his Australian tours. In 1899, at the age of seventy-five, he was off again to the same countries; in England the indefatigable missionary crowded seventy-one meetings and 2,500 miles' travel into fifty-three days. This ended his wider travels, but to the end he was moving about Australia and seizing any opportunity of a visit to the New Hebrides.

At the age of sixty-eight, he was addressing on average fifteen meetings a week; 'my only stimulant', he records, 'the ever-springing fountain of pure joy in the work of my Lord and Saviour Jesus Christ.' He regarded the time left to him to serve Christ as short, and packed as much work as he could into each day. Just before his seventy-sixth birthday, in a period of ill-health, he addressed, on successive Sundays, ten, eight and four different congregations, as well as at least one on every weekday. Frequently, while in America, he would travel hundreds of miles from one meeting to the next, without a meal. Even on a sea-voyage the absence of meetings merely meant more time for letter-writing. 'We had happy daily religious services', he records of one voyage, 'and I managed to secure about eight hours to myself out of every twenty-four for copying and translations, finishing my dictionary of the Aniwan language, and the Mission work on which I was constantly engaged.' So much activity could be carnal, but with Paton all was subordinated to a zeal for the Lord and His work that would not let him rest, and, in fellowship with Christ, never became mere activism. That such an amount of public speaking was possible is evidence not only of the missionary's capacity for work, but also of his popularity with every type of audience. An experienced local organizer in Sunderland remarked, after crowded meetings, 'Nothing and no one else would fill this hall.' Paton's 'Autobiography', which his brother James had wrung out of him and edited for publication, appeared in 1889 and opened the way into many places and hearts. It had an enormous sale, being translated into French, German, Italian, Welsh and Japanese. It made Paton, we are told, 'a household name in every Christian land.'

Paton greatly treasured his many meetings with individuals, who included many of his great contemporaries. George Müller, who gave him £50 for the Mission, made a particular impression on him, as also did C. H. Spurgeon. By the latter, Paton was introduced to a meeting as 'The King of the Cannibals' and Mrs. Spurgeon presented him with a copy of her husband's *Treasury of David* and '£5 from the Lord's cows'. (These were cows kept by Mrs. Spurgeon, who gave the profit to the Lord's work.) The friendship of the Hon. Ion Keith-Falconer, missionary to the Arabs in Aden, was a link with London which Paton particularly valued.

Paton's travels had many and varied purposes. In Australia he was generally the advocate of his Mission, as often also elsewhere. For much of the time, the building and supporting of the various *Dayspring*'s occupied him. He longed for a ship owned by the Mission, free from all sinful associations, to be the messenger of the Gospel among the islands. When the first *Dayspring* was wrecked in Aneityum harbour in a hurricane, Paton was given the task of raising money for a second ship, and was again successful. Later a third and larger *Dayspring* was also financed by his efforts and the purpose of building it carried through only by his persistence. Within two years, however, the ship was wrecked on an uncharted reef, a terrible shock to the aged missionary, who nevertheless set about securing a fourth vessel. To his intense disappointment, almost half the missionary synod disagreed with the project, and, in the interests of unity and peace, it was set aside.

Another errand, for the fulfilling of which Paton went round the world and became a delegate to various world Presbyterian assemblies, was the defence of his beloved islanders, both from the Kanaka* slave-trade and also from the sale of alcohol, opium and weapons. To this end he toured America, where he spoke with and influenced greatly two successive presidents, and also Britain, where his constant fight for the well-being of the New Hebrideans earned him in the House of Commons the title of 'The member for the Kanakas'. Fights with these vested interests made him many enemies, and libellous allegations were made and spread about his personal life and habits. Before his death, however, Paton knew that victory on the Kanaka issue, at least, had been gained. Nevertheless, this sort of concern, however dear to his heart, was never allowed to dominate his life and work. Writing half apologetically from New York about the time spent on these matters, he says, 'I am not losing an hour over it. My audiences range from 300 to 3,000 or more and a deeper interest is being awakened in foreign missions. I hope too that some are being led to Jesus for salvation.'

This quotation is typical of Paton's spiritual attitude and aims. He never permitted himself to be side-tracked by the need to raise funds for missionary work or to fight against social wrongs. 'In all my addresses', he wrote, 'I strove to combine the evangelist with the missionary, applying every incident in my story to the conscience of the hearer and seeking to win the sinner to Christ and the believer to a more consecrated life. For I knew that if I succeeded in these higher aims, then money too would be freely laid upon the altar of the Lord.' Again he asserts, 'The getting of collections, however anxiously desired for our Mission, was never my primary aim, but always the saving of souls by the story of the New Hebrides.' The sanctifying of the Lord's Day was another constant concern by precept and example. In San Francisco, among men and women going about their usual occupations, Paton, to the astonishment of his guides and even of his friends, insisted on walking the considerable distance between his three services.

So great was Paton's missionary concern that he was often taunted with being a man of one idea. Such taunts, he would

---

*Kanaka: the Hawaiian word for 'man', a name applied to natives of the South Sea Islands in general, especially to those set to work on the sugar plantations of Queensland.

[333]

respond, usually came from those who lacked even one idea, adding, 'My life has been dominated by one sacred purpose, but in pursuing it, the Lord has enabled me to be evangelist as well as missionary; He has enabled me, whilst seeking much-needed money, to seek for and save and bless many souls – has enabled me to defend the holy Sabbath in many lands – has enabled me to maintain the right of every child in Christian lands, or heathen, to be taught to read the blessed Bible and to understand it . . . and has enabled me also to do battle against the infernal Kanaka or labour traffic, one of the most cruel and blood-stained forms of slavery on the face of the earth.' In another place he records his achievements: 'I will write it to the praise of my blessed Redeemer; there are missionaries at this day labouring in every heathen land, who have assured me that they first gave themselves away to the glorious work while drinking in from my lips the living testimony from the New Hebrides, that the Gospel is still the power of God and the wisdom of God unto salvation; and there are individual Christians, and sometimes also congregations of the Lord, now zealously supporting missionaries to the heathen, who, till they heard the story of cannibals won for Christ by our noble missionaries on the New Hebrides, had foolishly branded the modern Christian mission to the heathen as the greatest imposture and failure of the century.'

So the veteran missionary travelled the world, but his heart was still in Aniwa. We have already recorded his visit to the island in 1886, but this was by no means his last; during the next six years he made several visits to the New Hebrides before going off to America and Canada. Wherever he was, his thoughts were on the islanders and their spiritual and bodily welfare. It was for them, as well as for his Lord, that he made his sacrifices and allowed himself to be dragged away from the islands. Further occasional visits followed his return to Australia, but it was not until 1898 that a longer visit could be paid to Aniwa. Even as he travelled he was correcting the proof sheets of his Aniwan New Testament and he took the finished translation with him to the island. His biographers describe how this 'fruit of an inspiring and beautiful old age' was produced. 'In trains, steadying paper on the back of his hand, at junctions waiting for connections, in station waiting-rooms, late into the night and long before dawn in houses where he was guest, often after two or three meetings, he never lost an instant. The manuscript went by post from all sorts of outlying villages, and the proofs came back, and were read and checked in the same tireless journeyings.' After many delays he arrived on Aniwa with his precious cargo. In a letter from the island he wrote: 'What a welcome we got! On the Sabbath we had a service of thanksgiving preceding the great event of the distribution of the complete New Testament. No one can realize my overflowing joy as I presented to each a copy of that Book, the divine teachings of which had raised them from their former savagery. They were intensely delighted with their prize. For this they had prayed and wrought for many years to pay for the printing and binding.' Not content with this, he spent several months instructing them, studying with them three or four chapters a week, especially the epistles, and first of all, 'Romans'. He spent much time also in going among the villages and in the preparation of hymns.

In 1902 came another visit to Aniwa, on which Mrs. Paton accompanied him. Here he gained new inspiration from the joy of the people at their return, and from their prayers for the blessing of God on him and themselves. This time he brought with him for distribution a new hymn book of one hundred and fifty three hymns and also a translation of the Shorter Catechism; all this was his own work. There was a severe drought during their stay but the old well of their early days was the unfailing supply for the whole island. Paton longed to stay there but, Mrs. Paton being taken ill, he had to return to Australia. He visited the island again in 1904, soon after his eightieth birthday, a wearisome journey even for a younger man, but Paton made it without hesitation to see once more his children in the Lord. Once there he had to be restrained from starting to rebuild the house! Soon, however, he had to leave and as he went tears filled all eyes, for they knew what he refused to admit, that this was his last visit. The doctors forbade any more such trips.

Nevertheless, we have not finished with Aniwa in the story of

God's work among the islands. On a communion Sunday on Aniwa during Paton's 1898 visit, the preacher addressed the people in the following words: 'Long ago Dr. Paton, the aged, was a young man and lived in Scotland. The light came into his heart and he said within himself, "I must not hide this light, I must let it shine." And so he left his own land and brought the light of Jesus to Aniwa. Aniwa was then a dark land, but now it is full of light. Men and women of Aniwa, don't hide your light, let it shine. There is a dark land across the sea there; take the light of Jesus there and let it shine till that land is full of light like your own.' This dark land was Tanna and it was in great measure through Paton's Aniwa that it received the light. God worked in many different ways to use Paton, after all, for the conversion of Tanna. Some time previously, about a hundred warriors had sought shelter on Aniwa, where, instead of being eaten, as would have happened earlier, they were treated kindly and fed, at great sacrifice, from the island's poor resources. All this greatly impressed the Tannese. Nevertheless, although missionaries returned to Tanna seven years after Paton's escape, for a long while they made very little impression on the people. In 1896 a new missionary was sent to the island, supported by 'The John G. Paton Mission Fund' in Great Britain, a direct result of the *Autobiography*. Dr. Paton visited the island in preparation for the new worker, reporting, 'We have talked with a big chief and some others and they are to consult with the surrounding chiefs and see if they are all agreed to have and protect a missionary living among them. They had, only a few days before, killed and feasted on a man and two women there. Two tribes are at war.' Thus, although some conversions had been seen, the island generally had not changed very much in thirty-four years and it was only with the coming of the new missionary that Tanna was, in any real sense, won for Christ. His name was Frank (Faranke to the Aniwans, on whose island he was born and bred), the third son of the aged missionary; and Lomai, the preacher at the communion service on Aniwa, was the young man's first convert.

In response to Lomai's sermon, Aniwan teachers with their wives were soon labouring on Tanna. Litsi Soré, daughter of chief Namakei and now Queen of the Aniwans, was among them. Her much-loved husband had been killed by a Tannese chief living on Aniwa and she became possessed with the idea of taking the Gospel to the murderer's people. So when Frank Paton went to Tanna, she and her new husband offered themselves, at the head of six or seven Aniwans, to go and help spread the Gospel. The ways of God's providence are often mysterious but sometimes, as here, we can trace the way His wisdom has taken. Failure and disappointment on the human level ultimately issued in the triumph of His Gospel and the manifestation of His glory.

VI.   Last Days (1905–07) and The Man of God

Paton continued 'indomitable to the end', renouncing the pleasure of the company of his beloved children and grand-children, who were his especial joy, to continue his journeys in Australia. In 1905 Mrs. Paton died, having been his companion and helper for forty-one years. She had given herself not only to her husband but also to his islanders; she was the first white woman who dared to live in their heathen midst and she won for Christ the many orphans entrusted to her care, who, to a great extent, became the leaders and teachers of Aniwa. She established a Christian home amidst the heathen darkness and, under God, this, combined with the preached Word, brought new life to the island. Her children bore testimony to her heroism and devotion to Christ, which aroused in them not only a deep love for her, but also a strong and permanent desire to follow in her steps. Margaret Whitecross Paton was always worthy of her great husband.

After his wife's death, Dr. Paton was welcomed into the home of his daughter-in-law's mother, but he was rarely there as he continued his long and tiring journeys through the Australian bush. One day, the horse drawing his buggy being scared by a train, he was thrown and knocked unconscious. He soon revived and insisted that the meeting to which he was travelling must be held. The assembled congregation saw a white-haired man, his head swathed in bandages, being helped into the pulpit to plead his cause. 'What have I been spared for', he argued, 'if it is not to use every remaining opportunity to plead for the perishing heathen.' From this accident he never fully recovered, although he continued his preaching and speaking, often in much pain. His last message was delivered in a church where two of his sons had ministered; here, for three-quarters of an hour, he captivated his hearers, pleading to the end the cause of his dear islanders.

His youngest brother, Dr. James Paton, editor of the *Autobiography* and treasurer and director of 'The John G. Paton Mission Fund', pre-deceased him by a month. Thus many of his earthly ties were loosed, but still his Aniwans silently called for his help. He pleaded to be allowed to go to Aniwa in the following January (1907), but instead his condition grew worse. Sometimes he became delirious and all his mental wanderings concerned the islands and the Mission. To visitors he spoke of his unclouded peace within. 'With me', he would say, 'there is not a shadow or cloud, all is perfect peace and joy in believing.' With fervent prayers for his children and their children, that there might be 'not one wanting' in Glory, he gradually slipped into unconsciousness and on January 28, went to be with the Lord.

For well over fifty years in a variety of ways and in many different places, John G. Paton had been a preacher of the Gospel. He was widely known for his adventures and his courage, famous and well-loved in thousands of Christian homes. The outstanding impression of him is not that here was a great preacher, though he could and did hold great congregations spellbound, nor that here was a courageous adventurer and traveller, though in this he excelled most explorers, but that here was a man of God. His simple godliness was noticed by ministers and children, by hostesses and cabbies. It was expressed not only in his deep communion with his Saviour, which has already been noted, but also in a constant spirituality, as he lived and walked with and before God. When his mission in Scotland in search of support for the *Dayspring* was hindered by jealousies in Australia, his thought was: 'Thus our God throws us back upon Himself.' The fear of the Lord ruled every aspect of his life, including his deepest wishes, as is shown by his feelings during a later dispute over the *Dayspring*: 'I do therefore most earnestly pray and hope that there may be unity, at whatever cost to my personal predilections; for the spectacle of a disloyal minority undermining and destroying the work of the majority is enough to bring on our cause the contempt of men, if not also the curse of God.' His desire for a ship owned by the mission, without any commercial interests being involved, sprang from the same concern for the glory and blessing of God above all things. He wanted a vessel unstained by slave-blood and unpolluted by the sale of firearms and alcohol.

Naturally, we expect to see such godliness accompanied by much prayer, and this we find. Nothing is so revealing in this respect as the islanders' attitude to prayer and to Paton's prayers in particular. On one occasion Frank Paton was having a difficult voyage from Tanna to Aniwa. With him was an Aniwan teacher who, looking longingly towards the dangerous reef and white breakers of his own island, said, 'The old man will be standing upon the rocks all the time and his heart will be saying, "My son is in the boat away out there", and then he will be praying hard to Jesus to help us and bring us safe to land.' And so it proved. Even the half-heathen Nowar of Tanna, watching the enemy advance said, 'Missi, sit down beside me and pray to our Jehovah God, for if He does not send deliverance now, we are all dead men.' Prayer characterized the Aniwan church as it did the church's founder. Together they prayed for the recovery of a Christian chief, who meant much to the young work on Aniwa, and health was restored. 'I am a firm believer in prayer', he often said, and illustrated the power of believing prayer with many stories. One concerned the missionary himself: while in Sydney, he received a letter from Antas, a converted chief on Malo Island. His father and the rest of the tribe had resolved to starve him out of his new religion; all food was made 'taboo' for Antas and the few other believers. Paton instantly prayed and began to think. He remembered a man in Sydney who had promised to do his best to give any practical help which was needed urgently. Paton, however, could recall neither his name nor his address, a most unusual thing for him. so he went out into the street, wondering how best to go about finding him. The man himself solved the problem by crossing the road just ahead of Paton, who ran to catch him and enlist his aid in sending some much-needed rice to Antas and his friends. 'Who says that God does not answer prayer?' Paton concluded.

Dr. Samuel Zwemer writes: 'The life of John G. Paton is one long record of answered prayer. By prayer he was led into missionary service; by prayer he was preserved on his long voyages; by prayer he dug wells and found fresh-water where others failed; by prayer he checked the hand of the assassin; by prayer he found the right words for his Gospel translations; by prayer he influenced the lives of young and old during his furloughs in Scotland and America. Only in eternity, in the presence of the innumerable company of the redeemed, can the result of such a life of prayer be measured.' Paton was confident that, as one of God's chosen children, he could address his Heavenly Father on any subject and be heard. He prayed with the simple childlike trust which God desires, and the Lord did great and wonderful things for him.

It has often been pointed out that the confidence in God's election, so dear to the hearts of the Covenanters and their spiritual descendants, leads not to antinomianism and idleness, but to that fear of the Lord which promotes diligence and self-sacrifice. In Paton we find a notable example of this. It was a hardship to his spirit that his body needed food and sleep, that hosts and hostesses must not be deserted too soon at their own table, that he might return to his work. He begrudged every second not spent directly in the work of the Lord. When in Chicago, he occupied a room overlooking a street along which a great procession passed for the opening of the great World Fair. Paton was busy with correspondence and although he heard the noise and knew the reason for it, he saw nothing of the great spectacle. The organizers of his meetings were attacked on occasion for being cruel to him; one lady said that if Dr. Paton sank under his work, they would be responsible for his murder! In fact, of course, they were doing their best to restrain the missionary from overtaxing his willing but failing body. His last letter,

[340]

written from the severe pain of his death-bed, contained only one complaint: 'Here am I lying, unable to work and there is so much to be done.' Money, as well as time, belonged to the Lord and his biographers record 'at least one authenticated case', where Paton, no longer young, had slept under a bush, rather than 'waste' the Lord's money on hotel expenses. Any gift received for the Mission was carefully acknowledged and used; any gift pressed upon him for his own use was promptly and unalterably refused. No critic must be able to say that he had gained anything personally from his efforts.

The amazing thing is that in all these experiences – success on Aniwa, popularity round the world, answered prayer in every place, love and near-worship from many, young and old – Paton always retained his childlike humility. It was only through the determination and unceasing pressure of his brother James that Paton ever consented to supply the material out of which his autobiography was fashioned. His argument was: 'Am I so to take the glory due to my Lord as to write what I have accomplished when He has done it all?' He was eventually convinced that the book could be written for God's honour and praise, and so it was compiled and published with this introductory note, 'What I write here is for the glory of God ... Latterly the conviction has been borne home to me that if there be much in my experience which the Church of God ought to know, it would be pride on my part, and not humility, to let it die with me.' He was given the honorary degree of D.D. by the University of Edinburgh. Mrs. Paton recalls it as a thrilling occasion when honour was paid to her husband – but, characteristically, the event is not mentioned in the *Autobiography*.

It is equally characteristic of Paton that, often in his meetings, he did not mention his own work at all, telling rather of his colleagues' achievements, and this to such an extent that one newspaper referred to him as the agent of the London Missionary Society! The display of enthusiasm which greeted him everywhere troubled him, for he feared that it came from a spirit of flattery for the man, rather than admiration for the work done by the Spirit of God through him. In 1894 he was asked to speak to the

Young People's Auxiliary of the Baptist Missionary Society, a meeting described by his biographers as 'the most magnificent of all the wonderful gatherings.' Paton left afterwards in a cab, where, after a few moments' silence, he buried his face in his hands and wept. In response to his companion's anxious enquiry, he said, 'Dear brother, I am not ill. I am only weeping because I fear I have not made sufficiently good use of the great opportunity placed in my hands this afternoon.' After an address in Naples, a hearer reported: 'Never shall we forget the veteran missionary's simple and graphic story. One wonders if he is at all aware how brave a man he is.' When he was dying, if anyone spoke of his past achievements, it only gave him pain, and thus it had been all his life. This humility also showed itself in a childlike lowliness in public. Once, as he advanced up a station platform, the guard held open invitingly the door of a compartment. 'Thank you, sir', said Paton, 'is it third class?' On discovering that it was first-class he went on, 'Missionaries never travel first-class; third please', and all this with the same bared white head and tone of regard which caused a London cabby to ask who he was, and to add, 'I shan't forget 'im in a 'urry.'

Nevertheless, the lamb could become a lion when roused to the defence of his beloved islanders or the no less beloved Gospel. He fought long and tenaciously against the Kanaka traffic; he was known and cursed by the evil white traders in the islands, but nothing moved him from his righteous anger against sin. He was the same in a very different and strange experience which befell him in America at a Temperance Union which he had been asked to address. An earlier speaker, a Unitarian ('or rather an infidel', says Paton), occupied most of the time, and this in sowing the seeds of class-hatred and unbelief. He had just parodied the Lord's Supper when Paton interrupted him, branded his teaching as blasphemy and an insult to Christ, and, finally, summoning the audience 'to remember that we must all appear before the Judgement Seat of Christ, implored them and Dr. Blank amongst the rest, to seek pardon and acceptance at the feet of Jesus now, that they might find their Judge was also their Saviour in the last awful day.'

Paton's resolution in witness and rebuke was normally accompanied, as we would expect, by a tact and mildness that turned away wrath. On one voyage, where the language of his fellow-passengers was unusually profane, he felt compelled to protest, telling them how wounded he was to hear them cursing the name of God and taking in vain the name of Christ. One of them, a banker, replied with an angry oath, to which Paton responded: 'Dear Sir, you and I are strangers. But I have pitied you very tenderly ever since we came on board for your heavy trouble and hacking cough. You ought to be the last to curse that blessed Name as you may soon have to appear in His presence. I return, however, no railing word. If the Saviour were as dear to your heart as He is to mine, you would better understand me.' Not only did Paton hear no more oaths, but the banker later met him and invited him warmly to his home.

Paton lived through the period when Modernism was gaining its crippling hold upon the church, but he made no concessions to it. He had been grounded in the doctrine of the Westminster Shorter Catechism; this was what he taught his people in Glasgow and Aniwa, and this was what he believed to the end. Before leaving Scotland for the last time, he confessed his undying allegiance to 'the grand old Covenanting truths of the Scripture.' To his converts he taught simple, sound, positive doctrine. That he was no mean theologian can be seen from his clear distinction between regeneration and conversion, which occurs, incidentally, in his description of the conversion of one who tried to murder him on Aniwa: 'Truly there is only one way of regeneration, being born again by the power of the Spirit of God, the new heart; but there are many ways of conversion, of outwardly turning to the Lord, of taking the actual first step that shows whose side we are on. Regeneration is the sole work of the Holy Spirit in the human heart and soul, and is in every case one and the same. Conversion, on the other hand, bringing into play the action also of the human will, is never absolutely the same perhaps in even two souls – as like yet as different as are the faces of men.' There is no trace of a developing theology in Paton's life. He was born into a home and church environment of godly and living orthodoxy, and his early faith, though deepened and matured, never altered.

Hence Paton held fast, amid the liberal theology current in his later years, to the truth he had believed and preached from his youth. In America he was asked how missionaries teaching the 'second probation' doctrine would succeed with his cannibals. He replied: 'How can they succeed on such terms anywhere? Our cannibals would say, "If we have a second chance hereafter, let us enjoy our present pleasures and risk the future".' To believe it but not preach it he roundly condemned as hypocrisy. His view of the Scriptures was equally clear and definite. In a letter from Aniwa in 1904 he wrote: 'Friends of the Bible need not fear the effusions of the Higher Critics, Advanced-View-Men and Unbelievers. The Word of the Lord endureth for ever. It is God's Word – man's only infallible rule of faith and practice in all things. The Book that converts cannibals and changes them into servants of God, can change any people.' The knowledge of these views is essential to a correct understanding of Paton's work. It is useless to describe or admire Paton's triumphs if we think that any message would have done, and that the missionary's doctrine is immaterial and, in the modern manner, may be safely ignored. This is utterly false. Paton was, quite rightly, convinced that only the evangelical Gospel, based on the infallible Scriptures, was 'the power of God unto salvation'. Without it, diligence, courage and self-sacrifice will achieve nothing.

Further, Paton believed firmly in the sovereignty of God in the sphere of providence, as well as in salvation. This confidence was the strength of his purpose; he was convinced and often said that he was immortal till his work was done. It was this same doctrine, as he taught it to the Aniwans, which, far from stultifying missionary zeal, as is commonly supposed, led to their evangelizing of Tanna. Indeed, Paton's trust in his sovereign God, combined with his faith in the true Gospel, was the source of the godliness, the compassion for the lost and the courage in adversity which made him both a man of God and a great missionary of the Cross.

To Paton these words of praise and commendation would have been extremely painful. It is fitting, therefore, that we should conclude with the words with which his autobiography closes:

'Oh, that I had my life to begin again! I would consecrate it anew to Jesus in seeking the conversion of the remaining cannibals on the New Hebrides. But since that may not be, may He help me to use every moment and every power still left to me, to carry forward to the uttermost that beloved work. Doubtless these poor degraded savages are a part of the Redeemer's inheritance, given to him in the Father's eternal covenant, and thousands of them are destined through us to sing His praise in the glory and the joy of the heavenly world! And should the record of my poor and broken life lead anyone to consecrate himself to Mission work at home or abroad that he may win souls for Jesus, or should it even deepen the missionary spirit in those who already know and serve the Redeemer of us all – for this also, and for all through which He has led me by His loving and gracious guidance, I shall, unto the endless ages of eternity, bless and adore my beloved Master and Saviour and Lord, to whom be glory for ever and ever.'